The Finnish Volunteer Battalion of the *Waffen SS*

The Finnish Volunteer Battalion of the *Waffen SS*

Wilhelm Tieke

Pen & Sword
MILITARY

First published in Great Britain in 2024 by
Pen & Sword Military
An imprint of Pen & Sword Books Limited
Yorkshire – Philadelphia

ISBN 978 1 39900 298 1

A CIP catalogue record for this book is
available from the British Library

Typeset by Mac Style
Printed in the UK by CPI Group (UK) Ltd, Croydon, CR0 4YY.

MIX
Paper | Supporting responsible forestry
FSC® C013604
FSC www.fsc.org

Pen & Sword Books Limited incorporates the imprints of After the Battle, Atlas, Archaeology, Aviation, Discovery, Family History, Fiction, History, Maritime, Military, Military Classics, Politics, Select, Transport, True Crime, Air World, Frontline Publishing, Leo Cooper, Remember When, Seaforth Publishing, The Praetorian Press, Wharncliffe Local History, Wharncliffe Transport, Wharncliffe True Crime and White Owl.

For a complete list of Pen & Sword titles please contact

PEN & SWORD BOOKS LIMITED
47 Church Street, Barnsley, South Yorkshire, S70 2AS, England
E-mail: enquiries@pen-and-sword.co.uk
Website: www.pen-and-sword.co.uk
or
PEN AND SWORD BOOKS
1950 Lawrence Rd, Havertown, PA 19083, USA
E-mail: Uspen-and-sword@casematepublishers.com
Website: www.penandswordbooks.com

Contents

Introduction

Amongst the formations of European volunteers who fought on Germany's side during the Second World War, the Finnish *Volunteer-Bataillon* of the *Waffen-SS* has a special place.

In 1966, history professors George H. Stein and H. Peter Krosby began to study the reasons for the formation and later disbanding of the *Bataillon*.[1]

A special contribution was made by Professor Mauno Jokipii, Jyväskylä, who researched the complete relationship between the *Bataillon* and the development of the war, and presented this in detail.[2]

Unfortunately, the research results are not available to the German reader due to the language barrier. It is therefore a great joy that Professor Mauno Jokipii has generously given permission for the three studies to be published in this book in the German language.

The men who actually sacrificed, suffered and put their lives on the line are often forgotten when historical studies are prepared. The Finnish volunteers fought in the *SS-Panzergrenadier-Division* "*Wiking*" as a living pledge of the comradeship of brothers-in-arms. They felt responsible to their legacy from their fathers, who had fought on Germany's side in the First World War as the *"Königlich preußischen Jägerbataillon Nr. 27"*. Their deployment in the ranks of the *Waffen-SS* was a controversial issue in Finland. Finnish government circles would have welcomed a Finnish formation as the successor of the *27. Jäger* in the German *Heer*. On page 447 in their study, Stein/Krosby wrote:

> The young Finns served as loyally and competently in the *Waffen-SS* as their countrymen at home in the Finnish army. But politics ruled behind the front.

1. Stein/Krosby: "Das Finnische Freiwilligen-Bataillon der Waffen-SS – Eine Studie zur SS-Diplomatie und zur ausländischen Freiwilligen-Bewegung", in "Vierteljahrshefte für Zeitgeschichte", 1966, Volume 4.
2. Mauno Jokipii: "Panttipataljoona", Verlag Weilin & Göös, Helsinki 1968.

When in September 1944 the Finnish Parliament decided to end the war the former volunteers were in the ranks of the Finnish army. There, they fulfilled their duties loyally toward their people and fatherland, even though tragic developments resulted in them having to fight their former brothers-in-arms.

This book does not glorify war; it portrays it as it really was. Whoever has survived the horrors of war and the hell of battles as a frontline soldier can only warn the next generation of this. The history of the Finnish *Volunteer-Bataillon* in the *Waffen-SS* presented here testifies to the sacrifice of the Finnish volunteers who fought on the German side, and also for the retention of Finland's freedom.

Thanks to all collaborators who contributed to the creation of this book.

Wilhelm Tieke
Gummersbach, October 1979

Finland, Country and People

The origin of the name Finland is contested. In addition to other words the English word "fen", which means marsh or swamp, builds a bridge, especially because the first part of the Finnish word "Suo-mi" means marsh and Finland has many large areas consisting of marshes and swamps. With pride, the Finns call their country, their homeland, "Suomi". Suomi, the land of lakes, forests, and swamps, with its taciturn people, hides from the stranger secrets, temptations and riddles.

In old records Finland is portrayed as a "country between the west and the east, but somewhat more northerly". The Roman classical writer Tacitus described it as more northerly, whereby he probably considered Finns and Laplanders to be the same, which of course is not correct. In the new encyclopaedias Finland is described as a north European state between Scandinavia and the eastern European lowlands, between the Baltic Sea and the northern Arctic Ocean, with an area of 337,009 square kilometres.

In 1975 Finland had a population of 4.7 million. Of those, 7 per cent are of Swedish origin, the so-called Finland Swedes. Approximately 1,500 Laplanders living in the far north still lead a wandering nomadic life, living off reindeer herds. Correspondingly, the Finnish and Lapland languages are used. The greater part of Finland's population considers itself to be evangelical Lutherans. Finland is a large country, greater than the Federal Republic of Germany, but sparsely populated in relation to central Europe. There are 13 people per square kilometre. It has a relatively good road and rail network and a capable air transport system. The communications system reaches even the most remote places by radio and telephone.

In addition to modern cities, wide open areas and isolated villages, there are many single dwellings. The living quarters and barns of the farmers are made mostly out of wood. A red coat of paint and the white painted window and door frames provide a great contrast in the landscape.

Each family has a bathhouse, a Finnish sauna, sometimes a winter sauna near the house and a summer sauna near a river or lake. A steam bath in the sauna can be devastating, breathless, or invigorating. Large, round, granite stones are heated, usually over a birch fire, and then water poured over the stones. The resulting mixture of steam, heat, and the spicy odour of the wood is taken in by the open pores of the body and the harmful body products are driven out.

Treatment of the skin with birch branches increases blood flow. There follows the sudden cooling of the body with cold water or in the snow. Proverbially, the Finnish sauna contributes greatly to the health of the people.

North to south, Finland extends 1,100 kilometres from north of the Polar Circle to the Gulf of Finland. East to west, it stretches from Lake Ladoga to the Gulf of Bothnia, a distance of nearly 500 kilometres. Its border with the Soviet Union is 1,246 kilometres long.

Finland is an ancient area covered with Ice Age deposits. The mountainous north has an arctic character with sparse vegetation, thin forests, and large marshes (tundra) covered with reindeer moss and small dwarf birches or polar birches. As one travels farther south, the terrain becomes flatter, changing into the country of "a thousand lakes" and forests up to the islands and skerries in the Gulf of Finland and the Aland Islands. From the high north to the south the country is covered mainly by birches, then pine trees, and then spruce trees. Near the southern shores, there are even deciduous forests consisting of oak, maple, lime, ash, and elm.

In addition to productive farming and the associated raising of live stock, mainly in the southern coastal areas and the river lowlands in the centre of the country, Finland lives off its forests and the related wood-processing and cellulose industry.

Approximately 55,000 fish-containing lakes and many rivers provide the second basis of the Finnish livelihood. After the ice melt, the logs cut down in the winter are put together as rafts and are floated down the river to the saw mills and pulp and paper factories. Furniture factories and shipyards process most of the wood; large shiploads with cut timber, paper and veneer sail to all the countries of Europe, providing for a healthy exchange for imports, which Finland needs.

Finland's climate in the north is arctic, with long winters and short, but beautiful warm summers. Its centre has a continental influence, and the coastal area is influenced by the Atlantic. Although Finland is on the same latitude as southern Greenland it has a substantially better climate because the warm Gulf Stream flows along the coast of Norway, influencing the climate of all of Scandinavia. The summer lasts only 60 days in the north of Finland, in the south nearly four months. When the sun reaches its highest point during the middle of June, Helsinki, the capital city, has a mid-summer day of 19 hours and the street lights are not turned on for 14 days. The mid-summer time in Utsjok, the most northerly habitation in Lapland, is 71 days without one hour of night. On the other hand, during winter, when the sun is at its lowest, the sun does not rise above the horizon for 51 days. In Helsinki night and twilight are 16 hours long, and only at noon does a bright gleam indicate daytime. But there is seldom a deep dark because the snow reflects the light in the atmosphere like a mirror. A unique experience for strangers are the northern lights, which suddenly appear in the sky at heights of 100 to 150 kilometres and produce a fantastic display of colour that can last for minutes or hours.

Forests and lakes, light and shadows, the light of the short, nearly tropical summer and the gloominess of the northern winter affect the mood of the Finns. They turn the Finns into taciturn, reserved people, influence their life style and character, which many central Europeans can only understand with great difficulty. As soon as a Finn recognizes the stranger as a friend, the icy reservation and the apparent impenetrability of the Finnish soul melt and disappear as rapidly as the summer ice melt on the Finnish lakes and rivers. Then there are no limits to his kindness and hospitality.

The Finns are a freedom-loving people, joined with nature, made from hard wood, a people which has maintained its national cohesion, culture and living space through all the tempests of time. Industrious, non-demanding and of good character, the Finns and Finland have gained fame, honour, respect and recognition all over the world as craftsmen, master builders, musicians and poets.

The symbol of Finnish spirit, that of Finnish self-assertiveness and national pride, is the beautiful and well-maintained Olavinlinna castle. It is located in the Finnish countryside of Lake Saimaa on the Karelian narrows, not far from the present border with the Soviet Union; a border that has been contested and fought-over since time immemorial.

The Coming into Existence of the Finnish People and Country

Along with Hungarians and Estonians, the Finns belong to the Finno-Ugric language group. Their original homeland is to be found in the area of the lower Volga, where German tribes (Goten) lived as neighbours. From there they wandered in all directions and were partly absorbed by other splinter and ethnic groups. Already in early times, one part of the original Finns wandered to the northwest and lived in today's Baltic region next to Germanic tribes, from whom they obtained part of their culture and language, as well as the plough.

At the turning point in history, the settling of today's Suomi-Finland took place across the Gulf of Finland by two tribes from the Baltic area, which had in part mixed with Germanic tribes. The third Finnish tribe, the Karelians, crossed over the Karelian land narrows to Finland and settled eastern Finland up to the White Sea. The Laplanders living in Finland were pushed to the north. Germanic immigrants, who came from the area of present day Sweden, mixed with the two western Finnish tribes. This helps to explain the difference in physical and mental characteristics between western and eastern Finns (Karelians).

Additional tribes, identified in part by the names of the countryside, developed from the three original ones, hindering the creation of a unified state. The large area and very low population density added to the difficulties.

In the meantime, next door, Russia and Sweden developed into nations, pushing beyond their natural boundaries. The Finn settlement area became a contested object between their geopolitical goals. Although the people of Finland ended up between two mill stones, over the centuries they did not give up their language, culture, and sense of national identity, maintaining the basis of a future Finnish state.

As so often happened in history, the churches were also used for power politics. The Swedes undertook their first crusade to Finland in 1157 and, by the power of the sword, converted the western Finn heathens to the Roman Catholic religion. The eastern Finns (Karelians) were converted by the Principality of Novgorod to the Greek Orthodox faith.

The split-up Finns were unable to resist the encroaching powers and ended up in the power struggle between Russia and Sweden, with the Swedes initially gaining the upper hand. Under Birger Jarl, the second crusade was launched in 1249, expanding Swedish influence farther to the east. The third crusade in 1293 brought the Karelian narrows also under Swedish control. It was secured against Novgorod and defended by the border fortress of Viborg (Viipurinlinna).

In 1323 the Peace of Schlüsselburg laid down the new spheres of interest between Sweden and the Principality of Novgorod, which went from the inner end of the Gulf of Finland (opposite Kronstadt) in a northerly, and then in a northwesterly direction to nearly the northeastern end of the Gulf of Bothnia. As a result, the entire Karelian land narrows ended up under the control of Sweden. In 1475 the Olavinlinna (Olofsburg) water castle on Lake Saimaa was constructed for the defence of the southeastern border.

After this territory came into their possession many Swedes immigrated into Western Finland, settling mainly in the fertile strip of land formed by the Gulf of Bothnia and Gulf of Finland. They provided the upper farming class and most of the government officials. As a result of those settlements and the mixing with Finns, the bond with Sweden became more pronounced. Western Finland became the Swedish border province of "Österland" and from 1362 participated in the Swedish elections. Österland became a Swedish Duchy and eventually a Grand Duchy.

The Finns adopted the Lutheran belief during the reformation. Under King Gustav Adolf, Sweden became a super power and intervened in the developments of central Europe. After the Peace of Stolbowa in the year 1617, eastern Finland, the sovereign territory of Novgorod, later that of the Muscovites (greater Russia), and Ingermanland (Estonia), became Swedish territory. That was the pinnacle of Swedish expansion.

Under Peter the Great, Russia became a superpower and slowly pushed the former Swedish super power back in the Baltic region. In 1703 Nevanlinna (today Leningrad) became Russian territory, and so did the Karelian land narrows with Viipuri (Viborg) after the Peace of Uusikaupunki (Nystadt) in 1721. After another war and the Peace of Turku in 1743, the Russians advanced the border in Finland to Kymijopki. Finally, all of Finland was lost to Russia after the Swedish-Russian War of 1808/09.

Following the Peace of Hamina (Fredrikshamm) in 1809, Finland became a Grand Duchy of the Russian Empire and, simultaneously, the Tsar became the Grand Duke of Finland. After 500 years of being

Sweden's equal partner, Finland received a new type of government. It became an autonomous state, with a Governor-General appointed by the Tsar as his representative. At the beginning of the nineteenth century Finland went through a quiet developmental transformation. Swedish remained initially the official language. The capital was moved from Turku to Helsinki.

However, a strong Russification process then set in, re-awakening the slumbering Finnish nationalism. Elias Lönnrot collected the ancient Finnish folk songs and heroic sagas, combining them into the Finnish national epic *Kalevala*. It was published in the Finnish language in 1835. Johan Wilhelm Snellmann published the first newspaper (*Saimaa*) in the Finnish language and ensured in 1855 that the Finnish language had equal status with the Swedish language. That resulted in the Swedish language being gradually eliminated. The Finnish-Swede, Johan Ludvig Runeberg, laid the foundation of Finnish poetry with his ballad *Fänrik Stals sägner*; the first poem became the Finnish national hymn.

Finland's special position was not satisfactory to many leading Russians. When Tsar Nicholas II mounted the throne in 1894 the people of Petersburg had a new ruler who introduced new politics into Finland. In 1899 Nicholas issued a manifesto. Its intent was that Finland was to be completely Russified and also was to lose its internal independence. The Finnish army was disbanded, and from then on Finnish youth was to serve in the Russian army. However, many escaped compulsory military service by fleeing into the forests.

In 1904 the disliked Russian Governor-General Bobrikow was shot by a Finn. The Russo-Japanese war of 1904/05 over dominance in Manchuria and Korea resulted in a Russian defeat. That and the revolution in 1905 against the Tsar and his governor shook up the Russian empire and provided the Finns with breathing space. However, in 1912 Nicholas II continued with his Russification plans. A law made the Finns citizens of the Russian Empire. The outbreak of the First World War brought a glimmer of hope to the Finnish people's aspiration to independence.

Finland's Position during the First World War

The efforts at Russification, which emanated from the Petersburg circles around Tsar Nicholas II and from the General Governor in the Grand

Duchy of Finland, General Alexandrowitsch Seyn, forced the Finnish people into a progressively more passive resistance. Arbitrariness, imprisonment and banishment were the replies of the Russian rulers. When the activities of the old Finnish guard of the freedom movement waned, the youth of Finland took their place, especially students and young academicians.

After the assassination of the successor to the Austrian throne on 28 June 1914 in Sarajevo the rivalries of the European powers changed to open warfare and plunged the blooming European continent into a catastrophe.

The Finnish archaeologist doctor Herman Gummerus was carrying out his research in the small town of Spalato on the Dalmatian coast. When he was informed of the assassination, he knew what would happen. He hoped and suspected that the event would lead to freedom for Finland.

Dr. Gummerus, who had been sentenced to six months imprisonment for insulting the Tsar of Russia, and who had decided to leave Finland to escape the prison sentence, decided to return to Finland as quickly as possible. He returned, passing through Berlin and Stockholm, where he spoke to leading personalities and made contact with expatriate Finns, under the name of Aberg on a small Swedish steamer and lived underground with his brother Johannes. Dr. Gummerus, alias Aberg, left his hiding place during the evenings and nights and met with old friends at the domicile of Freiherrn Adolf von Bonsdorf. But what they reported was depressing. The organization of the Finnish freedom movement was smashed and its leaders were either in jail or on the run. In expectation of good business with the Russian army, respected businessmen behaved in a reserved manner. There were divergent opinions amongst the most active freedom loving Finns. One group hoped for a victory of the Entente, of their democracies, which could have influenced the Tsar to give Finland its freedom. The larger group saw freedom for Finland only in a victory of the Central Powers, Germany, Austria and Italy, and thereby victory over the Russians. No decision was reached during those nightly meetings. All were of the same opinion, to wait and observe developments and approve Dr. Gummerus' decision to live in Stockholm and become the contact man for the Finnish freedom movement, especially with Germany.

The Swedish metalware dealer, Sven Aberg, alias Dr. Gummerus, passed the border control at Torneo without any difficulties. After reaching Swedish soil at Haparanda, he considered Finland's fortunes more dismal than ever.

Herman Gummerus sent a factual, comprehensive report on the situation of Finland to the foreign affairs department in Berlin. He believed that, with his candid report, he had buried his hopes for a free Finland for the foreseeable future.

During the night of 30/31 July 1914, there was hectic activity in the Russian war ministry on Saint Isaac's square in Petersburg. War minister Suchomlinow issued the prepared mobilization orders for the Tsarist armed forces. As part of that process, the Governor-General of the Grand Duchy of Finland, General Seyn, activated the prepared measures for Finland. The railroad timetables were cancelled, sea traffic was halted, the outer Aland Islands were evacuated by civilians and the coastal defences were occupied. The lights in the lighthouses were extinguished, the harbours were protected by mine barriers, and border traffic to Sweden passed only through Torneo. Press censorship was introduced, as was a curfew starting at 2100 hours. Anyone found on the streets had to identify himself. Resistance to the orders was punished with imprisonment. With the enacting of the mobilization decree, Finland became a war zone. Russian troops marched into Finland and behaved as conquerors.

In 1899 Tsar Nicholas II abolished the old Finnish military service regulations, according to which the Finns carried out their military service in purely Finnish units, under Finnish leadership while defending the borders of Finland. In 1904 the Governor General was shot by a young Finn, who was then killed himself. According to the new Russian military regulations, Finns had to serve in Russian regiments and could be deployed on any and all borders of the large Russian Empire. The Russian military regulations were ignored by the Finnish people. The communities did not issue any levies. Where they did take place, the young people simply fled into the forests or to other countries to evade the call-up to military service.

Then however, with the mobilization, the Russians attempted to enforce the military regulations in Finland. That, once more, pushed the Finnish youth to renewed resistance.

A few days after Dr. Herman Gummerus had left Finland and sent the depressing report about Finland's situation to Berlin from Stockholm, a few young Finnish students and academicians in the Ostrobotnia student club met in Helsinki. They were to evaluate the suggestion that the student organization of their country be divided into two sections, based on whether their mother tongue was Swedish or Finnish.[1]

The cleverly chosen topic was only a ruse to fool the Russian secret service. In reality, the students and academicians had no intention of splitting into two groups, thereby offering the Russian secret service even better opportunities for intervening.

The leader of those assembled, Master's degree holder Väino Kokko, spoke with passion of what all assembled were thinking, and of what animated them: The battle for Finland's freedom!

They had recognized that, to shake off the Russian yoke, they would not receive any sparks from the old freedom fighters, who had been worn out by punishments, imprisonments, and Siberia.

The "provisional central committee for an activist movement" was established around midnight on 27 October 1914. Finland's youth had seized the initiative into its own hands! The movement grew steadily but desire alone could not bring success: there was a lack of money and of military training to carry out sabotage activities against the hated Russians. The movement sent out feelers to Sweden and Denmark but received negative replies from all government offices; only individual, private citizens were willing to provide support.

It was decided to start a new initiative. On 2 December 1914, in Stockholm, the delegates from the Finnish freedom movement, engineer Bertel Paulig and student Walter Horn, presented to the German, von Hellberg, the request that 150 young Finns be militarily trained in Germany.

By chance, Dr. Gummerus ran into the delegates from the Finnish "activist movement". A careful evaluation of their plans resulted in a comprehensive agreement! Gummerus, the representative of the "old guard", placed himself without reservation on the side of the youths. They presented their plans to the German military and naval attachés, and received from them an agreement for a favourable evaluation.

In the meantime, a certain Miss Gerlach in Berlin was in the process of tracking down and documenting all Finns living in Germany. Those activities waned because German authorities created difficulties upon

1. Heinz Halter, "Finnische Jäger erkämpfen die Freiheit", page 12.

difficulties for Miss Gerlach, who until the outbreak of war had been a teacher at the German colony in Helsinki. At the end of November 1914 she received new impetus from the public prosecutor Adolf Fredrick Wetterhoff, a Finnish Swede by birth who had German citizenship. Together with the Finnish academician, Johannes Sundvall, they created the "Finnish department", where, from then on, all the threads of the Finnish freedom movement came together in Germany. The tasks of the "Finnish department" were:

1. Collaboration with German troops because only with Germany's help could Finland obtain its freedom.
2. Creation of a reliable client support system in Finland to provide the basis for German military action.
3. Expansion of the freedom movement in Finland.
4. Military training of suitable Finns.

At home and abroad, the Finnish freedom movement steadily gained more active and passive supporters. News and reports on the progress of the movement were exchanged through Stockholm. Doctor Gummerus was one of the most active couriers and advocates.

In January 1915 Adolf Fredrick Wetterhoff established the German-Finnish committee in Berlin. In addition to Wetterhoff, its members included *Kapitän zur See* Brüll, *Hauptmann* Nadolny of the General Staff, and counsellor Weber. A new phase began in the Finnish fight for freedom; concrete plans were created, reports and requests were sent to German offices. The decisive document arrived in Stockholm on 1 February 1915 from the Prussian War Ministry in Berlin:

> the offer to send 200 young Finns to Germany for military training is accepted. Training has the following purpose: to prove the sympathies of Germany for Finland, to inform them of the culture and spirit of Germany, and finally, in the case of Finnish activities or a Finnish rebellion, to have the ability to carry out military assignments.[2]

2. Halter, loc cit, page 18.

The Prussian War Ministry then provided the command structure and required obedience based on German principles. Additionally, training was initially limited to four weeks. To keep it secret it was classified as a "Boy Scout Training Course"; the participants were to receive Boy Scout uniforms.

On 2 February 1915 the lawyer Harald Ohquist, who had just finished his studies a few weeks before, received at his home in Helsingfors (Helsinki is the name used today by the Finns, Helsingfors is the old Swedish name) a telegram from Stockholm, which read as follows:

> News from your father indicated definite improvement. The doctor hopes for a complete recovery in two weeks.

This coded telegram led to the exodus of Finnish youth to Germany for military training. On the next day twelve students and young academicians disappeared from Helsingfors. They made it to Sweden by different routes and met by chance in Stockholm, Odengatan No. 19, at the home of the German representative von Hellberg.

The "Prussian Jägerbataillon Number *17*"

Fake companies communicated with coded telegrams between Berlin, Stockholm, and Finland. Only insiders knew that. On the southern edge of the Tiergarten, at Landgrafenstraße No. 20, was located the "Finnish department". In the Finnish border town of Torneo, a nice lady by the name of Reuter worked as a relay station, passing along the unusual telegrams and letters to the Finnish middle men. In Stockholm it was Doctor Gummerus through whom all reports, directives, and requests had to pass. A well-organized support system took over the Finnish volunteers and passed them along in stages; their secret routes from Finland to Germany passed through Stockholm, Gjedser, Warnemünde, or through Tralleborg and Saßnitz. The right officer was then also found in the German *Feldheer* (field army). As a former boy scout, *Major* Maximilian Bayer guaranteed the Finns good military training.

On 25 February 1915, a cold winter day, *Major* Bayer waited with mixed feelings at the small "Lockstedter-Lager" railroad station for the arrival of the first Finnish volunteers. Nineteen Finns arrived and on the next day an additional thirty-six. That was the beginning!

Bayer's initial concerns with respect to discipline and obedience disappeared after the first contact with the young Finns. Technically, the Finns were Russian subjects and therefore could not become German citizens. Under those circumstances, the soldiers rights and care, intimately associated with being incapacitated, were usually resolved to the detriment of the young Finns.

Lockstedter-Lager was an old troop training area in Schleswig-Holstein but only the initiated knew the secret that it hid. At the gate entrance to the blocked-off section was a sign that read:

Boy Scout Training Course
Lockstedter-Lager.
Entry Prohibited!

During the following days one could see young men dressed in German scout uniforms, wearing the broad-brimmed hats (one brim raised), undergoing military training.

Soon the number of volunteers in scout uniforms had risen to 170. Therefore, initially, two companies could be formed; the first under *Hauptmann* Knaths and the second under *Hauptmann* Bade. *Pionier* training was undertaken under the guidance of *Hauptmanner* Just and Heldt, with special importance being given to that branch because it was anticipated that there would be sabotage activities and demolitions carried out against Russian military installations in Finland.

Major Bayer was satisfied with the training results, but, in spite of all the volunteers' efforts, the training goals could not be achieved in the allotted four weeks. Bayer requested from Berlin that the course be lengthened. On 16 April 1915 the Chief of the German General Staff approved the extension of the training course and raised the number of participants to 1,000 volunteers.

While training continued at Lockstedter-Lager, *Major* Bayer constantly drove to Berlin to report on the progress of his troops, and also to remove the many political difficulties which went against the grain of his concepts of what a unique unit in World War One should be.

During the middle of August 1915 Kaiser Wilhelm II approved the combining of the Finnish volunteers into a regular *Bataillon*. On 26 August 1915 the Prussian Minister of War, Wild von Hohenborn, signed the document that became the "birth certificate" of the Finnish forces in the German *Heer*, with the new designation: "*Ausbildungstruppe Lockstedt*" (training troop Lockstedt).

According to orders to be created was:

> an immobile formation…, which would gradually attain the strength of a *Bataillon* according to *Stärkeanweisung D II 3* (table of organization D II 3),

with four *Jägerkompanien*, one machinegun company, and one *Pionier* company. Command and training were to be according to German principles, the language of command was to be German, the field-green *Jäger* uniforms were to be without troop numbers, the pay and rations were to be the same as German troops. Under point 3 it stated:

> With respect to duties and administration, as well as judicial concerns, the troop is under the direct command of the deputy *Generalkommando* of *IX. Armeekorps*. The highest army command will determine its future deployment.

Point 2 was the most important point of the constitution order and pointed out to the Finnish volunteers the great risks of their endeavour:

> The troop is designated to accept foreigners who report voluntarily for admission. The accepted foreigners will not become German citizens. The army administration accepts no responsibility with respect to them earning German citizenship. It also does not accept responsibility to provide support should anyone become wounded in the German *Heer* and therefore become an invalid. Relatives also may not make any claims against the German Reich in case of death or becoming an invalid. This has to be explained to each applicant clearly and be confirmed by him in writing. The foreigners must also be clearly informed that when they accept service with the German Reich their duty is to support it with all their powers, to obey all orders of their superiors and to subordinate themselves to all the German government and military laws, as well as any in effect during the time of hostilities.

Bringing the Finnish unit to the level of a *Bataillon* required increased personnel. An apparently harmless telegram from Stockholm reached a book dealer in Helsingfors on 30 August 1915 with the following content:

> Immediately send 2,000 copies of the ordered book.

Two thousand books represented the 2,000 volunteers for the Lockstedter-Lager.

A mass migration of Finnish men began under the eyes of the Russian secret police. There was a network of 87 recruiting and facilitating stations. During three years 700,000 Finnmarks were received as donations. The glowing spark had spread across the entire country. The Russian government and military authorities were powerless because the Finnish people were silent.

The old border crossing methods no longer sufficed for the new demands for Lockstedter-Lager. Large groups illegally crossed the border in the northern Finnish forest and swamp regions. There, German and Austrian soldiers who had escaped from Russian PoW camps were also helped along; a total of 1,500 men. When Russian border surveillance increased in that area the Finns found another way, across the ice.

During the winter of 1915/16 the Gulf of Bothnia was covered with a thick layer of ice. The new illegal route that the recruited Finns used was located at the narrowest part, the so-called throat, between the Finnish city of Vaasa and the Swedish city of Umea. The ice route was approximately 80 kilometres long and marked by nearly invisible rods jammed into the ice. On foot or skis, six to eight Finnish men passed along the secret route daily. Located in the middle of the ice desert was a crude, hidden tent that served as a resting station. On a number of occasions the illegal border crossers had to shake off, or kill in battle, pursuing Russians from the Nikolaistadt fortress. It was not difficult to cross the Swedish border after that.

In Stockholm, at Karlevägen number 14, from engineer Heldt, who ran a fake company, the volunteers received papers and tickets for the trip to Germany.

On 13 April 1916 the volunteer troop at the Lockstedter-Lager already consisted of 1,523 men. A total of 1,900 men were entered on the rolls of the *Bataillon*.

In addition to the general training, officer and NCO training courses were also given so that the Finns could eventually command their own units. The rank designations derived from the Boy Scouts, *Oberzugführer* and *Hauptzugführer* (company commander), were retained. *Oberleutnant* Rainer Stahel took over the machinegun company. On 17 March 1916 an artillery *Zug* with two 10.5 cm field howitzers was also established.

During a large exercise in the spring of 1916, in front of Prince Heinrichs and other high ranking German officers, the Finnish volunteers proved their expertise, receiving great praise and recognition from the high ranking German officers.

On 9 May 1916, in addition to a flag, where the blue-white colours of Finland were combined with Finnish and German themes from history, the *Bataillon* received its official designation:

Königlich Preußisches Jägerbataillon Nr. 27
Royal Prussian *Jägerbataillon No.* 27

After a farewell parade on 31 May 1916, the mobilized *Bataillon* was entrained at the Lockstedter railroad station and transferred to the front. The *Bataillon* consisted of four *jäger* companies, a machinegun company, a *pionier* company, and a field howitzer platoon. The German core personnel consisted of 39 officers, 53 NCOs, and 111 enlisted men. The Finns provided 27 platoon leaders, 39 *Gruppenführer*, and 1,134 *jäger*. Only the sick and a small training cadre remained behind at Lockstedt.

On 23 June 1916 *Preußisches Jägerbataillon Nr. 27* took over a sector on the small Misse River, west of the Mitau-Riga rail line.

A Russian offensive started on 16 July, penetrating the positions of the right neighbour, the 6. Reserve-Division, in the Eckau-Keckau area. On 25 July the Finnish *jäger* helped to clean up the dangerous penetration of the front with a counterattack.

On 11 September 1916 *Jägerbataillon Nr. 27* was relieved and took over the position of *Jägerbataillon Nr. 1* at Kneis, on the Gulf of Riga. With that, the Finns came closer to their homeland than any other unit on the German Eastern Front.

An internal crisis, created by rumours of a separate German peace with Russia and the inactivity that the quiet front sector brought with it, was overcome. *Major* Bayer was able to have *Brigadegeneral* von Wyneken relieve the *Jägerbataillon* with a battalion from *Infanterieregiment 332* so that he could prepare the Finns for their main task, the liberation of Finland. The *Bataillon* took up quarters in the Hansa barracks in Mitau.

On 18 December 1916 *Major* Bayer and the official and military departments agreed to continue to support the Finnish freedom movement, leave the *Bataillon* in its present form and strength, and to integrate the *Bataillon* into the fighting German *Heer* only when the deployment and eventual casualties were in sync with the general aspirations of obtaining Finland's freedom.

On 5 January 1917 *Major* Bayer, well liked by all Finns, had to turn over his *Bataillon* and take over *Reserve-Infanterieregiment 259* on the Western Front because its commander was killed on 25 October 1917 at Nomény in Lothringen. *Preußisches Jägerbataillon Nr. 27* was taken over by the most senior officer, *Hauptmann* Knaths.

Soon after Bayer left the *Bataillon* the Russians penetrated a German *Landsturm Bataillon* on the Aa and compressed the German front. *Jägerbataillon Nr. 27* was thrown into the front and helped to master the crisis. The *Jägerbataillon* was transferred back to Mitau on 18 January. It was to be deployed during a far ranging German counter-offensive but that became moot because the German offensive ground to a halt in its early stages.

The *Bataillon* remained at Tukkum from 10 February to 24 March 1917 and was transferred to Libau on 25 March to continue training.

A leader of the old Finnish freedom movement, Pehr Evind Svinhufvud, returned from exile in Siberia and the Finnish provincial parliament named him as head of the senate.

In the meantime everybody in Finland was talking about *Jägerbataillon Nr. 27.* Its existence substantially contributed to preventing the planned Russian introduction of compulsory military service in Finland in 1916. The national movement, the so-called *Jäger* movement, which had an independent Finland as its goal, continued to grow.

All nationalistic Finns knew that developments had to take place quickly. The Finnish quest for freedom continued to grow, and expressed itself through sabotage activities and open rebellion against the Russian military. Russia was forced to keep in Finland extraordinarily strong troop contingents, which were needed on the German-Austrian front.[1]

The first *Schutzkorps* units were formed in Finland. Weapons and ammunition entered the country along many secret routes. In the depths of the forests, in rapid two-week courses, Finnish farmers and workers were trained in weapon handling. The largest of the training camps was located in the village of Vindala. In the primeval forest, over 40 kilometres from the nearest railroad station, it was commanded by Paul Gerich, a former Tsarist general of Finnish birth. The graduates of those courses built the *Schutzkorps*. All that took place under the cover name of "the new forest department" and the "AK" (Aktionskomité).

The hour for deployment in the homeland was getting closer for *Jägerbataillon Nr. 27.* The planned landing of the *Bataillon* at Vaasa was postponed because the German army command had received reports

1. Dieter Aspelmeier, "Deutschland und Finnland während der beiden Weltkriege", Verlag Christoph von der Ropp, Hamburg 1967, pages 25–27.

from Finland indicating that the preparations for armed activity and the landing were not yet completed. As well, new power structures were in the offing in Russia.

The *Chef* of *4. Kompanie*, *Hauptmann* Ausfeld, rebelled against the monotonous training program in Libau and infected other Finns with his disobedience. Ausfeld was ordered to Berlin, where he convinced the men from the war ministry that the time had come to train the Finns in all the hardships of army life so that they would be capable of independently creating a Finnish army. The Finns received training as general staff officers, company and battalion leaders, paymasters, drivers, training leaders, weapon specialists, and battery mechanics. In that way *Jägerbataillon Nr. 27* practically became the framework for the subsequent Finnish armed forces. Ausfeld became the new commander of the Finnish volunteer *Bataillon*.

In the meantime, events in Russia moved rapidly. Although the peace-leaning Tsar turned over the government and leadership of the army to Alexander Kerenskij, a Russian politician, the collapse of the Russian army and the war weariness of the Russian people could no longer be halted. Long suppressed social opposition appeared openly.

The Russian Wladimir Iljitsch Lenin, a Russian revolutionary living in exile in Switzerland, who had by then been able to establish many secret contacts in Russia and increase the number of his supporters, prepared the revolution in Russia that would make world history a little later. In the factories and with the troops, workers' and soldiers' councils were formed. With help from Germany, Lenin returned to Russia and, on 25 and 26 October 1917 in Petersburg and on 30 October in Moscow, toppled the Kerenskij government. The Tsar and his family were murdered in Ekatarinburg. Lenin became chairman of the Council of People's Commissars and founder of the Soviet Union. As a result, new possible relationships emerged for the Finnish independence fighters.

Lenin was ready to end the war between Russia and the Central Powers. Peace negotiations were started at Brest-Litowsk, resulting in the Finns delivering a memorandum to the German government in Berlin. Two points in the memorandum were totally ignored by Germany: The inclusion of White Sea Karelia as part of the to-be-created independent Finland, and the release of Finland from its share of the war reparations to be paid by Russia. The recognition of Finland as a sovereign state, a contract on the future relations between Germany and Finland, as well as the financial and territorial questions relating to Finland's separation from Russia, were later resolved basically in Finland's favour.

The demand of a "speedy and complete liberation of Finland from Russian military occupation" was directly expressed in the Brest-Litowsk treaty. It stated in Article 6, paragraph 3, of the German-Russian Peace Treaty:

> Also Finland and the Aland Islands are to be evacuated soon by Russian troops, and the Finnish harbours by the Russian fleet and Russian naval forces…Russia is to cease all agitation and propaganda against the government or the institutions of Finland.[2]

Under German pressure through the Brest-Litowsk Peace Treaty of 3 March 1918, the Soviet Republic recognized the independence of Finland. However, it did not have in mind a Finland governed by its citizens, but rather a Finland according to its own image. Trotsky declared

> It has not been proven that Finland's independence corresponds to the will of the Finnish people.[3]

Russia continued to send additional Red Brigades to Finland, even after the signing of the peace treaty. The German government constantly demanded the withdrawal of Russian troops from Finnish soil. Finally, in a letter dated 24 March 1918, it threatened to take measures of its own to ensure that the conditions in the treaty were met.[4]

The Soviets repeatedly promised to withdraw their troops from Finland. They declared "that they would take no steps that would limit the national rights and independence of the Finnish people". Lenin wished to avoid a flagrant violation of the Brest-Litowsk Peace Treaty because he felt that his rule in Russia would be threatened by it.[5]

The demobilization of the Russian army was officially ordered but many soldiers remained at their old posts as "volunteers". They formed a

2. Dieter Aspelmeier, loc cit, page 33.
3. ibid, loc cit, page 30.
4. ibid, loc cit, page 34.
5. ibid, loc cit, page 34.

Russian "worker and peasant army", supposedly independent of Moscow or Petersburg. Quite a few joined the Finnish Red Guard, which, to avoid the conditions in the Brest-Litowsk Treaty, gave Finnish citizenship to some.[6]

The Soviet effort to create a Finland in its image was supported by the Finnish communists and social democrats; they formed the Finnish Red Guard. Triggered by powerful social conflicts, they supported a Finnish republic with ties to the Soviet Union. Gösta von Uexküll wrote about this: "To the Finnish workers and the other classes, Finland's thin Swedish upper class, in whose hands lay most of the economic power, was the class enemy. The hate against the "class of exploiters" was stoked by two sources: social and national. If the Finnish workers and small farmers, and the Swedish estate owners and citizens of means, had not had a common enemy in Russia, then it probably would have come to open warfare even before 1917.[7]

In the face of the common enemy, the national and social differences among the Finns took a backseat. The state's just-obtained independence was at stake; its preservation was the most important goal for a majority of the Finns. But, with Russia's help, the "Reds" were in power in the more densely settled area of southern Finland. The excesses of the Red Brigades piled up. The Finnish population defended itself against them. Finnish officials no longer went to work. Government broke down and, in a dictatorial fashion, was kept afloat by the "Reds".

In the meantime, the "White" Finns, under senate president Svinhufvud, governed in Vaasa, in central Finland. Svinhufvud was friendly toward Germany and managed to obtain weapons from it to arm the Finnish *Schutzkorps*. On 26/27 October 1917, the steamer *Equiti* brought from Danzig-Neufahrwasser to the coast near Vaasa, thirty machineguns, 6,500 rifles, a large number of pistols and hand grenades, plenty of ammunition and large quantities of explosives, as well as eight motorcycles. At a secret meeting point near Västero Island, the ship was taken over by the Finnish pilot Karl Rönnholm. It was brought safely, through skerries, Russian coast guards and mine barriers, to the coast, where it was unloaded by Finnish workers and farmers. The weapons

6. ibid, loc cit, page 35.
7. Juho Kusti Paasikivi, "Am Rande einer Supermacht" (The first edition appeared under the title: "My Moscow Mission 1939–41"), Holsten Verlag Hamburg 1966, page 12.

were brought to safe hiding places. A second trip by the *Equiti* (from 3 to 16 December 1917) failed due to lack of sufficient preparations. During both trips, Finnish men (advance troops from *Jägerbataillon Nr. 27*) stepped on native soil.

Those men and the weapon deliveries acted as a signal, secretly passed along by word of mouth. The strengths of the secret *Schutzkorps* increased rapidly. The insurrection, or, if you will, the civil war, began in central Finland. However, in southern Finland the "Reds" with Russian bayonets were in control, with nothing available to oppose them. Once more, Germany helped. On 12 November 1917, submarine *UC 57*, commanded by *Kapitänleutnant* Wißmann, sailed with weapons, ammunition, communications equipment and plenty of explosives. The load was picked up by a cutter on the coast of southern Finland, near the Loviisa skerries, and was brought on to land. With it, an additional eight Finnish *Jäger* reached home soil. Their mission was to blow up the important Petersburg-Helsinki rail line; it was only partially successful. *UC 57* did not return. Later, a memorial for the U-boat crew was erected near the Loviisa skerries.

On 8 January 1918 General Carl Gustav Emil Freiherr von Mannerheim, born a Finnish-Swede, an imperial Russian guards officer, returned to Finland. Mannerheim had commanded a Russian cavalry corps and was surprised in Odessa by the Bolshevik revolution. He made an adventurous trip back to help his homeland with its liberation. On 16 January 1918, Mannerheim was designated by Svinhufvud as the supreme commander of the *Schutzkorps* in the Pohjanmaa (Österbotten) area. He set up his headquarters in Vaasa.

The clashes between the Russians and the Finns, between "Reds" and "Whites" increased daily. The open conflict, a civil war, that Svinhufvud was trying to avoid broke out.

On 25 January 1918 Svinhufvud turned to the Soviets and demanded that the violence against Finnish men and women had to cease. Pokrowskij, Lenin's commissar for military issues, replied that the Soviet government was duty bound to support the Finnish proletariat in its battle against the Finnish bourgeoisie. Lenin then sent additional volunteers to help the approximately 30,000 Red Finns. With the support of their bayonets, Kullervo Manner became president of the Finnish Red government.

During the night of 28 January 1918 General Mannerheim disarmed all the Russians in his area of jurisdiction. Svinhufvud elevated Mannerheim as supreme commander of northern and central Finland, and charged him with maintaining security and order. As a result, on 28 January, the Russian 42nd Army Corps stationed in southern Finland, including the Finnish Red Guard (total strength about 80,000 men), declared war on the White Finnish Guard.

Open warfare began in northern and central Finland. The south, and above all the capital city of Helsinki, were still suffering under the suppression by the Red Russians and Finns. But there also, a *Schutzkorps* (white Finns) of approximately 2,000 men was created secretly. It was ready to strike at any time.

Developments in Finland demanded the help and deployment of the Finnish *jäger*. The farewell parade of *Jägerbataillon Nr. 27* was held in Mitau on 10 February 1918. The *Bataillon* was released by Germany and taken over by *Oberstleutnant* Wilhelm Thesleff, a Finn, in the name of the provisional Finnish government. The *Jäger* were then officially Finnish soldiers. Captains Ausfeld and von Coler, *Oberleutnant* Stahel, and four additional officers from the German cadre were taken into Finnish service.

The *Bataillon* boarded a ship in Libau. The transports *Arkturus* and *Castor* cast off on 13 February 1918 and brought the Finnish volunteers to Vaasa, Finland. Three years of training and combat were behind them. They were the basis for the creation of a Finnish army. The volunteers, on Mannerheim's orders, became the officer cadre for his *Schutzkorps*. Only a weak *Jäger* formation remained together and was filled up with young Finns.

The 12,000 men of Mannerheim's White Guard were opposed by 80,000 men from the Red Guard; an unfavourable force ratio. Svinhufvud called on Germany for help. On 24 March 1918, in a note, the German government threatened the Soviet Russians that it would take measures to bring about the conditions in the Brest-Litowsk Treaty with regard to the withdrawal of troops. The Soviet Union was once more urgently requested to withdraw its troops and the Red Guard from Finland. As that did not happen immediately, it was used by the Germans as a reason for intervening in Finland.

In the meantime *General* von der Goltz assembled the designated German *Ostseedivision* in the Danzig area for intervention in Finland.

With a special formation as an advance party, Meurer landed on the Aland Islands. During this operation a number of Russian coast guards were taken out. Ships, as well as large amounts of weapons and ammunition, were captured. The German advance formation continued its advance. On 4 April 1918, after the Russian Hanko harbour garrison had surrendered, the German *Ostseedivision* landed in Hanko harbour with 9,000 men, eighteen cannon, ten mortars, sixty-nine light, and ninety-eight heavy machineguns.

The Red Guards, who had turned against the White Guards in the north, became increasingly involved in heavier battles and there was the danger that they would be cut off from their supply lines.

Mannerheim's White Guard and the German *Ostseedivision* continued to improve their coordination and finally forced the Red Guards into a hopeless position.

After the red warships indicated that they would not fight, German warships *Westfalen*, *Posen*, and *Beowulf* entered Helsinki harbour and landed 400 men. By 15 April they had brought all of Helsinki under White control.

In the meantime, another formation, the landing detachment *Brandenstein* (*Infanterie-Regiment 255*), which had boarded the ice breakers *Tarmo* and *Wolhynetz*, suddenly landed on the Finnish south coast and captured Valkom and Loviisa in a coup de main.

In the meantime, Mannerheim's White Guard was in position along the line north of the Petersburg-Viipuri-Lahti rail line, approximately between the villages of Heinola-Hurja-Toupolsari-Tali-Raasuli. Mannerheim tied up the main Red forces and subsequently defeated them; 20,000 Russian entered the prison camps of Lahti and only small groups escaped to Russia. Finland had fought for its freedom with German help.

The former Finnish *Jäger*, as well as the rest of the Finnish nation, began the reconstruction of their country, with the *Jäger* taking over the most important command positions in the new Finnish armed forces. On 16 May 1918 the White Guard paraded in Helsinki in front of Mannerheim. Gösta von Uexküll wrote:

> Finland's independence was saved, but the price was high. It began with a hunt for all *Reds* in the country. Even the victories achieved in the field against the "outside enemy inside" had a hateful aspect to it. It poisoned the political atmosphere for years and kept alive the enmity between *White* and *Red*.

But the decision for Finland as an independent state and against the Soviet Republic had been made, for always. Even for the underdog Finnish workers, Helsinki was the true capital and not Petersburg or Moscow. Mannerheim had preserved them from the lot of Soviet citizenship, whether they wanted it or not, and thanked him.[8]

There were differences of opinion between Svinhufvud, the Germanophile, and the coolly calculating Mannerheim, whose sympathies were more with the western powers, especially Great Britain, as to which way the Finnish government was to proceed. Because of that, on 31 May 1918, Mannerheim, at the peak of his fame, resigned from his position.

Pehr Evind Svinhufvud, who had already declared the independence of Finland on 6 December 1917, became the first Regent of Finland. The Versailles Peace Treaty nullified the treaty of Brest-Litowsk. Svinhufvud's friendly attitude toward Germany boomeranged on Finland. The western powers refused to recognize Finland or establish diplomatic relations with it. The pro-western Mannerheim was remembered and was instructed by Svinhufvud to travel to England and France.

During November and December 1918 Mannerheim negotiated alternately with the governments in London and Paris. In the meantime, the Finnish government resigned. On 27 November 1918 a new government was formed; none of the previous members were present. On 12 December the Finnish parliament approved the resignation of Svinhufvud as Regent and designated Mannerheim, in his absence, as the new Regent. As a result, the rejection of Germany was complete and a pro-western policy was introduced. When Mannerheim returned to Finland from England he had secured Finland's food supply by the western powers. Diplomatic relations with Finland were established one after the other with France, Great Britain, and the United States, starting in the beginning of March and the beginning of May 1919.

In 1919 Stahlberg became the first state president of Finland. The economy of the country bloomed. The wounds of the civil war slowly healed over. Understanding and far-sighted Finns made every effort at reconciliation and unification of the Finnish people, especially the labour leader Väino Tanner, who had been a "Red" during the civil war.

8. J.K. Paasikivii, loc cit, page 10.

> For a long time, the chances that he would be able to reconcile the workers with the 'White' general Mannerheim and lead them to a parliamentary democracy seemed minimal at best. But Tanner did not become discouraged. He took up the fight with the radicals and won the Finnish worker's soul in the end.[9]

On the basis of its long suffering history, maintaining its national identity in opposition to its eastern neighbour, during the twenties and thirties Finland orientated itself toward the west, especially England and France.

9. J.K. Paasikivii, loc cit, page 12.

The Russo-Finnish Winter War 1939–1940

In spite of all the tensions in Europe during the thirties the Scandinavian countries were able to maintain their policy of neutrality. This changed for Finland when in 1938 the Soviet ambassador in Helsinki made contact with the Finnish foreign ministry. He made demands with respect to protecting the approaches to Leningrad by building Soviet strongpoints on the southern coast of Finland. The Finnish Republic declined but was aware of what might come its way in case of a European conflict. It was easy to recognize the Soviet efforts to control the Baltic Sea. Finland looked for a closer relationship with the Scandinavian countries and started planning with the Swedes to jointly fortify the Aland Islands. That, however, was terminated in the spring of 1939 due to Soviet protests.

Through the German-Soviet Non-aggression Pact of 23 August and 28 September 1939, and especially with the secret protocol of 23 August 1939, the German-Russian spheres of interest were staked out, whereby Finland and the Baltic states fell into the Soviet sphere of influence.

The Finnish statesmen saw what was coming. Mannerheim, who was being considered as the supreme commander of the Finnish armed forces in case of war, was inclined to accede to the Soviet demands. Finland made great efforts through all channels to obtain clarification and to find out from where help could be expected. The Scandinavian brother countries expressed their desire to maintain their neutrality and England and France were far away. Germany showed no interest in Finland; in the summer of 1939 the relationship between the two states was more than cool.

The deterioration of the German-Finnish relationship had started with the ascension to power of the national socialists, to which most Finns had an open antipathy, so that the old friendship with Germany slowly disappeared. In the thirties the Finnish economic

> circles began to steadily orientate more toward England because the English bought from Finland five times more goods than the Germans.[1]

With the outbreak of the Second World War on 1 September 1939, the situation worsened for Finland because it could then hardly expect help from the western powers. With German agreement, during the German-Polish war, from 17 September on the Soviet Union occupied the eastern part of Poland. Poland was divided between Germany and the Soviet Union. Consequently, the Baltic states (Lithuania, Latvia, and Estonia) were forced to sign a "mutual assistance pact", which, in practical terms, meant their incorporation into the Soviet Union. On 18 October 1939 the Russians occupied the bases agreed to by Estonia in the pact, and did the same in Latvia on 29 October. As a result, the Soviet Union had secured the southern approaches to Leningrad with bases in Ösel, Dagö, Baltischport, Libau, and Windau.

In an effort by the Soviet Union to then also gain fleet and air bases on the Finnish southern coast, it demanded on 5 October 1939 that the Finnish government send a delegation to Moscow to negotiate. State councillor Juho Paasikivi led the delegation to Moscow, with instructions from his government to refuse any border changes. There were fruitless discussions regarding leasing some islands in return for Finland being able to fortify the Aland Islands.

Negotiations began on 12 October 1939. The Finns rejected a mutual assistance pact along the lines of the Soviet-Estonian pact. The Soviets then explained in detail their demands, which represented a major infringement on the sovereignty of Finland:

1. Conceding Hanko as a base for Russian naval and air forces;
2. Turn over the islands in the Gulf of Finland;
3. Moving the Finnish border near Leningrad to the north, for which a section of Russian territory in central Finland would be given in return.

1. Dieter Aspelmeier, loc cit, page 81.

Finnish agreements to the fortification of Suursaaris and the separation of a narrow strip of Karelia, as well as stressing Finland's neutrality, did not satisfy the Soviets. On 13 November the negotiations were broken off without any results.[2]

Basically, Finland was on its own. England and France, which offered the prospect of help, were far away. Except moral support, no help could be expected from the militarily weak Scandinavian countries. On 15 October 1939 Sven Hedin, a Swedish researcher of Asian studies, who had intervened as a middle man without any mandate, found out in Berlin from Hermann Göring:

> The fate of the Baltic states is already sealed. Finland will be annexed by Russia.[3]

When Sven Hedin called on the German foreign minister von Ribbentrop in Berlin in the spring of 1940 to try and arrange peace between Finland and Russia, he too was rebuffed.[4]

On 26 November 1939, Soviet foreign minister Molotov asserted that Finnish artillery had fired on Russian border troops near Mainila in the Karelian land narrows and demanded that Finnish troops move back 25 kilometres behind the border. On 27 November 1939 he cancelled the non-aggression pact signed between Finland and Russia in 1934. On 29 November Russian troops opened fire on Finnish border troops in the high north, in the Petsamo area. On 30 November 1939, without a declaration of war, Soviet military formations crossed the Soviet-Finnish border on all other front sectors.

Finland was prepared for the dispute with Russia. Reservists were called up for training. The occupation of the border fortifications was nearly completed by the outbreak of fighting. Weapons and equipment, however, were only available in insufficient quantities. Finnish "Lottas", female auxiliaries, moved into offices, with staffs, into hospitals and other positions, so as to free up battle-capable men for the front. A defensive will and self-sacrifice in the battle for freedom permeated through all the people of Finland.

---

2. J. K. Paasikivi, loc cit, page 60f
3. Sven Hedin, "Ohne Auftrag in Berlin", Tübingen und Stuttgart 1950, page 47
4. ibid, loc cit, page 75f

Nine Finnish divisions and 160 aircraft had the difficult task of defying the assault of twenty-eight Russian divisions, numerous special units, 800 aircraft, and a far superior naval force. The outcome of this struggle was already clear from the beginning but Finland hoped that through a valiant fight it could influence the political conditions for an acceptable peace. During the hour of greatest danger, as before in 1917/18, General Carl Gustav Freiherr von Mannerheim again took over the supreme command of the Finnish armed forces.

The *schwerpunkt* of the battle was, as had always been in history, the Karelian land narrows between Lake Ladoga and the Gulf of Finland. There, Finland had created the Mannerheim Line; a thin, 125 kilometre-long fortified line studded with ninety-six concrete bunkers. North of Lake Ladoga was the Salmi sector, and continuing northward were the Lieska, central Finnish, Salla, and Petsamo sectors. The sectors north of Lake Ladoga mainly blocked the terrain sectors with access paths (there could be no talk of roads there) and protected Finnish cities and important traffic networks. They lay in the forests, river, and lake regions or in the barren northern tundra. There were strongpoints between the main positions, which limited themselves basically to observing the area in-between. The land border with Russia was 1,560 kilometres long. The deployment of naval forces was prevented by the onset of a severe winter and the associated icing up of the Arctic Ocean and the Gulf of Finland.

According to Mannerheim's plan, the Finnish covering detachments at the border were to carry out a fighting withdrawal to enable the additional construction and occupation of the Mannerheim Line positioned farther west.

On 1 December 1939 the main assault by the Soviets was launched in the Karelian land narrows with one armoured corps and twelve divisions. The Russian air force simultaneously launched a bombing attack on Helsinki. At the behest of Moscow, in the evacuated Finnish border town of Terijoki, the communists under O. V. Kuusinen created a shadow government designated as the "People's Government of the Democratic Republic of Finland". On the following day, it asked for help from the Soviet Union and concluded a friendship and a mutual assistance pact. After the Second World War the Soviet Union practised this successfully with a variety of central European states.

After a brief pause in the fighting, the Soviets attacked again between 7 and 17 December with three divisions in the Taipale sector, and from 17 December in the Summa sector with six divisions. However, the positions defending Viipuri (Viborg) held; it is there that on 23 December the Finns counterattacked, which so impressed the Soviets that they halted their offensive in the Karelian land narrows.

The Finns had two divisions in the 100 kilometre-long Salmi sector north of Lake Ladoga. They had expected the deployment of, at the most, three Russian divisions there because of reduced mobility due to the lack of roads in the forest and swampy region. However, the Russian 8th Army deployed seven divisions, a tank brigade, and heavy artillery. It achieved a deep, surprise penetration, and got behind the Mannerheim Line. The Finns were barely able to hold their own and suffered heavy losses until finally reserves were brought up from the main front and coastal defence. With help from the Finnish IV Army Corps, they were then able to hold a defensive line. In an attempt to split Finland apart in the centre, the Soviet 9th Army, with five divisions, advanced on the three sectors in central Finland in the direction of the Gulf of Bothnia. Mannerheim had to rush some of his reserves from the south to the north. A special tactic was developing: the splitting up of enemy forces, creation of small pockets, and the destruction of those surrounded. With these tactics, in a ten day battle near Tolvajärvi, Colonel (later general) Talvela smashed the Soviet 139th Rifle Division with seven Finnish battalions and four batteries, thereby preventing a far-ranging Russian encirclement.

At the same time a Russian division had overrun two Finnish battalions at Suomussalmi and continued its advance toward the west. Mannerheim sent regiment Siilasvuo to help. On 11 December 1939 it counterattacked and brought the Russian advance to a halt, even though the Russians had brought up an additional division. New Finnish reinforcements arrived to intervene in the developing heavy battles, amongst them *Pak* companies, which sent the remainder of the Russian 163rd Rifle Division to flight at temperatures of minus 40 degrees Celsius. Subsequently, the Russian 44th Rifle Division was attacked by these new tactics and destroyed completely. The Russians left 5,000 Russian dead and numerous weapons and equipment on the battlefield, with 500 Russians being taken prisoner.

Russian forces that had advanced on Salla were surrounded by small Finnish forces and forced to flee. The severe winter caused the Russians great difficulties. With respect to their climatic, weapons, and battle adaptations, the hardy Finns were far superior to the Russians.

Following these battles, the three sectors in central Finland became quiet.

In the far north the Russians attacked with the 14th Army, which consisted of three divisions and a tank brigade. Weak Finnish forces had to evacuate Petsamo but repelled the Russian attackers near Lake Inari during the arctic winter.

The Finnish forces in the northern sectors went over to the attack at the beginning of 1940 to destroy as many Russian forces as possible, thereby freeing up reserves for the main front in Karelia. At the end of January 1940, formations of the Finnish IV Army Corps destroyed the surrounded Russian 54th Rifle Division, which was being supplied by air, north of Lake Ladoga. The Soviets were learning from their bitter experiences and were able to prevent additional large losses, thereby having the ability to tie up Finnish forces on all front sectors. Only negligible reserves were freed up for the main front by those actions.

The Finnish armed forces had fought valiantly on all fronts but the Russian leadership had also learned and wanted to avoid any mistakes during a new offensive. Stalin named Marshal Voroshilow as the supreme commander for the entire Finnish front. Marshal Timoschenko, with the 2nd Army Group consisting of the 7th Army and the 13th Army, was attached to him. His mission was to break through the Karelian land narrows. Marshal Stern commanded a second Army Group, consisting of the 9th, the 14th, and the 18th Armies, which assembled on the eastern Finnish border. All Soviet troops were trained and familiarized with the special conditions associated with fighting in Finland. The Finns observed with concern the exercises of the Russians in front of them, especially in the area of cooperation between infantry and armoured units. Air reconnaissance and artillery activities increased substantially in the land narrows. The Finns recognized with concern what was coming toward them.

On 1 February 1940 the expected new Russian offensive was initiated in the Summa sector with heavy artillery fire and rolling air attacks. Russian tanks and infantry attacked at noon. The Finnish front still held.

A second assault followed on 6 February; that time the Russian infantry was mounted on tanks, which also pulled behind them armour-shielded sleds carrying infantry. New flame-throwing tanks forced the Finnish defensive troops into completely new critical situations. The Russians succeeded in making a large penetration north of the Summa position, in the Lähde sector, which was temporarily closed again by a Finnish counterattack. After constant new and heavier Russian attacks, the Finnish IInd Army Corps had to relinquish the Summa sector and move 15 kilometres west to an intermediary position, which was attacked on 18 February 1940 by Russian forces that had closed up. The situation became extremely precarious. A Russian breakthrough began to emerge along the centuries-old and embattled border at Viipuri. A new Army was created by General Erik Heinrichs with the last reserves. Its task it was to protect Viipuri.

In the meantime General Mannerheim ordered the withdrawal of the I Army Corps and the II Army Corps to a barrier line, which just enclosed Viipuri. It was the shortest front line between Lake Ladoga and the Gulf of Finland and was adjacent to lakes and rivers. But the Russians did not attack that line; they decided on an encirclement of Viipuri across the frozen Viipuri Bay.

The last defensive battle of the Finns began on 2 March 1940 in the Karelian narrows. Armoured and infantry forces, totalling four divisions, attacked the southern flank of the cornerstone, Viipuri, across the ice. Fourteen battalions, the last Finnish reserves, were thrown into the battle. A day-long battle ensued for Viipuri.

Simultaneously, farther west, from the previously-occupied island of Suursaari (Hogland), a powerful Russian force attacked Kotka across the ice and threatened the Finnish capital. The Finns were only able to counter those forces with a quickly assembled force of older recruits and underage youths. Supported by a few coastal batteries, they fought bravely.

From the beginning, it had been clear to Mannerheim and the Finnish political and military leaders that the war could not be won without outside help. The Scandinavian countries did not help officially because they wanted to hold on to their neutrality and were concerned over the survival of their countries in case of conflict. England and France, which had substantially helped to stabilize Finland and supported it in world politics during the twenties and thirties, did prepare an expeditionary corps. But a quick transport to Finland was thwarted through indecisiveness, weak conviction, and diplomatic difficulties with the transit across Sweden, until it collided with German troops that were occupying Norway. German troops were fighting at Narvik, the vital ore shipping harbour, against the previously landed British-French expeditionary corps. It remains to be seen whether in the creation of the expeditionary corps the needs of the Finns were at all dominant, or whether it was the desire to occupy northern Norway on the northern flank of Europe.

It was from a sense of solidarity between the Scandinavian people and the besieged brotherly Finland that small contingents of volunteers from Denmark, Sweden, and Norway, as well as a Hungarian formation, fought on the side of the Finns. The Swedes provided the largest group with a 6,000 man contingent, including approximately 600 Danes and 600 Norwegians. Commanded by Colonel Lindner, they were deployed in the Salla sector. The former Danish officer, von Schalburg, who had grown up in Russia and where his parents had lost all their possessions in northern Russia during the October revolution, also fought with the Finns.

Many Swedes also moved to Finland to help with farming and in industry, replacing Finnish men that had joined the armed forces.

During the last battles in the Karelian land narrows, a Finnish delegation travelled to Moscow on 6 March 1940 to enter into peace negotiations. The Finnish representatives signed the cease-fire on 12 March. Large sections of Karelia and northern Finland, including the Petsamo region, had to be ceded to the Soviet Union. Additionally, Hanko was leased to the Russians as a naval and air force base for thirty years. Since Russia had to consider the existing general situation in Europe, and because Finland wanted to be open to all sides, the Finns ended up with a relatively favourable peace, which permitted them to maintain their national independence. Four and a half million Finns paid a high price for that: 27,000 dead and 40,000 wounded. The Soviet losses were many times that.

The unequal battle lasted until 12 March 1940. On 13 March Mannerheim informed his troops that fighting had ceased. In his last order of the day, he acknowledged with pride, justifiably so, the accomplishments of his troops; but he also reminded them of the bitterness that had arisen with the Finnish people because of the empty promises and the lack of meaningful help from the outside:

We have the proud knowledge that we had a historic mission, which we continue to fulfill, to protect western civilization, which has been our inheritance for centuries, but we also know that we have paid to the last penny the debt that we owe to western civilization.

A Straw for Finland

The Background which Led to the Creation of the Finnish *SS-Bataillon* during the Winter of 1940/41

by Professor Dr. Mauno Jokipii

One of the most difficult chapters of Finland's history is the so-called in-between peace, which lasted from the peace treaty with Moscow in March 1940 until the attack by German troops against the Soviet Union in the summer of 1941. In the foreign policy of a small country 15 months are a brief moment, during which seldom-important events take place. For the above-mentioned time frame the exact opposite is true. On the basis of intensive research during the last ten years, one can clearly identify five different phases in which the direction of Finnish foreign policy changed:

1. Recovery during spring and summer of 1940
2. Renewed threats of war by the Soviet Union in August/September 1940
3. Negotiations phase with the goal of a union with Sweden from the fall of 1940 until January 1941
4. Phase of a threatened new war with the Soviet Union
5. Relaxation phase in the spring of 1941

The relaxation phase (5) started once Germany took a public position on Finland. That brought about a change in the Soviet Union's foreign policy, which peaked in April 1941 with the attempt to re-establish friendly relations with Finland.

There were obvious changes in policy within a few months. For the observer, who considered that time frame as a homogeneous interval, the changes are hard to explain. It appears that the relevant political steps by the Finns were initiated by the special situations occurring during that time. The historical research, looked at from the international point of view, provides comprehensive agreement in the evaluation of the Finnish events during the second half of 1940.

During May/June 1940 Germany was tied up by its attack in the west. It is true that the cease-fire with France took place on 25 June 1940, but the preparations for a landing in England, "Operation Sea Lion", tied up German forces in the west. On the other hand, Russia took advantage of the secret clauses in the non-aggression pact of 1939 with Germany. It used June and July of 1940 for bolshevize the Baltic area. On 20 July 1940 Estonia, Latvia, and Lithuania were declared to be Soviet republics.

That was the run-up to the expected conflict with Germany. Because Finland was placed on the same level as the Baltic States during the base negotiations in the fall of 1939, in general, the entire world expected that the Soviet Union's grip on Finland would be tightened. There were clear indications of that. The Soviets then demanded a share from the nickel mines in Petsamo and took a hard line with regards to the disbanding of the Finnish-Soviet friendship organization. Various departments from the German embassy, and military professionals, reported (from Kaunus in Lithuania on 24 July, from Reval on 2 August, and from Helsinki on 8 August) to the foreign affairs department in Berlin that Finland would soon be attacked again. The Finnish ambassador in Moscow, Paasikivi, determined on 10 August that people in Stockholm were very concerned about the fate of Finland. On 15 August, Witting, the Finnish foreign minister, reported to the German ambassador in Helsinki, Wipert von Blücher, that the Soviet Union had increased its divisions on the border from 15 to 22.

In spite of that, the generally expected attack on Finland did not come. The question as to why it did not come to an attack is easily explained by the fact that Germany, although formally an ally of Russia, began to show a renewed interest in the Scandinavian region. One indicator of that were the agreements reached with Sweden in the summer of 1940 and Finland on 22 September 1940 (practically already on 19 August). Those so-called transit agreements permitted German railway and motor vehicle troop transports to transit from the Finnish and Swedish harbours on the Gulf of Bothnia to northern Norway. Because Germany was neither able to win the air battle over England or to overcome with its fleet the mighty English fleet, on 12 October 1940 Hitler gave the order to postpone "Operation Sea Lion" until the following spring. In January 1940 the final order was issued to completely cancel "Operation Sea Lion". As a result, from October 1940 on Germany had the ability to become active in areas other than toward the English Channel. That changed situation was clearly recognizable during negotiations with the Soviet Union (12 to 13 November 1940), when Hitler declared that Finland was under Germany's protection.

Sweden's and Finland's desire to stay out of the confrontations between the super powers is quite obvious from the plan for an alliance in the fall of 1940.

In August 1940, that plan, which coincided with some previous concepts, was again latched onto by the Swedish minister for religious affairs, Gösta Bagge, and the industrialist S. Pahlsson, when they presented it to the Finnish defence minister, Rudolf Waldén. The Swedish king was to be the head of the alliance and Mannerheim the supreme commander of the combined forces. Sweden's participation was to be a guarantee that there would be no revenge politics from the Finns, while the combined armed forces would be a strong guarantor of Finland's and Sweden's neutrality. On 25 October 1940 the Finnish government accepted that suggestion in principle. With that confirmation, the Swedish government decided to work on the plan's details. There was the appearance that, although only the closest government circles were informed about the plan, a Scandinavian federation was in the offing.

Already during that stage the Soviet Union, which had heard about the plan through diplomatic channels, clearly indicated its reservations. The Finnish ambassador in Stockholm, Wasastjerna, brought up the federation plans with the Soviet ambassador in Stockholm, Mrs Kollontaj. After making enquiries with Swedish sources, Mrs Kollontaj immediately sent an alarming report to Moscow. On 6 December Molotov ordered Paasikivi, the Finnish ambassador in Moscow, to the Kremlin at midnight. He recommended that Finland think about the consequences of such an agreement, which, according to Soviet opinion, would alter the power structure in Scandinavia.

When Germany, which had its own reasons for not wanting an independent Scandinavian federation, declared that it could not support such a plan because of the disapproving position of the Soviet Union, the plan had to be abandoned. In the middle of January, the new Finnish government of Rangell, formed after parliamentary elections, responding to a question from the Swedish government, stated that it was still interested in the plan but, considering the present circumstances, saw no sense in continuing the negotiations at that time. The intervention of the great powers with respect to Finnish neutrality in the framework of a Scandinavian federation pulled the rug out from under that plan. Finland, should it in future be again put under political pressure, would have to choose between the great powers.

During the final phase of the federation negotiations, for the first time there were occasional efforts made at recruiting Finnish volunteers for the German armed forces. The German *Waffen-SS* was especially interested. During the in-between peace period at the end of 1940, the *Waffen-SS* numbered approximately 150,000 men. That was not even ten per cent of the strength of the German *Wehrmacht*.

At the beginning of December 1940 the *Waffen-SS* made great efforts at recruiting in occupied Norway for *Regiment* "*Nordland*" (later *Division* "*Wiking*"), in which only volunteers from Scandinavia could serve. From related correspondence, it becomes clear that an effort was made to also recruit Swedish and Finnish volunteers through Norway. It met with minimal success.

However, at the beginning of January 1941 the *Waffen-SS* recruiting station sent one of their representatives, the Swedish businessman Ola Vinberg, to Helsinki. Without informing the German embassy in Helsinki, which was symptomatic because the *SS* attempted to deliberately keep the foreign affairs department from any responsibility in those activities, Vinberg made inquiries as to whether there would eventually be volunteers from the Finns for *Division* "*Wiking*". In March he declared to the *Chef* of the *SS-Ergänzungsamt*, *General* Berger, that he had compiled a list of 700 men, of whom 40 were pilots in the reserve. However, he had to destroy the list of names because the Swedish police had arrested him in Malmö on his return.

That action, which by-passed the official diplomatic channels, had the result that Himmler, the German *SS* leader, and Berger placed great hopes in the recruiting action, which was officially set in motion two months later. The German ambassador in Helsinki, Blücher, who had been by-passed in that action, sent a telegram to the foreign affairs department.

In it he attempted to downplay the hopes that many Finns were ready to be recruited.

From the standpoint of official Finnish policy, the inquiry carried out at the beginning of January 1941 was very dangerous. If the Finnish government, which had been trying to maintain a balance between Germany and the Soviet Union, had known about Vinberg's business trip and its associated goal, it would most likely have been prevented it at that stage.

In January/February 1941 the relationship between the Soviet Union and Finland was once more severely disturbed by a second threat of war from the Soviet Union. That time, the disagreements over the nickel mine in Petsamo were the basis for the conflict. There had already been negotiations regarding the ownership of the mine in 1940 but this time it rose to the level of a great nickel crisis. The mine belonged to an English-Canadian nickel concern, which had most of the shares of Petsamo-Nickel-AG. During the summer the Finnish government had already committed itself to sell 60 per cent of the year's production to Germany and 40 per cent to the Soviet Union, because the two states had agreed amongst themselves on those numbers. Therefore, as that would have hurt English interests the Soviet request to dissolve the old company and form a new Finnish-Soviet one was rejected.

During the tough and prolonged negotiations the high point came on 12 November 1940 when Wyschinski declared to Paasikivi that making laws was reserved for human beings and therefore laws could be changed if necessary. The idea that the Finnish government was defending the legal position of the English-Canadian company did not impress the Soviet Union. On 14 January 1941 the same Soviet representative declared that the Soviet Union's patience had come to an end. A week later Finland received an ultimatum, limited to two days, which would run out on 23 January 1941.

The situation was really serious. The Soviet Union suddenly recalled its ambassador from Finland and issued an export ban. Mannerheim wanted to send two divisions to Finland's south-eastern border on 23 January 1941, when the secret services reported Soviet troop concentrations there. However, President Ryti's cold-blooded attitude prevented that action from being taken, which would definitely have aggravated the dangerous situation.

Because Germany had declared through various diplomatic channels to the Finns that it also was interested in the Petsamo nickel mine, quite understandable because nickel was rare in Europe and was needed by the steel and weapons industry, the Finns attempted to have Germany support them publicly over the tense nickel negotiations brought on by the ultimatum. That, however, was not given. For that reason, at the beginning of February, Paasikivi, the Finnish ambassador in Moscow, suggested to the Finnish government that it give up the Petsamo area since it had caused nothing but problems. Contrary to the unofficial German recommendations, the Finnish government's position stiffened during the middle of February. A Finnish-Russian nickel company should have only been agreed to if Finland would have had the controlling interest. Wyschinski considered that an insult and protested on 19 February 1941. On 20 February the poorly informed Paasikivi requested to be relieved as ambassador because he considered the new position of the Finnish government as inconceivably brusque.

The Soviet Union, however, retreated from its demand. On March 15, during a friendly speech, Molotov touched on the topic and in an indirect way turned to Paasikivi to find suitable steps so that the situation could be cleaned up. The Soviets had withdrawn from their previous threats.

Although the nickel crisis passed without the greater public being aware of its serious character, it nonetheless had fateful consequences. Finland, which had just been forced by Soviet objections to give up on closer Scandinavian co-operation, was then forced for the first time to look for security guarantees from the only remaining direction, namely Germany. The western powers were too far away and, as an example, did not help get the Finns out of a desperate situation by suggesting to the English-Canadian company that it sell its share to the Finnish state.

It was also during that time that the German request was made to recruit for a Finnish volunteer battalion. On 1 March 1941, the *Chef* of the *SS-Ergänzungsamt*, *General* Berger, took the request to Kivimäki, the Finnish ambassador in Berlin. Following diplomatic protocol, also because there was the appearance that the *SS* had once again tried to circumvent its own foreign ministry, Kivimäki immediately informed the German foreign ministry. It was only on 9 March that the German foreign ministry wrote to Blücher, the German ambassador in Helsinki, to try to get agreement for the plan from the Finnish government.

On 8 March in Helsinki the presence of Kivimäki was announced for the same issue. *Oberst* Dahm, who was responsible for the practical aspects of the recruiting programme, was to arrive in Helsinki on the next day. On 11 March 1941 Blücher had his first conversation with the Finnish foreign minister, who had already been informed on the issue much earlier by Kivimäki.

By 5 March 1941 the nickel crisis had definitely had a happy outcome, but it may be assumed with some certainty that the issue still disturbed some members of the Finnish government. Paasikivi reported from one of his former trips to Helsinki that Ryti was convinced that the Soviet Union's ultimate goal was the destruction of Finland. Although Germany had given unofficial assurances of support, a public statement, which could have been pointed out to the Finnish population, was strictly avoided by Germany. Finland had once more opposed the eastern superpower on a very insecure basis. What would happen if the situation became serious once more and Germany left Finland in the lurch? Reliable agreements did not exist. Therefore, it was important for Finland to ensure German support in case of a new crisis. Under those circumstances, it was very difficult for Finland to refuse permission for Germany to recruit volunteers. They would be a pledge and a guarantee for continued collaboration.

Finland grabbed at a straw and gave permission for the recruiting of volunteers on its territory. At this time, the political and military leaders, Ryti, Rangell, Witting, Mannerheim, and Waldén, were all of the same opinion regarding that issue.

With respect to National Socialism, the agreement to permit the recruiting of *SS*-volunteers did not necessitate any change in Finland's policies. This can be proven with many details. The matter was not handled publicly or by state offices, but rather by a private Finnish committee, whose chairman was to be the former *jäger*, *Oberstleutnant* Ragnar Nordström, from Loviisa. After Nordström rejected that offer, the former chief of the secret police, Esko Riekki, a council member from Helsinki, was chosen; he too was a *jäger*.[1]

Riekki did not belong to the so-called "activists" that had started the matter, but who only acted clearly as a recipient of orders from the

1. former member of *Jägerbataillon Nr. 27.*

government or the foreign affairs department. On 29 March 1941 the Finnish foreign minister declared that he knew nothing officially of the matter:

> Any other attitude would be dangerous for Finland.

Although the gentlemen met several times a week and quite openly discussed politics, the matter itself was not touched upon again in the manner of the old school of genuine diplomatic self-discipline until an article on it appeared in the London *Times* on 5 June 1941.

The Finnish army was also kept officially out of the matter; the few active officers who reported as volunteers took leave from the military. Recruiting for volunteers was carried out in Finland because Finns wanted diplomatic support in the future, but they did not want to annoy other countries and therefore carried out the recruiting in complete secrecy.

Since their formation on 25 March 1941, Riekki's committee had issued a number of conditions to the Germans for the recruiting process. For example, the Finns were not to be deployed against the western powers. They were not to be combined with other volunteers from other German occupied countries. The soldiers' oath was to be in general form, and not sworn to the German leadership. In other words, they did not just agree to everything. The conditions delayed the recruiting about three weeks, until the middle of April 1941. As Dahm had noted, by then the conditions were not agreed to by all responsible Finns. Some right wing extremists on the committee would have been satisfied with far fewer conditions, and Riekki had to back off. On 16 April he declared to the German ambassador Blücher that the conditions had only been suggestions. After that explanation a reply was awaited from Berlin. It arrived only on 28 April. The Germans respected many of the Finnish requests. Such an agreed-upon contract was then followed by the actual recruiting. Already approximately on 4 April 1941, a recruiting station was established under the cover name of "*Ingenieurbüro Ratas*" (engineering office Ratas).

However, it must be pointed out that the Finns tried to have the service of the volunteers take place with the ideologically neutral *Wehrmacht,* rather than with the *Waffen-SS*; then the Finnish unit could have continued the tradition of *Jägerbataillon Nr. 27.* However, a change was not possible because the initiative had been taken by the *Waffen-SS* and preparations were already far advanced. To the German leaders (if not the diplomats) such a path appeared to be the proper way to go. Although the *Waffen-SS* was not that active politically, from Hitler's point of view it was an elite formation and was associated with the united Europe concept.

The *jäger* tradition was still being discussed later on. On 10 June 1941 the Finnish military attaché in Berlin was informed that *Feldmarschall* von Brauchitsch had also expressed the desire to have a Finnish formation in the *Heer.*[2]

However, as that offer came too late, it was not possible to realize. From the other side, the Riekki committee tried, through Blücher, to have the Finnish *SS-Bataillon* carry the "*Jägerbataillon*" designation. Although the commander of *SS-Division* "*Wiking*", Felix Steiner, amongst others, recommended it, that consideration was rejected.

Riekki was able to ensure that the future Finnish recruits, where all parties were to be represented, including the social democrats, were vetted thoroughly by the state police. A police official in the "*Ingenieurbüro Ratas*" took over those duties. Initially, that was an effort to prevent the possible entry of communists into the volunteer *Bataillon*. However, at the same time many right-wing extremists were also rejected. That caused substantial agitation in the small group of Finnish national socialists, amongst them the Kalstagruppe and the Snellmangruppe. Nevertheless, with a strong hand, Riekki enforced the policies he considered right. That manner of selection was a sign that the *Bataillon* would not be sent to Germany to have the men politically indoctrinated. Riekki reiterated that the troop had to be completely apolitical and had to represent their country only as good soldiers.

The decision with respect to the volunteer matter took place at a fateful time. The Germans had been on the move since 16 April 1941. The affirmative reply, one that could not be reversed without offending the Germans, arrived on 28 April 1941 in Helsinki.

It was during the same week in April that the great change in the Soviet Union's Finnish policy took place. In place of ambassador Zotov, who

2. On 17 November 1941 the OKH ordered (Ch. H. Rüst. u. B.d.E.-20737-AHA Ia/I): "To strengthen the traditional link with the Finnish army, which was renewed during this war as brothers-in-arms, *III./IR 92* received, as the traditional unit of the former *Jägerbataillon Nr. 27*, the designation *III. (Jäg.) Btl./Inf.Rgt. 92 (Jägerbataillon Finland)*." During the war IR 92, later (GR) (Grenadier Regiment), belonged to *60. Infanterie-Division (mot.)/Wehrkreis XX, Danzig*.

had been recalled in January from Helsinki, the Soviet Union sent a new man, ambassador Orlov. His most important assignment was to improve relations with Finland. Orlov presented himself to Ryti on 23 April.

In spite of his friendly appearance, he of course could not suddenly remove all obstacles to a better understanding that had been created by the winter war and the threat of war in the previous year and a half. Orlov's appearance was acknowledged but one suspected that it was tactical because the trade relations did not improve, although the lack of grains was a special concern for the Finns. Therefore, Orlov's important declaration that the Soviet Union no longer had any objections to a union with Sweden was ignored. When the Swedish foreign minister Günther spent some time in Helsinki on 6 May 1941, that matter was no longer discussed seriously, although Witting assured him that Finland had no plans for revenge.

Finland's interest in peace was obvious. It had not taken any measures to protect the civilian population or initiated any economic measures in preparations for a defence. On 9 May 1941 Blücher expressed his criticism of that inaction to the Finnish foreign ministry.

Russian troops occupied Bessarabia (Romania) in the summer of 1940. Stalin then demanded the Romanian Bukovina and issued further demands in the Balkans. The mistrust between Stalin and Hitler grew constantly and put an end to German-Soviet cooperation. At the same time, Germany saw a Soviet threat to the Romanian oil fields at Ploesti; Germany was dependent on Romanian oil. In the summer that consideration finally triggered plan "Barbarossa", the attack on the Soviet Union. Germany had already begun planning the operation in August 1940 (first draft on 5 August). The final draft (no. 21) was confirmed on 18 December 1940. The contents were kept extremely secret. Even the neighbouring states, whose support was expected, were only informed of the plans during the last few months.

The "dose of reality", as Arvi Korhonen put it, began only at the end of May 1941. On 20 May, Schnurre, the special representative, met with Finland's president Ryti.

With special emphasis, he pointed out that Molotov had demanded in November a "liquidation of Finland" in favour of the Soviet Union. Hitler did not support that. From that point on the relations between Germany and the Soviet Union had deteriorated and there now was the danger of war. If Finland were to be attacked now by the Soviet Union it could expect German military help.

And so, without asking for them, at the end of May 1941 Finland obtained the military guarantees that it had tried in vain to obtain during the winter crisis.

On 25 May 1941, during negotiations in Salzburg, Finland received news from the officers' delegation, led by *General* Heinrichs, that a war between the great powers was in the offing. That was confirmed on the following day in Berlin by the highest military circles (Jodl, Brauchitsch, Halder). From 3 to 5 June the negotiations were continued in Helsinki with a German officers' delegation (*Oberst* Buschenhagen and *Oberst* Kinzel). According to protocol, a theoretical situation was spoken of where Finland would have to carry out a defensive war against the Soviet Union. However, the negotiating partners understood clearly that Germany was planning an attack on the Soviet Union. The Finnish political and military leadership then declared that Finland would only participate in the planned military activities if it was attacked.

After all the rumours, lasting the entire spring of 1941, of a war between the great powers were confirmed as true, the Germans became immediately active in the matter of the *SS* volunteer battalion. There can be no doubt that the German delegation, which arrived in Helsinki at the beginning of June, was asked through Heinrich for the return of the *SS* volunteers, especially the reserve officers. Mannerheim reacted to the new situation in the following way. He now needed all his men. The Marshal recalled later that he had initially opposed the sending of the *Bataillon*, but at the beginning of June 1941, three weeks before the outbreak of the German-Soviet war, had changed his opinion. It could perhaps be said that his changed position toward the *SS-Bataillon* was a sure sign of an impending war.

But, at that point in time, it was too late for the return of the *Bataillon*. From 6 May to 5 June 1941 the approximately 1,200 men had been sent by ship (in five transports) to Germany. When Buschenhagen and Kinzel left Helsinki on 6 June the entire *SS-Bataillon* was already in Germany. The "old fighters" from the Russian-Finnish winter war were on their way by rail from the Heuberg (near the Swiss border) troop training area to Silesia and the assembly area of *Division* "*Wiking*". On the other hand, the young soldiers of that same transport (the first three transport groups) travelled by a different train to the training centre at Wien-Schönbrunn. The fourth transport had just arrived at Stralsund, where the young soldiers were being fitted out for the trip to Vienna. The fifth transport was still at sea from Turku to Danzig; it also was to be forwarded to Vienna.

It became obvious that the later wishes for a return could not be agreed to by the Germans. In addition, psychologically speaking, the wishes, requested officially a few days later through the military attaché to the embassy in Helsinki, did not come from the right source. The *Waffen-SS* command had already assigned the older trained Finnish men (first wave) to the *Division "Wiking"*, which consisted of volunteers from all over Europe, and had sent the young untrained volunteers (second wave) to the training centres. The Finns were informed about that only when the separation into two groups could no longer be reversed; in other words, upon Riekki's arrival in Berlin on 9 June. At that point the "first wave" was already on their way to participate in operation "Barbarossa".

From the standpoint of the *SS* leadership, the separation was an advantage because, after all, it wanted to lead a crusade with all of Europe against the Soviet Union. Because the largest number of the *SS*-volunteers came from German-occupied countries, the volunteers from Finland (from a politically independent state) were very important. Therefore, the point that the Finns had been with the foreign volunteer formations of the *Waffen-SS* from the beginning could be brought up later. That may have been true, but there were some drawbacks for the so-called "division men", as the approximately 400 Finns (amongst the *SS* volunteers who had taken part in the summer of 1941 as part of the *Division "Wiking"* during the Ukrainian campaign) were referred to. Everything was too rushed. Inadequate knowledge of the German language and insufficient training with German weapons and German command principles created hindrances. Finnish officers and NCOs had to accept initially lower ranking positions in combat.

At the same time, contrary to original plans, the Finnish *SS-Bataillon*, whose training had begun in Vienna, was assigned German officers. Meanwhile, Finnish officers, with rifle in hand and practically without any function, participated in the Ukrainian campaign as guests. The propaganda implications of those measures should have been carefully investigated in the summer of 1941. The Finns fighting as part of

Division "Wiking" were only reunited with other Finns in January 1942, when the completely trained Finnish volunteer *Bataillon* was deployed in the southern sector of the *Ostfront*, on the Mius River. At the same time, the surplus officers and NCOs, approximately 100 men, were sent back to Finland.[3]

The question of whether the Finnish *Bataillon* was necessary from the Finnish point of view, can be asked. If the changing month-to-month situation or eventual intentions of revenge (considered as unjustified), or nationalistic dreams, are taken into account, then the answer to the question must be in the negative. However, when the *Bataillon* and its creation are investigated, and the general background events are taken into account, the measure seems understandable.

At the beginning of March 1941, when Germany was looking into the possibility of creating the *Bataillon*, the nickel crisis around Petsamo had not yet been resolved. During the crisis Finland was forced to find some public support from somewhere. It was therefore very difficult for Finland to turn away the first offer from Germany. There certainly had to be serious reasons why Ryti and Mannerheim, Anglo-Saxon-leaning men, decided to agree to the formation of the *SS-Bataillon*.

In my opinion, the great tragedy of the Finnish SS-*Bataillon* was that, from the new political perspective, two months after the decision had been made with respect to its creation, it was no longer important. From then on, it was only a sort of representative *Bataillon* in the army of brothers-in-arms; as was, for example, a Russian representative unit fighting in France during the First World War. During its creation, an important assignment was being planned for the new "Finnish Jägerbataillon": The fatherland was to be saved by a living pledge, whereby the politicians of the great powers were obliged to come to their aid in a crisis situation.

If the Finns had found out about operation "Barbarossa" at the end of February 1941 instead of at the end of May, the *Bataillon* would have never been created. That is also the entire reason why the formation of the *SS-Bataillon* was not dealt with under the auspices of the war crimes processes. The agreement to its formation stemmed from the nickel crisis in February and not the need to launch operation "Barbarossa".

3. See documentation in the appendix.

The formation of the SS-*Bataillon* can only be understood as a reaction to the stresses that Finland was experiencing during the time of the in-between peace. It was the only straw to clutch at for neutral Finland, desperate to get the support of at least one great power.

Recruiting Finnish Volunteers and their Transport to Germany

The report by Professor Jokipii illuminates the background for the creation of the Finnish *Volunteer-Bataillon*. The report also points to the intertwined ways of diplomacy and the struggle for authority between the German foreign ministry and the *Ergänzungsamt* (replacement office) of the *Waffen-SS* under *SS-Brigadeführer* Gottlob Berger.

Hitler's and Himmler's ideas to create a "Greater Germanic Reich" can be seen imbedded in the activities of the *Chef* of the *Ergänzungsamt* of the *Waffen-SS*. However, as the war went on those ideas were discarded, piece by piece, because the lack of soldiers resulted in the exploitation of the manpower reserves of all of Europe. As already mentioned, during the creation of the *Bataillon*, the concept of a "Greater Germanic Reich" was brought up because the greatest part of the Finnish population is of Ugric origin; only the Finns with Swedish roots are Germanic. Berger, who was always desperate to recruit and prepare the necessary replacements for the *Waffen-SS*, was already not really that fussy with respect to the Finnish *Waffen-SS* volunteers. Stein/Krosby write about that:

> Only twelve per cent of those checked out spoke Swedish! It appears that *Hauptsturmführer* Tack, the race and suitability specialist, did not give much thought to the usual requirements of the *Waffen-SS* with respect to racial purity.[4]

The report by Stein/Krosby also contains sound and exact details regarding the recruiting, medical examinations, and composition of the volunteers. According to their report, 1,326 Finns had been examined by 20 May 1941 and 1,084 found to be suitable. Of those 15.7 per cent were school boys, 14.4 per cent secondary students, 20.2 per cent workers, 15.7 per cent farmers, and 34.2 per cent other professions. Approximately

4. Stein/Krosby, "Das Finnische Freiwilligen-Bataillon der Waffen-SS", in "vierteljahreshefte fü Zeitgeschichte", 1966, Volume 4, Page 442.

one-third came from the larger cities of Finland, two-thirds from the smaller cities and the countryside.[5]

Of those volunteers, 125 officers, 109 NCOs, and 850 enlisted men (trained and untrained) were found suitable. The disproportion between officers, NCOs, and enlisted men is obvious. That caused difficulties later on because not all officers could be accommodated within the *Bataillon*, and many were sent back to Finland. Only a few of the volunteers had any idea of the shady tricks carried out behind the scenes. They were merely genuine actors in the spotlight on the stage. With youthful élan, or with the experience of older men, they participated enthusiastically in an endeavour that they believed would ensure freedom and independence for their people and their country.

The first of the volunteers, recruited from all parts of the country, were given tickets by go-betweens to Helsinki. They were assembled there by the "*Ingenieurbüro Ratas*" in inconspicuous buildings, and checked out in groups by a medical commission. *Hauptsturmführer* Dr. Tack, who checked them for suitability, and Dr. Weiß, the examining physician, were part of the commission. The examination was strict. Men were rejected for even minor problems and sent home.

On 6 May 1941 the first intake of Finnish volunteers was sent by rail from Helsinki to Turku. The volunteers, arriving in Turku in groups and individually, were assembled for a few hours in an inconspicuous holding area. During the evening 116 Finnish volunteers embarked on the motor ship *Adler*, which sailed for Danzig during the same night. The young Finns wore lifejackets as was standard procedure during military transports. Along the way, an alarm brought a little excitement. A Russian submarine was supposed to have been seen, but nothing happened.

The MS *Adler* arrived in Danzig harbour on 7 May. The Finnish volunteers were directed by a German central office to travel to Stralsund by rail, where they were put up in an *SS* barracks.

On 14 May a second transport from Turku arrived in Danzig with 255 men, and on 23 May a third one landed with 330 Finnish volunteers. They then carried on to Stralsund.

In the meantime, the volunteer movement had become generally known in Finland. Large segments of the Finnish population and the army, the

5. Ibid, a.a.O., Page 441–442.

right wing circles and the farmer party, had a positive attitude toward the volunteer movement. The Finnish social democrats and communists rejected it, demanding the cessation of recruiting.

There were branch offices of the "*Ingenieurbüro Ratas*" in all the major cities of Finland. The volunteers came from all parts of the country and from all layers of society. Many of them fought in the Finnish-Russian winter war of 1939/40, but only a few of the volunteers knew the political background that brought about the formation of the *Bataillon*.

In Stralsund the Finnish volunteers received German field uniforms and sent their own civilian clothes back home. Then, some light military service started.

After a few days the Finnish volunteers were forwarded on to *SS-Freiwilligen-Division "Wiking"*, which was stationed in Heuberg, a troop training area in the Swabian Alps. There, the unit was practising large-formation tactics.

Of the 701 men from the first three transports, approximately 421, who had already been trained militarily in Finland or had taken part in the Finnish-Russian winter war, were distributed among the various units of *Division "Wiking"*, especially *III./"Nordland"*. Between ten to twenty Finns were distributed to the companies, where they were integrated into the continuing training. Those Finnish volunteers that had been officers or NCOs in the Finnish army had to first undergo a German basic training course as ordinary soldiers. Then, if they had proved to be capable, they were deployed at their Finnish rank in *Division "Wiking"*. The Finnish volunteers that were immediately integrated in *Division "Wiking"* (referred to as "division-men") were sworn in during a small ceremony.

The 280 Finnish volunteers that had not had any military training were sent from Heuberg to the Schönbrunn-Fasanengarten *SS* barracks in Vienna. Amongst them were a few Finnish instructors. Basic training began in Vienna. There, as well as on the Heuberg troop training area, language courses ran parallel with the training programme.

The fourth and fifth transports consisted of young, untrained Finns, who had to be trained. On 2 June 1941 the fourth transport (330 men) embarked on motor ship *Bahia Laura* and sailed from Vaasa to Stettin. On 5 June 1941 the fifth transport (220 men) was transported by MS *Adler* from Turku to Danzig. Those transports were immediately forwarded to Stralsund and then to Wien-Schönbrunn.

Following the fifth transport, the recruiting of volunteers in Finland ended. The members of the German examination commission (Dahm, Tack, Weiß) returned to Germany with the last transport. That transport was accompanied by a four-member Finnish delegation, which included Riekki, Aaltonen, Backberg, and Tamminen. They were to inspect the Finnish volunteers in Germany. Riekki and his three companions circulated amongst the Finnish volunteers and discovered that many of the negotiated conditions had not been kept by the Germans.

They especially protested the distribution of their people in groups to *Regiment "Nordland"*. The commander of *Division "Wiking"*, *Generalmajor der Waffen-SS* Felix Steiner, was able to convince senior civil servant Riekki and his companions that the "division-men" were considered as cadre. Once they had become familiar with German battle and command methods, they would be transferred back to the Finnish *Volunteer-Bataillon*. The Finnish *SS* Committee was also displeased by the fact that Finnish volunteers, contrary to Finnish desires, were in a unit consisting of volunteers from the German-occupied countries of Norway, Denmark and the Netherlands. The latter were reproached as collaborators in their homeland. The affected Finns wanted to keep an open relationship with those countries and England, and one of the conditions had been to keep "the Finnish formation as separate and as independent as possible".[6]

When senior civil servant Riekki and his companions visited the Finnish volunteers in Germany they did not know, nor did any of the volunteers of "*Wiking*", of the coming war between Germany and the Soviet Union. From that point of view, a rejection of the integrated *Regiment "Nordland"* is understandable. But, once the war against the Soviet Union began, that question (if it was even posed by the ordinary man) became meaningless and German propaganda spoke of a "European crusade against Bolshevism".

The "division-men" were soon integrated into *Gruppen* and *Züge* in the companies and batteries of *Division "Wiking"*, and, in their service and military training, did not lag behind any of the comrades from other European countries. Having learned the German military basics and proved their ability, the Finnish officers and NCOs were given the rank that they held in the Finnish army. In many cases the Finnish officers and

6. Stein/Krosby, a.a.O., Page 430, 431.

NCOs were kept on the staffs of "*Wiking*" companies and battalions as so-called *z.b.V.* (for special purposes) and deployed for special assignments, so as to strengthen their knowledge of German command methods.

The deployment of *Division* "*Wiking*" had already been incorporated into "Plan Barbarossa". Therefore, there was time pressure to integrate the Finns. Already after a few weeks, *Division* "*Wiking*" moved from Heuberg to the assembly area in Silesia.

There were special difficulties with verbal communication between the Germans and Finns; a foreign language could not be learned in a few weeks. That was also the basis as to why the Finns felt somewhat restricted in their authority as officers and NCOs. However, the language of command was German, and command was carried out according to German command principles. It is also understandable that the Finnish officers and NCOs felt like "guests" as *z.b.V.* However, based on their language difficulties and the associated errors, could they have been given greater responsibilities, which would have often involved life or death decisions? The Finnish officers and NCOs were to be the first to overcome their German language and command difficulties and to learn German command principles. Only then were they to command units. That is what was done with other European volunteers in *Division* "*Wiking*".

Deployment of the "Division-men"

The Finnish volunteers were treated as equal partners from the first day of their incorporation into the *5. SS-Division* "*Wiking*". In a well-meaning, comradely way, they were integrated into all the secrets of daily duty, and especially the many unit drills. In the commander of *Division* "*Wiking*", *Generalmajor der Waffen-SS* Felix Steiner, and the commander of *SS-Regiment* "*Nordland*", *Standartenführer* von Scholz, they found leaders and father figures, who, with their concern for the volunteers, made the settling in with their units easier. Many times, the Finnish volunteers stood side-by-side with their German, Danish, and Norwegian comrades. *Division* "*Wiking*" proved to be an experimental organization of a European military formation, where, for the first time, members from various European states fought together as equal partners. When considering a future united Europe, it must be kept in mind that the first integrated division was created under *Generalmajor der Waffen-SS* Felix Steiner. In it, young men from the various European countries grew into a solid military unit. From it come the first European leaders. As Finns or Danes, they commanded units that, for the most part, consisted of Germans.

At the same time as the Finnish volunteers arrived at the troop training area Heuberg so did contingents of Norwegian volunteers, who were also parcelled out to the units. In that way many groups, consisting of members from four or five nations, were created. The training at Heuberg was strenuous, but, to reach their goals as quickly as possible, the young volunteers tackled it with great enthusiasm.

As part of *SS-Division "Wiking"*, the Finnish "division-men" and their units moved from Heuberg to the Silesian assembly area. It was time for deployment. However, its intended location remained a mystery to the end. Cleverly spread rumours supported the assumption of a march through the Soviet Union, with whom Germany was allied.

From Silesia it goes to the assembly area by Lublin in Póland. From here it becomes certain that the tough training of the volunteers of *5. SS-Division "Wiking"* will find its crucial test in a war with the Soviet Union.

The deployment of *Division "Wiking"* in Russia has been described in detail in Peter Straßner's book, *"Europäische Freiwillige"*, and will not be repeated here in detail. From the first day, the Finnish volunteers, the "division-men", stood their man in the various units. Rawa-Ruska, Lemberg, and Tarnopol were places of their deployment. There followed the battles at the Slutsch near Satanow, the defence at the *Rollbahn "Nord"* up to Kiev, and finally the crisis on the Dnjepr by Smela, where Pihkala, the Finnish liaison officer and divisional chaplain, amongst others, found a soldier's death. The battles for Dnjeprodzershinsk and Dnjepropetrowsk followed.

Division "Wiking" withstood its most severe test in the Dnjepropetrowsk bridgehead. In their battle for their concept of a united Europe, the Finnish volunteers, amongst others, demonstrated their great soldierly courage, their fighting ability and self-sacrifice, embodying true Finnish soldierly virtues.

Pawlograd, the pursuit battles in the Stalino area, and the last thrust toward Rostov and Schachty were the conclusion to a stormy, terrain-conquering advance in 1941.

The longest and toughest endurance test was provided to the volunteers of "*Wiking*" when, in the process of attacking Rostov, the November 1941 Russian counterattack engulfed *Generaloberst* von Kleist's *1. Panzerarmee.* During that time, worn out and decimated during the summer offensive, the formations of "*Wiking*" repelled powerful attacks by the Soviets. In position at the focal point on the southern flank of the Eastern Front, *SS-Regiment "Nordland"* successfully stood alone against five Russian divisions and a tank brigade, thereby preventing the encirclement and destruction of the *1. Panzerarmee.* Especially successful during those battles was *Sturmbannführer* Plöw's *III./"Nordland"*, which had many Finns in its ranks. Balabanow was the breakwater. It was at Balabanow that the Finns confronted the attacking Russian tanks. They did not retreat until the bulk of *1. Panzerarmee* had taken up new positions behind the Tusloff sector. The next move was to the Mius sector, which became the final winter position.

The Finnish "division-men" entered the history of the *SS-Division "Wiking"* and German military history as true brothers-in-arms. Most of them were wounded. Many were killed and rest in simple field graves in foreign soil alongside their German, Danish, and Norwegian comrades. Their spirit and self-sacrifice continue to live on as a sign of their loyalty to their oath and to Europe.

Creation of SS-*Freiwilligen-Bataillon "Nordost"*

Finnish *Freiwilligen-Bataillon* of the *Waffen-SS*

The assembled Finnish recruit contingents at Wien-Schönbrunn quickly reached the strength of a battalion. *SS-Freiwilligen-Bataillon "Nordost"* was officially created on 15 June 1941. On 9 July 1941 the *Bataillon* was transferred to Stralsund by rail transport and was accommodated there in the *SS* barracks. *Hauptsturmführer* Collani became its commander. Young officers from *SS-Junkerschule Bad Tölz* and NCOs from the Lauenburg NCO school joined the *Bataillon.*

The soldiers were trained individually in Stralsund. Great emphasis was placed on the Finnish volunteers becoming comfortable with German military procedures and being acquainted with German mentality and cultural history. During a social evening, the well-liked radio announcer, Rolf Wernicke, and, among others, Lale Andersen, showed up. Lale Andersen sang her (soon-to-be famous song) "*Lili Marlen*", which made its debut in the summer of 1941. Rolf Wernicke bridged the various presentations and entertained with jokes. Later, at a subsequent drinking session in the officer's mess, he expressed his surprise to Collani that so few people laughed at his jokes. But he laughed the most when he found out that the majority of his listeners were Finns, many of whom did not understand a single word of German.

On 25 August 1941 *SS-Freiwilligen-Bataillon "Nordost"* was transferred to the better training facilities of the Groß Born troop training area in western Pomerania, and quartered there.

There was intensive training at Groß Born. Although the Finns received no favours, they participated enthusiastically. Command during field exercises was mostly by signals. Each *Gruppe* included a Finn that had at least some knowledge of German. When necessary, he acted as an interpreter.

The training followed a detailed plan. There was individual combat training from 26 August to 7 September. From 8 September to 28 September *Gruppe* and *Zug* training took place, and from 29 September to 12 October 1941 unit training within a company. The training of the Finnish volunteers ended with a number of battalion-sized exercises.

After the formation training, so-called *Jägerzüge* (as the *4. Zug*) were formed in each company of the *Bataillon*. As a result of that measure, the above-strength platoons were reduced to the normal war-time strength in the German army. *Untersturmführer* Toivo Vaaramo, a North Karelian woodsman, led that platoon in the *2. Kompanie*. The *Jägerzüge* were equipped with the Finnish Suomi MPi, which had been donated by the Finnish armed forces. The Suomi MPi was developed by Captain Lahti and the Finnish weapon specialist, Generalmajor Saloranta, who also developed shaped hollow charges and a light machinegun. In 1932 the plans for the Suomi MPi ended up in Russian hands because of the Finnish spy, Oberleutnant Pantikainen. Therefore, it is obvious why the Russian MPi, with its drum magazine and high rate of fire, is so similar to the Finnish Suomi MPi.

The *Bataillon* already had a musical platoon in Groß Born. It was created by *Obersturmführer* Tauno Pajunen and conducted by him. Pajunen composed a song for the *Bataillon*. The liaison officer, the connecting link between German and Finnish command positions, was the war-wounded, arm amputee, Finnish Oberst Levälahti, who listened to the concerns and needs of his Finnish countrymen and looked for German redress.

On 13 September 1941, *SS-Freiwilligen-Bataillon "Nordost"* was renamed as "*Finnisches Freiwilligen-Bataillon der Waffen-SS*".

In the meantime, motorcycles, cars, and trucks arrived for the Bataillon, so that its strength corresponded to a German, war-time, motorized battalion in the *Heer*. The technical leader of the *Bataillon*, *Untersturmführer* Konrad Bläss, as well as the *Schirrmeister* (technical sergeant of maintenance) and *I-Trupps* (*Instandsetzung*-repair), accepted the responsibility for them and completed their technical knowledge of the vehicles, especially the French cars.

The oath taking ceremony took place on 15 October 1941, a memorable day for the young Finns. The commander, *Hauptsturmführer* Collani, reported the *Bataillon*, lined up in an open square, to the commander of the Groß Born troop training area, *General* Thofern, to the Finnish delegation led by *Oberst* Horn, *General* Heiskanen and *Major* Riekki, to the gentlemen Aaltonen and Rautala, as well as to the ladies Kaila, Heiskanen, Riekki, Tuomola, Backberg, and others. Then the military attaché, *Oberst* Walter Horn, with a short speech (translated into German), handed over the flag brought from Finland to *Hauptsturmführer* Collani.

The flag was designed by *Major* Riekki, a 27 year old *jäger*, and checked for heraldic correctness by Professor Carolus Lindberg. Wives of former members of *27. Jäger* sewed it.

The flag had a blue cross on a white background. In the middle of the cross, on a red background, was the Finnish lion. In the left upper corner were the *SS*-runes and in the lower left corner the German Iron Cross. In the right upper corner ws the Finnish Cross of Freedom and in the lower right corner the *Jäger* Cross, the former insignia of the *27. Jäger*. Although competent German and Finnish armed forces specialists could not come up with a final decision regarding the continuation of the tradition of the *"Königlich preußischen Jägerbataillon Nr. 27"*, it became clear from the flag and the discussions that the *Bataillon* did continue that tradition.

Aaltonen also wrote:

> Finnish volunteers breathe life into the *Jäger* inheritance. They too, as were their fathers, are imbued with the glowing thought of fighting for a free and independent Finland. The Finnish volunteer *Bataillon* is also evidence of the strong will to defend Finland and the readiness to self-sacrifice by Finnish youth.[1]

After the flag hand-over by *Oberst* Horn, *Hauptsturmführer* Collani replied with the following speech, which was translated into Finnish:

> I accept the flag from your hand, *Oberst* Horn, which Finland has created for its *"Finnisches Freiwilligen-Bataillon der Waffen-SS"*. As a former member of *"Königlich preußischen Jägerbataillon Nr. 27"*, you are symbolically transferring the tradition of your old glory-covered *Bataillon*, a *Bataillon* in which your fathers, my *SS*-men, fought in difficult times for the greatness of Finland and were victorious. Finland's freedom is due mainly to its *jäger*.

1. B.S. Aaltonen, "Waffenbruder Finnland", Page 111.

> You cannot buy tradition; you have to fight for it. A man who is not willing to enhance this tradition with his life and actions should not talk of honour. It is our desire to lead a fight that will be a worthy addition to the deeds of the *jäger*, and which will add glory and honour to this flag.
>
> From now on, this flag will flutter before us in battle. Men that have voluntarily gathered around it in the recognition of a necessary shared battle will follow it.
>
> *Oberst* Horn, as commander of this *Bataillon* and as leader of your young Finnish soldiers, I promise you in this hour: 'We will all protect this flag with our lives. We will do everything to make certain that it will never be lowered into the dust. It is to flutter victoriously during battle in front of us and those who will follow. But there will always be a community marching behind it, whose highest principle is honour and loyalty!
>
> I now turn this flag over to its bearer, *SS-Unterscharführer* Hoffren. Be aware of the distinction and the honour which is given to you to carry this flag. Grasp its shaft and always remember that only death will relieve you of this task.[2]

To the accompaniment of the Defilier march played by an army band, flanked by two officers, Hoffren carried the flag past the assembled *Bataillon* and took up a position in the centre of the *Bataillon*. *Hauptsturmführer* Collani spoke once more and pointed out to the *Bataillon* arranged in an open square the meaning of the oath:

> Your oath is taking place during this solemn hour, in the presence of your superiors, and the representatives of Finland and of the German *Wehrmacht*. Our thoughts go back to the days when you arrived. They were weeks and months of hard soldierly work that lay between then and now. I did not know anyone of you to despair

2. The *Bataillon* took the flag along to the front. When it became obvious in the spring of 1942 that the unit was again going over to mobile warfare, the *Bataillon* commander asked the *Bataillon* doctor, *Obersturmführer* Dr. Bumke, to take the flag to Dnjepropetrowsk, where *Division "Wiking"* had established a supply depot. It is not known whether an effort was made to get the flag from there during the return of the *Bataillon* to Germany in April 1943. An inquiry was started in July/August 1943 as to the whereabouts of the flag and finally an inquiry was ordered. All efforts to find the flag again remained fruitless.

over the difficult tasks. You fulfilled your duty with an iron will and have become good soldiers. A group of you have already proven yourselves through special achievements and are wearing the insignia of officers and NCOs. Another group will follow soon. It is through your energy and devotion that the training has progressed so well and that the *Bataillon* will be moving soon to the front.

The oath of allegiance, which you are about to undertake, does not relate to a process that is over at the end of your training period. It has the meaning of an outwardly ceremonial strengthening of loyal fulfillment of already existing duties. The soldier's set of professional ethics finds its religious basis in the taking of the oath. Soldierly virtues and the oath have always been two inseparable concepts.

Each and every one of you feels the righteousness and greatness of your task in this hour. This loyal relationship is sealed in a solemn ceremony by the invocation of God. Your decision to fight for the freedom, greatness, and new order in Europe receives the highest consecration through your vow.

From now on, your soldierly life is always to be based on the principle: Honour and loyalty. The honour of the soldier is in the unquestioning deployment of his person for the *Führer* and the community in which he lives.

Our fighting community requires a comradeship that has to prove itself especially during needs and danger. I expect from you that you will faithfully fulfill this comradeship.

Before you, in front of our flag, stand the sons of former soldiers of *Preußischen Jägerbataillon Nr. 27.* They will take an oath for you on the flag and you will all be loyal to your oath, as was the Finnish *Jäger* during the World War, and fight until our great European goals are realized.

The flag was lowered. Four young Finns placed their left hand on the flag and raised their right hand for the oath. The assembled companies came to attention at the same time upon the command "*Stillgestanden*!" in a position that touched every heart, which underlined the solemn procedure. One officer of the *Bataillon*, his left hand also resting on the flag, spoke the oath in sections. The Finnish youth repeated after him:

> I swear to you, Adolf Hitler, as *Führer*, loyalty and courage. I vow to you, and the superiors that you designate, obedience until death, so help me God.

The German and the Finnish national anthems sounded. The flag was carried to the head of the *Bataillon*. The high ranking German and Finnish officers reviewed the front rank of the *Bataillon* and then went to the grand stand. One after the other, the companies moved off and performed a march-past in front of the guests of honour.

They marched past the grandstand full of pride. Company after company. In front were the company commanders. The platoon leaders were in the first *Rotte* (rank) of the platoons on the outside right. Eyes were turned toward the honour guests, who greeted every company as it marched past. The companies were then dismissed and went to their barracks.

Present in the grandstand were representatives of state and party, from the *Kommandoamt*, the commander of Groß Born, from the Finnish side Oberst Horn, Oberst Leválahti and Major Riekki, and as the representative of the Lotta-Swärd-organization, Baroness Ruth Munk. After the march-past, under the guidance of *Hauptsturmführer* Collani, the above-named personalities viewed the barracks and the impeccably drawn-up vehicles of the *Bataillon*.

A day, which the Finnish volunteers would not soon forget, came to an end. With the conclusion of their training and the taking of the oath, the young Finns and their *Bataillon* were ready for combat. The day came closer when the *Freiwilligen-Bataillon* would leave for deployment at the *Ostfront*.

On 15 October 1941 the *Bataillon* had the following organizational and command structure: *Bataillon Kommandeur*: *Hauptsturmführer* Collani; *Adjutant*: *Untersturmführer* Hirt; *1. Kompanie*: *Obersturmführer* Hoy; *2. Kompanie*: *Obersturmführer* Pallesche; *3. Kompanie*: *Obersturmführer* Hartmann: *4. Kompanie*: *Obersturmführer* Pleiner.

In conclusion, one can say the following about the creation and training of the Finnish *Freiwilligen-Bataillon* of the *Waffen-SS*:

The German authorities placed special emphasis on good and comprehensive training. Initially, that was made somewhat difficult by language problems. The training plans and times corresponded to the normal German ones, which meant a shortened peace-time training program.

Therefore, it is not correct when the historian Aspelmeier writes:

> Approximately 400 men went to Germany in May and June 1941 and, after a short training period, were deployed in the southeast as the "Finnish *Freiwilligen-Bataillon* of the *Waffen-SS*.[3]

Compared to the training periods for other German units, that must be considered as a long time. What German unit at that time had seven months available for training?

Deployment Readiness and March to the *Ostfront*

After a stormy advance through southern Russia during the summer of 1941, as part of *1. Panzerarmee* commanded by *Generaloberst von Kleist, Generalmajor* Steiner's *SS-Division "Wiking"* reached the area south of Stalino. Begun before the beginning of winter, the attack on Rostov on the Don was halted by a powerful Russian counterattack. The *1. Panzerarmee* was forced to retreat behind the Tusloff, and then finally into the Mius sector.

The Russian rasputitza (the rainy and muddy period, accompanied by frost during the night), which started in November, caused great difficulties for the German soldiers. They had no experience of the Russian winter. Tanks and vehicles remained stuck in the mud and then froze solid into the ground where they stood. Re-supply was interrupted and nearly came to a halt. Great sufferings began for German soldiers, with frozen limbs being the most common injury. They had to laboriously prepare new defensive positions in rock-hard ground.

Like all other divisions, combat and the winter had burned out the units of *SS-Division "Wiking"* to slag. Following the retreat, eight weak companies were formed from the fifteen previous companies of "*Nordland*". The *III. Bataillon* and the regimental formations were disbanded and distributed amongst the *I. Bataillon* and the *II. Bataillon*. However, the weakened regiment had to occupy its normal frontal length and as a result

3. Dieter Aspelmeier, loc cit, page 111.

the units had to carry a double load. In spite of that the Russian storm troops were unable to overrun the German front.

After overcoming the initial shock of the retreat, the German command organizations got to work. They grabbed all reachable, whether trained or half-trained, equipped or partially-equipped, formations, often battalions, and sent them to the *Ostfront*, amongst them the Finnish *Bataillon*, to somehow reinforce the thin "front".

On 1 November 1941, the *Bataillon*, which had completed its training at the Groß Born troop training facility, was reported as ready for deployment to the *Kommandoamt* of the *Waffen-SS*. Its commander, *Hauptsturmführer* Collani, found out that the *Bataillon* was probably to be deployed on the southern section of the *Ostfront*, attached to *SS-Regiment "Nordland"*, part of *SS-Division "Wiking"*.

There was great activity in the companies' accommodations. The preparations for transport were in their last stages. Equipment, weapons, and ammunition, as well as the vehicles, were checked for readiness to the front, and all unnecessary items were left behind.

The necessary transport volume, with respect to personnel and freight cars, was reported to the Stettin transport command. The transport command notified the *Bataillon* leadership that there might be a delay in departure because of the existing transportation conditions.

On 13 November, after days of gruelling waiting, *Hauptsturmführer* Collani finally drove to the *Kommandoamt* in Berlin and found out that blown up stretches of rail and bridges, as well as the overloaded rail system in the Ukraine, were responsible for the delay in transporting his *Bataillon*.

On 21 November 1941, Finnish *Jägermajor* Kurkiala reported to the *Bataillon* in Groß Born as the new liaison officer for the Finnish army and government. Kurkiala, a minister by profession, was at the same time the *Bataillon* army chaplain. He was to also deal with the personal concerns and needs of the Finnish volunteers.

On 30 November the *Bataillon* finally received the order to get ready to march. Initially, it was to be transported by rail to Dnjepropetrowsk. The vehicles were to be brought by rail to Berditschew and from there they were to follow in a motorized transport. That directive made clear once more the severe demands on the rail network in the Ukraine. Supplying the front with food, weapons, and equipment had priority.

Dnjepropetrowsk was the eye of the needle of the southern sector of the *Ostfront*, through which all transports had to pass.

The first rail cars arrived at the railroad station of the Groß Born troop training facility on 2 December 1941 and the entraining of the *Bataillon* began. The first transport train departed on 3 December at 0755 hours, with others following in sequence. The sequence of the trains was as follows: *Bataillon* staff and *4. Kompanie, 1. Kompanie, 2. Kompanie, 3. Kompanie*. Since the possibility of air transport from Dnjepropetrowsk or Winniza was brought up sporadically, the rail cars with the vehicles were separated and combined in their own transport. The transports rolled through Graudenz, Warsaw, Lublin, and Rovno.

During the night of 5 December the transport of *2. Kompanie* was fired on. The train stopped. *Untersturmführer* Reubold jumped from the train and ran in the direction of the shots. *Untersturmführer* Ertel and a messenger followed him. They found Reubold lying on the ground with a stomach wound and carried him back to the train. There he is looked after by the *Bataillon* dentist, *Untersturmführer* Franke, who happened to be on the train. After hours of travel Reubold was taken off the train at Deblin and brought to the hospital, where he later died. To this day no one knows whether Reubold was hit by a partisan bullet or by the wild shooting coming from the train. However, *Untersturmführer* Ertel doubts that it was a partisan ambush because there were hardly any partisans in the area. He believes that it had to do with the locomotive personnel throwing coal off the tender, which was then to be collected by armed accomplices. *Untersturmführer* Reubold was the first to be killed from the *Bataillon*.

The troop transports arrived at the Winniza railroad station on 8 December 1941 and were unloaded. Accommodations were found in a barracks camp. The vehicles travelled to Berditschew and were unloaded there.

In Winniza it became certain that there would be no air transport because there were far too many more important air transport missions to be carried out. Therefore, the *Bataillon* had to complete the journey in a motorized land march in its own vehicles. The *TFK* (*Technische Führer Kraftfahrzeuge*, officer in charge of motorized vehicles) of the *Bataillon*, *Untersturmführer* Konrad Bläss, received the order to move the vehicles from Berditschew to Winniza as quickly as possible. They arrived in Winniza on 9 December.

> Motorized march to the front! Destination, Stalino in the Donez Basin!

These two apparently bland-sounding sentences from the march orders contain much more in them than appears. The duration of the march was estimated at ten days. A rail transport of more than one thousand kilometres took five days. A ten-day road march covering 900 kilometres would average 90 kilometres per day. That was nothing out of the ordinary, when considered against central European standards. However, the motorized march of the vehicle column of the *Bataillon* across the barely 100 kilometres stretch between Berditschew and Winniza gave the officers and NCOs a foretaste of what they and their drivers could expect along the 900 kilometre-long trip to the front. The autumn rainy period had turned every road into soft soap. The word "road" was a far too-elevated term for field paths without any substructure. During summer they consisted of rutted, dark earthen, trampled paths, which, with their long, grey dust clouds, marked the march of the columns. One of those "roads" then became a single strip of mud, with many of the loops and dips as traces of stuck vehicles that had churned up the ground underneath. The mud held boots and wheels tight, creating difficulties for men and machines. And still, it continued to rain!

The *Bataillon* leadership, especially the technical officers and the maintenance personnel, made all possible preparations to overcome the unusual weather conditions facing the motorized march. Mats were created out of logs tied together with wire. They could be placed under the wheels if needed. An advance detachment proceeded ahead of the *Bataillon* to prepare accommodations and to obtain provisions and fuel.

On 10 December 1941 the *Bataillon* departed Winniza on its motorized march. It passed through Uman and arrived in Kirowograd on 13 December. Winter set in abruptly. There was strong frost during the night. It thawed during the day. Already on the stretch to Kirowograd, the groups had to get out of their vehicles numerous times and push their stuck vehicles. The Russian winter made its appearance with frost and would demand all the strength that the men had in them.

The *Bataillon* remained in a school in Kirowograd for several days. The men were kept busy with light duties and cleaning up their surroundings; they were impatient and wanted to get to the front. They disliked cleaning the area. The term "Finnish volunteer-cleaning *Bataillon*" made the rounds. Impatience resulted in help from the bottle. Alcohol was drunk to excess. During the late evening a row took place in the accommodations of *2. Kompanie* and a scuffle began. *Untersturmführer* Ertel, a platoon commander in the company, had all the men of *2. Kompanie* assemble in the large hall of the school and carried out rifle drill for an hour until all the hot heads cooled off. At the front of the great hall, in Cyrillic script, hung the slogan "proletariat of all countries unite!" The Finnish volunteers translated that into German as "night time cooling-off drill".

On 23 December the march finally continued into the Alexandrija area, and reached Dnjepropetrowsk on 24 December 1941.

The advance detachment and the *SS-Division "Wiking"* depot had prepared everything in Dnjepropetrowsk. The companies of the Finnish volunteer *Bataillon* were accommodated in the Museum of the Revolution.

It was Christmas Eve. The men of the *Bataillon* assembled in a room of the museum for a Christmas celebration. *Bataillon* commander Collani and the military chaplain, Kurkiala, gave a speech. Christmas songs were sung. The thoughts wandered briefly to the homeland, to Germany and to Finland. The glow of lights and the Christmas packages underscored the festivities of the evening.

Then a relaxed mood set in, accompanied by melancholy and gallows humour. Wine and alcohol passed down the many throats. A large oil painting showed the entrance of the Red Army into Viipuri. Angered, some of the Finns began to mutter. A larger than life statue of Stalin made of gypsum was wrestled to the edge of the steps and pushed down. Stalin broke into thousands of shards. The Finns were satisfied, their anger was sated.

The Christmas holidays were free from duties. The days following were filled with light service and work, the maintenance troops worked on repairing broken-down vehicles. Due to the extraordinary demands on work conditions, improvisation played a large role. The *2. Kompanie* had an especially large number of vehicles broken down, which in some cases had to be repaired in the maintenance vehicle depot in Dnjepropetrowsk.

In the meantime, the commander of *SS-Division "Wiking"*, *Generalmajor der Waffen-SS* Steiner, and the *Oberbefehlshaber* of *1. Panzerarmee*, *Generaloberst* von Kleist, were discussing where the *Bataillon* was to be deployed. Both were in agreement that the *Bataillon* should be deployed in a quiet sector so that it could acclimatize slowly.

On 28 December 1941, while in Dnjepropetrowsk, the *Bataillon* received its order from *1. Panzerarmee* to continue its march to Stalino. The *2. Kompanie* was transported by rail from Dnjepropetrowsk to Jassinowataja because of its extraordinary large number of vehicle breakdowns. Departure took place already on 28 December. The men began to experience the icy cold of the Russian winter in unheated rail cars. The company celebrated New Year's Eve in Jassinowataja with a lot of alcohol.

On 1 January 1942, *2. Kompanie* received its orders in Jassinowataja. It was to start its march to Rutschenkowo, where it would bivouac. The *Bataillon* started its march on 2 January, a crisp, frosty, and sunny day, at -20° C. However, after two hours, it was recalled to its previous accommodations.

On 3 January the final departure took place for Rutschenkowo, eight kilometres southwest of Stalino. It was still colder than on the day before. During the entire march, an icy wind blew constantly into their faces. Hoar frost formed on the head protectors near the mouth. Many men remained behind, exhausted during the 30 kilometre-long stretch of road. Some only arrived in Rutschenkowo, a mineworker's settlement, on the next day. The *2. Kompanie* was directed to their accommodations by the advance detachment. The other companies of the *Bataillon* were still on the motorized march. Their arrival could not be predicted.

On 29 December 1941 the remaining companies started their motorized march from Dnjepropetrowsk. When the *Bataillon* left Winniza the Russian "Rasputitza" was in full swing with rain and muddy, bottomless roads. The increasing frost and snow, as well as obtaining fuel, become the greatest difficulties. The vehicle breakdowns increased because of the extraordinary weather conditions. The *Bataillon* advanced only in a step-like fashion, in some cases literally, only step by step. Pushing was always the last resort. Day-long rest periods had to be instituted to permit the vehicles to be repaired and to wait for fuel. Finally, a teletype was sent to *1. Panzerarmee*, in which the difficulties were laid out in plain language:

> "The march is to be continued only once the road conditions allow it. The one possibility to get vehicles started under these weather conditions, by warming up the motors in a heated hall, is being

> considered. Columns with snow ploughs and teams of oxen are active on the roads. The total number of vehicles out of action on 6 January 1942: 49 trucks, 11 automobiles."

On 8 January 1942, while still on the march, the *Bataillon* was attached to *SS-Division* "*Wiking*" by *1. Panzerarmee.* A teletype with similar content informed the *Kommandoamt.*

The difficult march passed through Nowomoskowsk, Snamenka, Pawlograd, Petropolje, and Slawjanka. On 11 January 1942, 34 officers, and 786 NCOs and men, arrived in Rutschenkowo, near Stalino; 131 men still remained behind with broken-down vehicles. Later on, the stragglers also arrived at the *Bataillon.*

The *Bataillon* had accommodations in the mineworker's settlement of Rutschenkowo, which they had to share with the civilian population. By Soviet standards, the settlement was relatively modern. According to a standard building plan, two families shared a kitchen. Each family had a large room to themselves, for living and sleeping purposes. Civilians and soldiers crowded each other in the rooms because of the harsh winter outside. It was a nightmare to maintain sanitary conditions. Wooden outhouses stood in a long row behind the houses. Washing was a luxury.

Idleness can cause unpleasant situations. The men had to be kept busy. Specific times were designated for polishing, mending and weapon cleaning. Formal training was around noon.

On 12 January 1942 the *Bataillon* received an order from *SS-Division* "*Wiking*" with the following content:

> On 17/18 January 1942 the Finnish Volunteer-*Bataillon* of the *Waffen-SS* is to march, in two march groups, to Amwrosiewka and become the motorized reserve of the division. It is anticipated that the companies of the *Bataillon*, in turn, will be given opportunities to gain front-line experience. Only then will the *Bataillon*, as a whole, be assigned to a front-line sector.

On 16 January the *Bataillon* shuttled from Rutschenkowo to Amwrosiewka. Amwrosiewka was the supply, as well as the accommodation, base of the "*Wiking*". After long weeks of front-line deployment, the battalions and companies of "*Wiking*" were alternately resting and de-lousing in

Amwrosiewka. The men from the *Bataillon* moved into these prepared accommodations. One day later the commanding general of *XIV. Panzerkorps*, *General* von Wietersheim, to which "*Wiking*" was attached, inspected the accommodations of the *Bataillon* and mentioned the imminent front-line deployment.

While visiting the quarters of the *Bataillon* staff on 18 January, the commander of *SS-Division "Wiking"*, *Generalmajor der Waffen-SS* Steiner, informed *Sturmbannführer* Collani and his officers of his intention to deploy the *Bataillon* during the night of 22/23 January on the northern wing of *SS-Division "Wiking"*. The *Bataillon* was attached to *Regiment "Westland"* and was to relieve a mobile *Bataillon* from the Slovakian division deployed in that sector.

On 19 January at 1430 hours, *Generalmajor der Waffen-SS* Steiner spoke to the Finnish volunteers in Amwrosiewka's theatre hall and explained to them the meaning of their deployment against Bolshevism, which also threatened Finland. He then proceeded to the factual aspects of their front-line deployment and expressed the hope that this *Bataillon* would also contribute to this European battle, and also establish a link to the deeds of *Jägerbataillon Nr. 27.*

Generalmajor der Waffen-SS Steiner, creator of the first integrated European troop formation of the Second World War, the *SS-Division "Wiking"*, led his volunteer formation well in southern Russia, and had won the hearts of his volunteers from northern and western European countries. His whole attention was then on the total care for the unified *Bataillon* of Finnish volunteers. It is true that the formation had a cadre of German officers, but those were to be slowly replaced by suitable Finns, as they became trained and gained experience.

The men from the *Bataillon* sensed the care and comradeship that met them, from the division commander on down to the last rifleman, in the *SS-Division "Wiking"*. They had found a larger military home and, from the first day, saw the "*Wiking*" as their division.

First Combat Deployment

On 20 January1942, at the command post of *SS-Division "Wiking"* in Kalinowo, *Hauptsturmführer* Collani and his company commanders were familiarized with the *Bataillon*'s first defensive sector. The *Bataillon* was assigned an approximately three kilometre-wide sector southwest of Golodajewka. The right boundary was: Krynka loop one kilometre northwest Kalinowo – village centre Nowo Bachmutzkij – southern edge Tschemokosewa – Balka-Golubjatschij; with left boundary: southern edge Belojarowka – southern edge Ochowtschik Brook to where it enters the Mius River – northern edge Shelobak.

Artillery in this sector: *2./SS-Artillerie-Regiment 5*, *II./SS-Artillerie-Regiment 64* (light batteries), *IV./SS-Artillerie-Regiment 5*, and the heavy *Heer Artillerie-Abteilung 844*.

Attached to the *Bataillon* were one *sIG* and two *lIG* from *13./SS-Regiment* "*Westland*".

Opposite was the 31st Rifle Division of the 9th Soviet Army, with parts of the 75th Rifle Regiment and the 248th Rifle Regiment. The enemy behaved passively.

Additional results from the discussion:

> The reserve company was to occupy quarters in Bischlerowka. It was assigned *2./Heeres-Pionier-Bataillon 60* to help with the construction of field fortifications. The *Bataillon* command post was in Nowo Bachmutzkij. The deployment of the *Bataillon* was to be as follows:
>
> Two companies with two platoons each (8 MG) in the foremost line. The remaining two platoons were to remain as the corresponding company reserve.

Relief:

1. In platoon formations within the companies;
2. In company formations within the *Bataillon*. Each company was to spend 20 days in the foremost position and rest 10 days in Bischlerowka.

> A sled column was to be organized to supply the positional companies. One *Zug* from *SS-Flak-Abteilung 5* would provide air defence in Nowo Bachmutzkij.
>
> The company and platoon leaders were to be guided into their positions at 1500 hours by Slovakian unit commanders. The position was good and provided a good view. It was positioned on the western

rim of the Mius flood plain. Field construction left something to be desired. The unit commanders were already having thoughts about it on the way back to Amwrosiewka.

On 21 January 1942 the companies of the volunteer *Bataillon* departed from their accommodations in Amwrosiewka. The *Bataillon* was moved in a motorized march as follows:

1. *Kompanie* with attached sMG *Zug* of *4. Kompanie* to Olchowskij;
3. *Kompanie* with attached sMG *Zug* to Nowo Bachmutzkij;
2. *Kompanie* with attached sMG *Zug* to Bischlerowka (reserve)

The trains of *1.* and *3. Kompanie* remained in the named places, while *2. Kompanie* was in Bischlerowka. The Finns immediately began the construction of saunas, the Finnish "fountain of youth"; their march route could be followed by the construction of their saunas.

Toward the evening of 21 January 1942, the positional companies moved into their designated sectors; the *3. Kompanie* into the right *Bataillon* sector, the *1. Kompanie* into the left sector. The men were loaded down with weapons and equipment. As daylight faded, they were guided through the trenches by their company and platoon leaders. German, Finnish, and Slovakian words, and field-grey and earth-brown uniforms marked the relief, which proceeded smoothly. The Slovaks shuffled their way back through the trenches. The Finns were alone, finally in the foremost front-line. Some of them were posted in front at listening posts, eavesdropping on the enemy. Strained nerves, thoughts, and feelings tested each soldier.

During the next few days the *Bataillon* sector was relatively quiet, an excellent situation to familiarize a young formation, without combat experience, with life at the front. Nonetheless, a day at the front is not as quiet as one might assume. A day at the front brings about many happenings of local importance to the platoons, the companies, and the *Bataillon*. To eventually recognize, and then frustrate, the intentions of the enemy, it was important to always be vigilant, and keep an eye and ear on the enemy. Although it is seldom mentioned in the large scheme of things, it did happen that sometimes large operations started out from the smallest of incidents, coincidences, or combat patrol evaluations.

During the morning hours of 23 January the pickets in the trench, at the front with the machineguns, observed a Russian soldier moving unobtrusively toward the Finnish positions.

They were wide awake and readied their weapons. But when the Russian made himself noticeable and raised his hands the pickets knew that they were dealing with a Russian defector. The Red Army soldier was captured and brought to the rear for interrogation.

One more event shook up the Finns on that day: The Finn, Onni Martikainen, from the *3. Kompanie* was killed by a sniper's bullet. He was the first soldier to be killed from the *Bataillon*.

The commander of *SS-Regiment "Westland"*, *SS-Brigadeführer* Phleps, known as Stolz, discussed with *Sturmbannführer* Collani the additional construction of field positions. On the next day, 25 January, Phleps showed up again at the *Bataillon* command post in Nowo Bachmutzkij to say farewell. Phleps returned to his home in Siebenbürgen to establish the *SS-Division "Prinz Eugen"* from *Volksdeutschen* Romanians. Phleps was already a general in the Romanian army and was the creator of the Romanian mountain troops. *Obersturmbannführer* Maack took over command of *SS-Regiment "Westland"*.

The positional companies gave special attention to the enemy-occupied villages of Golodajewka and Skeljanskij facing them. Skeljanskij was the sensitive spot in relation to the Finn's position. It was a long, stretched-out village, with single farm houses surrounded by fruit orchards, and was located in the low-lying terrain on the western side of the Mius River. Skeljanskij was occupied by parts of II./248th Rifle Regiment of the 31st Russian Rifle Division. However, the main Russian position lay on the eastern side of the Mius.

On 26 January, *Hauptscharführer* Eggers, platoon leader of *3. Kompanie*, was killed during a reconnaissance mission in Skeljanskij. German artillery fired harassing fire into the village after the return of the reconnaissance patrol.

On 27 January, during a heavy snow storm, Russian forces penetrated into Berestowo at the *I./"Westland"* and were thrown back across the Mius again. There was another attempt at a penetration on 30 January, somewhat farther south. That raised the alarm status for the *Bataillon* but *SS-Regiment "Westland"* dealt with the crisis on its own.

The hard Russian winter, with its alternating severe frost and snow storms, made living and fighting extremely difficult. The German field army was insufficiently equipped with practical winter clothing. The winter clothing, collected during special donation drives in the Reich, only arrived at the front when the winter was over. The men in the positions helped themselves. They wore Russian padded jackets and felt boots, as well as Russian fur hats. Self-preservation pushed aside all formalities. Hour-long guard duty in extreme cold or snow storms required a large amount of willpower. Tiny bunkers hacked into the earth, heated by home-made stoves from barrels or ammunition containers, were the accommodations for many days at the front. There was no washing or shaving for days. Sometimes, there was no change of clothes for weeks. Underwear and sweaters were full of lice. It is hard to describe what the frontline soldier had to endure and suffer during the first Russian winter. Added to that was the constant need for battle readiness.

During the last days of January enemy movements increased in the Golodajewka area. Golodajewka was occupied by the Soviet 75th Rifle Regiment. A combat patrol on Golodajewka was ordered by *Bataillon* to obtain some clarification regarding enemy movements.

The Finnish *Untersturmführer* Ingerö, a platoon leader in *1. Kompanie*, was chosen to carry out the combat patrol with his platoon. From their observations in their positions, Ingerö and his men created a profile of the Russian position with respect to Russian habits, guard rotation, and inspections by their officers. They memorized the minefields and free lanes, the wire barriers and the good crossings over the frozen Mius River.

Everything was ready by 28 January. Combat Patrol Ingerö, with machine pistols, pistols and plenty of hand grenades, advanced into the position on the left wing of *1. Kompanie*. A discussion with the groups in position took place as to how, when, and where the combat patrol would be going. The weapons were checked once more. Any unnecessary equipment that could have restricted the movements of the combat patrol was left behind.

It was past midnight, 29 January 1942 had already started. The clear star-spangled sky was a dim, midnight blue. There was some hissing and whispering among the men. Combat Patrol Ingerö crept into no-man's land. It slid silently down the slope from its position. Unnoticed, it passed by the Russian forward post on the right, on the western side

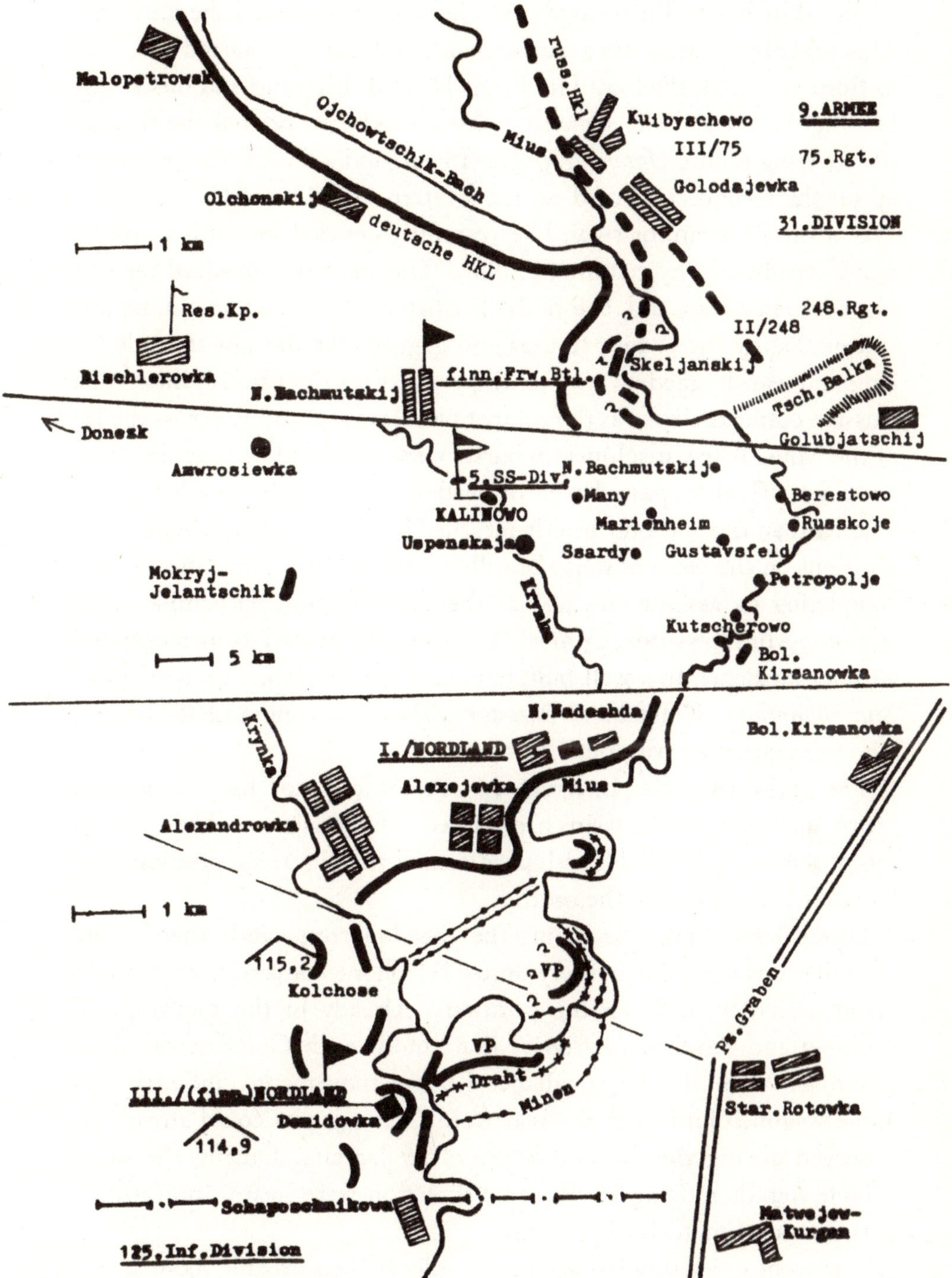

Winter position on the Mius, 1941/4.

of the Mius River. Then singly, cat-like, the men crossed the ice of the Mius and disappeared into a fruit orchard. Golodajewka started to appear in front as a dark shadow. The Finns lay still, listening and observing. Hissing, barely audible, *Unterscharführer* Kukkosen briefed the men of the covering group. *Untersturmführer* Ingerö and a few of his men snuck up on the recognized guard on the western outskirts of Golodajewka. Was it one Russian, or two? They carefully crawled forward, metre by metre, centimetre by centimetre. Now! The shadows advanced rapidly, like tigers in a leap, and, before the Russian could make a sound, he was surrounded by three, four figures and gagged. He did not struggle for long and was dragged away; a daring coup along the Finnish lines. The Russian outposts awoke as the combat patrol was returning across the ice of the Mius. A few machinegun bursts were sent in the wrong direction and a few rifle shots passed over the heads of the returning combat patrol. The Russian fire was only briefly returned by German weapons from the positions on the western range of hills near the Mius. After successfully completing its assignment, just as the new day rose with milky veils from the Mius lowlands, Combat Patrol Ingerö reached its own outposts without incidents. In a well-built bunker of *1. Kompanie* command post, *Sturmbannführer* Collani and *Obersturmführer* Hoy congratulated Ingerö, who subsequently gave a detailed report.

The prisoner was interrogated. According to his statements, approximately 1,000 Russians had arrived at Golodajewka, They were to attack the German and Finnish positions, or the Slovakian positions, the battalion's neighbour to the north.

Discussions took place in the headquarters and there were consultations with the artillery units. Telephone conversations brought about activities in the firing positions. Already in the morning, all German and Slovakian batteries that could reach Golodajewka fired in unison onto the large village. Enemy movements, infantry and panje wagon columns, to the rear from Golodajewka could already be observed during the evening hours of 29 January. During the night vehicle sounds moving in the same direction were heard, indicating a withdrawal of motorized vehicles.

The front quieted down again, but snipers then became more active. On 1 February, snipers located in Skeljanskij wounded two men from *1. Kompanie.* The Finns were trying to figure out how to eliminate them.

On 3 February the *Chef* of *2. Kompanie*, *Obersturmführer* Pallesche, was transferred to headquarters of *SS-Regiment "Westland"*. He turned the company over to *Obersturmführer* Ladau, a Finn.

In the meantime, a reorganization and a strengthening of the formations of *1. Panzerarmee* was also taking place on the southern sector of the front. It was the same at the *XIV. Panzerkorps*, to which *SS-Division "Wiking"* was attached. Replacements arrived. One by one, the *Panzer* divisions were withdrawn from the front and sent to the rear to be re-equipped with new tanks and vehicles. The entire German front was in a constant movement of relief and exchange. This went on within the *Armee*, the *Armeekorps*, and even within the divisions. As part of that process, and with agreement from *SS-FHA*, *SS-Division "Wiking"* was considering incorporating the Finnish volunteer *Bataillon* into *SS-Regiment "Nordland"*.

In November, having been forced to retreat, the *XIV. Panzerkorps* under *General* von Wietersheim occupied the Mius position on the northern wing of *1. Panzerarmee*. The *1. Gebirgsdivision* arrived at Dimitrowka (12 kilometres north of Golodajewka). The Mius front between Malopetrowskij and Skeljanskij was occupied by the mobile Slovak division, some of whose officers had already served in the Austrian K.u.K. army. The *SS-Division "Wiking"* took over the Skeljanskij-Alexejewka sector. Initially, the *16. Panzerdivision* was its southern neighbour. *General* von Mackensen's *III. Panzerkorps* defended the right wing on the Sea of Azov. That is how it looked up to the beginning of the reorganization of the German formations.

Let us now have a retrospective look of the movements within *SS-Division "Wiking"* up to that point:

As a result of the withdrawal movement into the Mius position, *SS-Regiment "Germania"* was in position at Berestowo on the northern wing of the division, *SS-Regiment "Nordland"* was in the centre at Kutscherowo, and *SS-Regiment "Westland"* was at Alexejewka. Each regiment had only about half of its personnel complement. Soviet attacks and the Russian winter forced the mixing of the battalions because every available soldier was slotted into the defence. The *I./"Germania"* even had to intervene outside the divisional boundaries. It had to help defend against a Russian assault on Dnjepropetrowsk from the Isjum area. The Soviets intended to surround *1. Panzerarmee* from the north.

In the process, *Bataillon Dieckmann* was completely burned out. As part of the reorganization, on 13 February 1942 the Slovak mobile division was withdrawn from both sides of Malopetrowskij. The northern sector was taken over by *I./SS-Regiment "Nordland"*, the southern sector by *II./SS-Regiment "Nordland"*. At the southern sector, near Olchowskij, the *Bataillon* had to take over an additional frontal width of two battalions from the Slovaks, which made it necessary to deploy the reserve company in the foremost frontline. The other regiments of "*Wiking*" were also assigned wider sectors. Without any interruptions, the relief took place in the old, well-tried manner.

The *Bataillon* departed from *SS-Regiment "Westland"* on 16 February 1942 and became attached to *SS-Regiment "Nordland"*. The anticipated command incorporation was thereby concluded. The left neighbour consisted of volunteers of *II./"Nordland"*, Germans, Danes, and Norwegians.

The commander of *SS-Regiment "Nordland"* inspected the positions of the Finns for the first time on 18 February. *Oberführer* von Scholz, already as a young officer highly decorated for bravery during the First World War with the Austrian K.u.K. army, someone who proved to be a wise and prominent troop leader during the Russian summer campaign of 1941, soon won the greatest of confidence from the Finns. Being uncomplicated and warm-hearted, in no time he won the hearts of the Finnish volunteers. Collaboration with Collani was excellent from the first day on.

The 18 February was a clear winter day, flying weather. Russian reconnaissance aircraft dared to approach the German *HKL*. Infantry fire greeted them. Late in the afternoon, seventeen machines overflew the front near Skeljanskij and Olchowskij and dropped leaflets urging German soldiers to defect.

On 19 February the *7./"Nordland"* relieved the battalion's *1. Kompanie* in the Olchowskij sector. As a result, the approximately seven kilometre-wide *Bataillon* sector again became smaller. The regiment designated the projecting overhang east of Olchowskij as the new left boundary, which was to be occupied by the Finns. The Russian had penetrated there once against the Slovaks.

The Skeljanskij-Golodajewka sector has already been described. North of there ran the *HKL* on the raised edges of the Ojchowtschik brook. Between the brook and the Mius was a good observable flood plain. The Russian positions were located on the ridge east of the Mius. Both sides pushed listening posts forward into no-man's land, which constantly changed their positions because the beaten paths were regularly mined.

During the following days enemy reconnaissance and combat patrols, as well as movements in the hinterland, increased along the entire divisional sector. The occupation of the German *HKL* was reinforced during the nights.

On 22 February the *Bataillon* had losses from artillery and sniper fire. At 1600 hours civilians ran out of Skeljanskij, 3 men, 17 women, and 23 children, and entered the Finnish lines. The first air raid started at 1900 hours on Nowo Bachmutzkij and was followed by others; 59 bombs fell. Thanks to good air protection, the *Bataillon* had only one wounded.

Skeljanskij, a critical point in the *HKL*, a stronghold of Russian snipers, a thorn in the eyes of the Finns. Skeljanskij, an inconspicuous village with spread-out single dwellings and orchards, located in no-man's land between the two main battle lines. It appeared quiet, deserted to the casual observer. But it hid treachery and deceit; the Russians had occupied it with advanced battle outposts, which the casual observer was unable to see. However, the Finnish observers were able to see any change in the village from their positions on the western ridge. During long hours of observation the keen eye notices changes in roof tiles, of ruins, and shrubbery. Powerful binoculars bring the changes closer to the eye and bring certainty that here or there a sniper has taken up a new position; even changing his position daily does not help him much.

At different times on 23 February, three Finnish reconnaissance patrols left toward Skeljanskij, guarded and protected by their comrades on the ridge. Skeljanskij, as it turned out, was more heavily occupied by the enemy than first thought. The last reconnaissance patrol left during evening twilight. The Russian were apparently in the process of carrying out a relief. Their inattentiveness supported the Finnish endeavour.

Lightning fast, a concentrated charge of hand grenades into an enemy occupied house was followed by a mighty detonation. Screams mixed with shots. The reconnaissance patrol returned without any losses. Another reconnaissance patrol was sent to Skeljanskij during the early morning of the next day. It snuck up using Finnish tactics. A different house was the target. A lightning fast entry; "Hands up-come along-quickly, quickly!" The Finns returned with four Red Army men.

They stated that the concentrated charge on the previous day killed five men and that a whole company had taken flight. A Russian battalion was then located in a small area in Skeljanskij. The Russians anticipated a German attack on Skeljanskij due to the increased reconnaissance activities and evacuated the village. They bombed Skeljanskij on the assumption that it was occupied by German-Finnish forces. When nothing then happened the Russians reoccupied the village on 25 February. The Finns had another soldier killed on 26 February by one of the snipers located in the northern part of Skeljanskij.

On the evening of 26 February a Russian loudspeaker blared music and a speech in Slovakian from the Golodajewka area. After 13 days the Russians still had not noticed that the Slovaks had been relieved.

During the past February and most of March, from both sides, there was alternating artillery fire, mortar fire, reconnaissance activity, and then the mutual deployment of snipers. Positions were improved. Skeljanskij, that nest of snipers, made its way again into the considerations of our own planners. A combat patrol had to teach the Russians a lesson they would not forget so easily.

A Finnish reconnaissance patrol reconnoitred a path for a combat patrol on 25 March at 0300 hours. The results of the reconnaissance patrol were evaluated at 1100 hours at the *Bataillon* command post in Nowo Bachmutzkij and the deployment of the new combat patrol was discussed with all participating unit commanders, including the artillery. *Untersturmführer* Ingerö, platoon leader of *1. Kompanie*, would again lead the combat patrol.

Ingerö assembled his men and explained their assignment and its execution. There was very little time available for preparations. Combat Patrol Ingerö departed at 2240 hours. There was a heightened degree of alertness, even in the positions on the ridge. Everything was still quiet at midnight. The witching hour started.

The first hour of 26 March had passed. Ingerö and his men had penetrated into the northern part of Skeljanskij. Explosions suddenly tore apart the eerie silence of the night. Russian anti-personnel mines blew up, killed one and wounded two of Ingerö's men. That woke everyone up! And then everything happened very rapidly: concentrated charges were thrown into two houses that were full of Russians. There were screams of those hit, shouts in Russian and Finnish. Everywhere, dark shadows were jumping around like ghosts. Machine pistols rattled, pistol and rifle shots whipped through the night. Hand grenades boomed like drum beats. The Russians, having overcome the moment of shock, defended themselves, and wanted to capture the Finnish combat patrol. One Finn was killed in hand-to-hand fighting, three others were wounded more lightly. Ingerö left last, having covered the withdrawal of his combat patrol.

Untersturmführer Ingerö reported the return of his combat patrol to the *Bataillon* commander at 0430 hours, *Sturmbannführer* Collani, who was already waiting for him in the position. Ingerö reported that two occupied houses were destroyed with concentrated charges, whereby it was estimated that twenty Russians were killed. Ingerö also reported his own losses. Two dead, one in hand-to-hand fighting and one from a Russian anti-personnel mine, and five wounded; which was a high price. All the dead and wounded were brought back.

Hours later, the Finnish *Obersturmführer* Ladau, *Chef* of *2. Kompanie*, was wounded in his own position by a surprise Russian artillery barrage. *Untersturmführer* Ertel took over the company on the orders of *Bataillon* but had to leave the position on the same day due to a lung infection. Ertel waited in the well-built company command bunker for the *Spieß*, who brought up the meals with a panje sled during the evening. Ertel had a high temperature and, to distract himself, played with young cats, which were running around the command post. Finally, the *Spieß* arrived with the meals.

Ertel climbed onto the sled and wrapped himself in blankets. The trip to the rear started but it soon became apparent that the small panje horses were so exhausted that they were unable to pull the light sled through the deep snow. Ertel was forced to get off and stumble behind the sled with a temperature of 40°C.

He was completely exhausted when he arrived in Nowo Bachmutzkij. Ertel spent three weeks in sickbay in Nowo Bachmutzkij, looked after by the *Bataillon* doctor, *Obersturmführer* Dr. Bumke, and Dr. Necker, before he was finally able to be transported to the field hospital in Mokryj Jelantschik. Those, by the way, were the stations for all sick and wounded of the *Bataillon*.

The effectiveness of the combat patrol against Skeljanskij can be judged by the fact that there were 19 defectors during the following few days.

During the following days and weeks it remained relatively quiet on the Finnish sector of the front. The Finns were eager for new action with the beginning of spring, coming after the hard winter that had demanded everything of them. Preparations were made for new offensives on both sides of the Mius. The rest and refitting of the divisions of *1. Panzerarmee* and the associated re-organization of positions continued.

On 22 April, regimental *Adjutant*, *Obersturmführer* Hans Meyer, brought the initial orders for the withdrawal of the *Bataillon* from the frontline and its possible future deployment. *SS-Regiment "Nordland"* was to take over the Alexejewka sector, with the "*Wiking*" expanding its frontal sector to the south, and thereby relieving parts of *16. Panzerdivision*.

At 2100 hours on 25 April 1942, the *Bataillon* was relieved in the Olchowskij-Skeljanskij sector by the *I./Schützenregiment 20* of the mobile Slovakian division. One after the other, the relieved sections were transported by the battalion's *MTW* (*Mannschaftstransportwagen*, personnel transports) to Many, where the last ones arrived on 26 April. After a few hours of rest, preparations for new deployment began to fill the day. By the late afternoon, the *Bataillon* was once again ready to march.

Frontline Sector Demidowka

The *Bataillon* assembled in Many. On 26 April 1942, after a few hours of rest and the replenishing of weapons, equipment, and ammunition, the *1.*, *3.*, and *4. Kompanien* were driven in *MTW* to Alexandrowka. Relieved last, the *2. Kompanie* followed a day later. In the meantime, the company and platoon leaders were briefed on the new sector. The companies went into position during the evening and relieved *II./Schützenregiment 64* of *16. Panzerdivision* in the Demidowka sector. At 2130 hours, *Sturmbannführer* Collani reported the completion of the relief operation to *SS-Regiment "Nordland"* in Alexandrowka.

The new *Bataillon* sector was characterized by the Mius loop. The right boundary, also the division boundary, proceeded along the northern outskirts of Schaposchnikowa. The right neighbour was the Württemberg *125. Infanterie-Division*, which had the jumping weasel as its tactical sign. The left boundary was formed by the Krynka River south of Alexandrowka. The left neighbour was *I./"Nordland"*.

The Mius River, which gave its name to the most southerly position of the German *Ostfront*, flowed in the *Bataillon* sector from the northeast and changed its path toward the south after the Krynka flowed into it south of Alexandrowka, and finally flowed into the Sea of Azov at Taganrog.

The new positions of the *Bataillon* were located on Hill 115.2 and Hill 114.9, which were a part of a hilly ridge west of the Mius, running parallel to the river. One part in the northern *Bataillon* sector was located on an easterly raised river bank, which blocked the Mius loop that penetrated deeply into the German front.

Fruit orchards located in the Mius valley near Alexandrowka, especially cherry trees, bloomed with wasteful splendour, and attracted the first bees and bumble-bees. Days later the valley was a sea of blossoms which made one temporarily forget the war for. Sprouting and blooming nature, the beginning of spring with its bright colours of the life force, let the memories of the dark and cold days of the Russian winter fade. All soldiers who experienced the first winter of the war in Russia were issued the medal "*Winterschlacht Osten 1941–42*". The broad red ribbon with its narrow black and the two narrow white stripes was to be recognition for surviving the deprivations and dangers, for the lack of many things and the sacrifice of health. That ribbon could not better express the numerous crises of the previous winter as this sentence:

> The red of the medal ribbon stands for Ivan, the black is the *Rollbahn*, and the white, that is we!

The command post of the Finnish volunteer *Bataillon* was located in a farmer's house in the centre of Demidowka. An observation post on the floor of the attic was constantly occupied. The already good overview became even better through a scissor telescope, permitting all enemy movements far into the hinterland to be recognized. Right beside the command post was a large communal cold storage cellar.

The regulations, demanding that the civilian population had to be evacuated from the battlefield and only the work force needed by the troops be allowed to remain, was in the main interpreted in a generous manner in Demidowka. Therefore, there were still women, old men, and even children in the village. They were employed as help with the field kitchens; they washed the clothing of the soldiers, heated the sauna and looked after cattle and fowl. Civilians that were directly employed by the companies were also listed on their ration lists and received the same rations as the troops.

There was constant work on improving the positions. A contest: "Who has the best camouflaged and best bomb-proof accommodations?" was started. New bunkers came into existence, one as a *Bataillon* command post. Everyone who arrived at the command post had to do some digging. The commander, *Adjutant*, and *Ordonnanzoffiziere* were of course also busy at work. Even the two caretakers, Lyda and Clava had things to do. The new bunker even had a door handle. The bunker was officially dedicated on 15 June 1942, the one year anniversary of the *Bataillon's* existence. Plenty of alcohol flowed and even a battery assigned to the *Bataillon* fired a celebratory volley, probably from its "black" reserve.

The Demidowka frontal sector was quiet. Only on the roads in the enemy hinterland was lively traffic observed. Defectors stated that there were three Russian regiments in front of the *Bataillon* sector but nobody was able to say what their intentions were. As a precautionary measure, *Sturmbannführer* Collani discussed additional defensive measures with his company and platoon leaders. The lively enemy air activity was very noticeable. Did the Russians fear a German offensive from this sector?

For example, the war diary of the *Bataillon* notes for 2 May 1942:

> 35 horse drawn carts, eight trucks, and three armoured-like vehicles were observed driving in the direction of the Rotowka settlement. In addition, there was lively traffic toward Matwejew-Kurgan, as well as on the road connecting M.-Kurgan with Stara Rotowka, including messengers on horses. Enemy reconnaissance patrols are checking out our own frontline.

On 12 May 1942, by order of the regiment, the *4. Kompanie* of the *Bataillon* was disbanded as part of the re-organization of the regiments and battalions of the German field army. The platoons from the machinegun company entered the rifle companies as the fourth (heavy) platoons. In addition to the four sMG (two sMG *Gruppen*) was also added a 8 cm mortar *Gruppe* with two mortars. The organizational structure permitted easier supply and tighter command. Under the previous organization the platoons of the machinegun company were greatly dispersed and supplying them was made correspondingly more difficult. The re-organization was completed by 15 May.

Simultaneously with the disbanding of the machinegun company, a new heavy company was formed, consisting of a *Pionier-Zug*, a 5 cm *Pak-Zug*, a *lIG-Zug*, and a communications platoon. The cadre for those platoons came from the corresponding specialist units. Finnish replacements were used to bring the unit up to strength. *Hauptsturmführer* Brückner took over the new heavy company on 4 July.

On 16 May, the Finnish General Talvela (successor to *Oberst* Horn) and a small retinue arrived at the *Bataillon* command post in Demidowka, where they were greeted heartily by *Sturmbannführer* Collani. Talvela had a look at the positions, spoke with his countrymen, and then went to the reserve company in Alexandrowka. There, he looked at the accommodations, the sickbay, the sauna, and the laundry facilities. Everywhere, there was openness, mutual affection, co-operation and fellowship. In a farewell speech the high-ranking guest acknowledged the high standard of training and the enthusiastic attitude of the *Bataillon*. On behalf of the *Bataillon*, *Sturmbannführer* Collani thanked him for the honour and promised that the men of the *Bataillon* would fulfill all the expectations. The *Bataillon* was the symbolic expression of Finnish-German comradeship-in-arms, as well as a connection to the traditions of *Jägerbataillon Nr. 27* during the First World War.

Smaller formations, such as *Bataillone*, which were usually attached to larger formations only limited by time, were too often given the most difficult assignments and regularly became "cannon fodder". For that reason, *Generalmajor* Steiner always made a great effort to attach such small units firmly to a regiment. Those concepts were finally carried out by the *SS-Kommandoamt* with the order from 23 May 1942: The Finnish volunteer *Bataillon* became the *III.(finnisches)/SS-Freiwilligen-Panzergrenadier-Regiment "Nordland"* and, simultaneously, the companies were redesignated as the *9.* (previously *1. Kompanie*), *10.*, *11.*, and *12. Kompanie* etc. *SS-Regiment "Nordland"* then had again three *Bataillone*. With the addition of a *Panzerabteilung*, the *"Wiking"* became officially *5. SS-Freiwilligen-Panzergrenadierdivision "Wiking"*.

At the same time, the previous *SS-Regimenter* became *SS-Freiwilligen-Panzergrenadierregimenter.*

From then on, the *Bataillon* was known to the men of "*Wiking*" simply as the "Finnish *Bataillon*", and everyone knew which unit was referred to. Mockers, and even some of the Finns themselves, named the *Bataillon* "nearly independent" *Bataillon*, while "Finnish" remained in brackets in the official designation, and the Finnish lion, symbol of the Finns, was surrounded by the tactical regimental sign. Some Finns considered the incorporation of their *Bataillon* as surrendering some of their independence.

In the meantime, the reserve company carried out regular training behind the heights by the Mius River. Special stress was placed on working together with the heavy weapons. During quiet periods, even the companies positioned in the frontline carried out training behind the heights and only left small defensive forces in their positions.

A new offensive was being prepared on the German side. There was also something happening with the Russians. Both sides kept an eye on each other and small actions were responded to with counteractions. It is understandable that, with increased reconnaissance activity and combat patrols, the Russians made every effort to find out as early as possible the intentions of the Germans so that they could frustrate them. During the night 20/21 May 1942, a Russian combat patrol, in company strength, was recognized in time by *I./"Nordland"* and was repelled. The Russians left behind 25 dead, as well as a mine detector (there was a minefield in front of the position) and numerous weapons. Prisoners stated that the combat patrol had the assignment to create unrest in the German front and to bring back prisoners so that they could draw some conclusions from their interrogations. The highest alert was then ordered by regiment. For such purposes, the Russians had formed combat patrols consisting of young, battle experienced soldiers, who were then deployed in various locations. That was probably done because most of the Red Army men were not up to such challenges, or were too tired of war.

At 0200 hours on 3 June, the *Chef* of *10. Kompanie*, *Obersturmführer* Hilker, reported by telephone to *Bataillon* the sounds of battle and explosions of mines at the battle outposts, and the presence of a 5-man enemy reconnaissance patrol on the banks of the Mius River. At 0210 hours Hilker added more details to the first message, namely that three enemy reconnaissance patrols had appeared at the battle outposts in front of the Mius loop; one ran onto mines, the others were just being driven off by fire. A Russian remained lying within the mine barrier and was brought in. *Obersturmführer* Hilker, called "Bobby", was a well-known pentathlon athlete before the war. He led his company with calm and circumspection.

The company was then in the left sector of the *Bataillon*. The main position of the *Bataillon* was west of the Mius, while the company command post was in a Kolhoz on the Demidowka-Alexandrowka road. There was a strong outpost on the eastern heights by the great Mius loop. It was the repeated target of Russian reconnaissance and combat patrols. But the Finns were alert and parried every attempt at penetration. On the left, along the same line, but west of the river, was an outpost of *3./"Nordland"* (*I. Bataillon*).

In the name of the *Bataillon*, and in solidarity of the Finnish volunteers with their homeland and with the Finnish supreme commander *Feldmarshall* Mannerheim, *Sturmbannführer* Collani sent a telegram to Mannerheim, wishing him well on his birthday on 3 June. On 14 June the *Feldmarshall* thanked them appropriately in a return telegram.

The *Bataillon* celebrated one year of its existence on 15 June 1942. In an order of the day the regimental commanders and *Sturmbannführer* Collani honoured the achievements and the deployment of the *Bataillon*. The daily orders ended with the expectations that the *Bataillon* would also loyally fulfil its assignments in the future. As already mentioned, the new command bunker was dedicated.

The testing of the German front continued. On 17 June, at approximately 2100 hours, a 30-man strong combat patrol was recognized in front of the right *Bataillon* sector. It was driven off with heavy defensive fire.

And again the outpost position: On 2 July, at approximately 1000 hours, *Sturmbannführer* Collani, who just happened to be at the outpost, recognized three Red Army men in front of the wire obstacle. Collani shouted to them. They threw away their weapons and surrendered. One day later, toward morning, an enemy reconnaissance troop triggered a flare barrier. The outpost pickets answered with fire. The Russian reconnaissance troop withdrew.

Our artillery fired daily the usual harassing fire. On 25 June one battery fired so-called "Goebbel's shells" at Stara Rotowka. The shells, made out of cardboard, burst open upon impact and released leaflets that urged soldiers to defect.

The Russians, with the employment of civilians, had dug an antitank ditch during the winter and spring. The mighty undertaking with pick axes, shovels, and spades began at the outskirts of Stalino and ended at Taganrog. Who could count the curses, the blisters on the hands, the many drops of sweat? Who could even guess how many thousands of cubic metres of earth were moved by hand?

The Finnish volunteers saw that antitank ditch grow daily. It could be quite easily identified in front of their position, running from Matwejew-Kurgan to settlement No. 3.

The attack of the northern wing of *Heeresgruppe Süd* began on 28 June 1942, in the direction of Woronesch, but did not develop the way that the German high command had anticipated. Time pressed and became short, if the large operational goals of 1942 were to be achieved. They were clearly defined: Stalingrad with the lower Volga area and the Caucasus with its oil fields. On 13 July, *1. Panzerarmee* received the order to attack Rostov as part of the Caucasus offensive and to open the Don crossings for the assault to the south.

As part of the framework of the German *V. Armeekorps* (Wetzel), which was located in the front on the lower Mius, and has located going from south to north the *298.*, *73.*, and *125. Infanterie-Division*, which were supposed to create the first gaps. *General* Kirchner's *LVII. Panzerkorps* (both *Armeekorps* were combined into *Armeegruppe* Ruoff) was brought up to follow through, with the "*Wiking*" also being attached to it.

On the basis of those plans and the fact that the front at Isjum had already started to move, the *125. Infanterie-Division* had to take over part of the "*Wiking*" sector. On 8 July, the "*weasel*" division, with parts of *Grenadierregiment 419*, took over the right sector of *III.(finnisches)/SS-Freiwilligen-Panzergrenadier-Regiment* (*10. Kompanie*), and on 13 July the remainder of the frontline. *Bataillon* Collani transfered to Mokryj Jelantschik to rest. The other *Bataillone* of *Regiment* "*Nordland*" prepared in Alexandrowka and Alexejewka for the new offensive.

It became apparent that a substantial part of "*Wiking*" was not ready for deployment at the beginning of the Caucasus offensive because it lacked many motor vehicles and had to wait on the Mius until the new vehicles arrived from the homeland. That applied to the entire *SS-Regiment*

"*Westland*" and for the *III./SS-Regiment* "*Nordland*" and *III./SS-Regiment* "*Germania*". From 16 to 19 July, the *III.(finnisches)/*"*Nordland*" turned over its vehicles to *I.* and *II. Bataillon*, which were to participate in the attack on Rostov.

The *III.(finnisches)/*"*Nordland*" made themselves comfortable for a long stay in Mokryj Jelantschik. The impatience of the young Finns grew. *Sturmbannführer* Collani declared a three week training program. There was hope that the *Bataillon* would then rejoin the *Regiment*.

Mokryj Jelantschik

From 13 July to 10 August 1942 the *III.(finnisches) Bataillon* of *SS-Freiwilligen-Panzergrenadier-Regiment* "*Nordland*" was stationed in Mokryj Jelantschik. The first days were taken up with repairing weapons and equipment. Specialists had their training improved in special courses to deepen their skills and knowledge. Courses were provided for *Pioniere*, communications personnel, and messengers. The latter were intensively trained in map reading, skills with the compass, and how to orientate in terrain, even during the night under the most difficult of conditions. Driving schools trained replacement drivers, and the designated drivers had technical training, and were given practical hints with respect to motors and vehicles.

The platoons and companies practiced battle drill, which peaked with company and *Bataillon* exercises. The special training on the 5 cm *Pak*, the light infantry howitzer, as radio and telephone operators, and as *pioniere*, continued and concluded with formation exercises.

Hauptsturmführer Brückner, in 1941 the *Chef* of *1./*"*Nordland*", commanded since 4 July 1942 the newly-created *12.* (heavy) *Kompanie*. He was at the same time the deputy *Bataillon* commander. He soon won the respect and affection of his subordinates of the new twelfth, as he did with the old *1./*"*Nordland*", addressed their concerns and needs, and helped to find remedies. During a live fire exercise of his heavy weapons, *Hauptsturmführer* Brückner was severely wounded on 1 August 1942 by a round landing short and later died in the field hospital. The heavy company was later taken over by *Hauptsturmführer* Ladau, a Finn, who had recovered from wounds that he suffered on 26 March.

The Russian summer showed its best side in Mokryj Jelantschik. There was plenty of free time and time for sports. The regiment's musical platoon played music. Mokryj Jelantschik was a beautiful village, located in the low lands of a brook by the same name, surrounded by gentle hills. Mokryj means "moist" in Russian. The Finnish volunteers had a good and warm relationship with the locals. The volunteers sat with the women and girls during the beautiful summer evenings on benches in front of the houses, gossiping and singing.

Hygiene and bodily care were a top priority. Inoculations and health services were supervised by the medical officers, Dr. Bumke and Dr. Necker. The *Bataillon* dentist, Dr. Franke, examined teeth and fixed the bad ones. And of course, there was a Finnish sauna in Mokryj Jelantschik.

At the beginning of August, during a number of large exercises, the *Bataillon* trained using all weapons and communications equipment that it had under its command. That concluded the training.

Reports arrived daily from the Caucasus front, keeping the *Bataillon* informed about the fighting and progress of *SS-Regiment* "*Nordland*" and Division "*Wiking*". Of course all the volunteers in Mokryj Jelantschik were feverishly waiting for new deployments. As more and more vehicles started to arrive from the homeland vehicle parks at the beginning of August, deployment became more certain.

On 8 August 1942, the Finnish *Bataillon* had again available 78 trucks, four "Steyr" and four "Krupp" vehicles as prime movers for the heavy platoons of *12. Kompanie*, one Kfz. 17 "Mercedes" commander's vehicle and nine "Opel-Kadett" cars for staff and trains leaders. The trucks were "Mercedes" and "Klöckner-Humboldt-Deutz-Diesel" types.

On 9 August the *Bataillon* received the order from regiment to move up into the Maikop area. The day was one of hustle and bustle. Vehicles, weapons, and equipment were gotten ready and loaded. And then it was farewell from the local population. There were some hidden tears in the shiny eyes of girls as once more melancholic Russian and Finnish songs were sung during the evening; songs of home, songs of love, of Erika and Lilli Marlen.

Caucasus and the Maikop area

The lower Volga with Stalingrad and the Caucasus oil were the triggering objectives for the German 1942 summer offensive. The Allied supply convoys going through Iran were to be cut off as part of the mission.

Harry Hopkins negotiated with Stalin, on behalf of Roosevelt, over the Allied lend-lease deliveries. During those discussions it was decided to open a second transport route, in addition to the the Arctic Ocean route, and send transports through Iran, which would have to be occupied for those purposes. The British Prime Minister Churchill justified those steps with the sentence:

> "The laws are silent during war."

On 25 August 1941 two British and three Russian divisions marched into Iran and conquered the country after four days of fighting. With that, the second supply route for Allied aid was created.

During 1942, after the route was opened, approximately 30% of total deliveries to the Soviet Union passed through Iran. In 1943 it was 1,606,979 tonnes, representing 33.5% of the aid. It is quite understandable that one of the German goals, in addition to capturing the Caucasus oil fields, was to shut off that flow of materiel.

The main goal, however, was the capture of the Caucasus oil fields and the important fertile food growing Kuban area. Oil was the magical product that mesmerized Hitler and his entourage. Without oil and its derivatives, such as gasoline, no tank or aircraft motor would run. Oil, processed right on the spot, eliminated the long supply routes and made the gigantic supply system superfluous. The bold dreams went even farther: In a great oil pincer, the entire Black Sea area and Asia Minor were to come under German hegemony. The northern arm of the pincers was to come across the Caucasus and the southern one through Africa/Egypt, where the German *Afrika Korps* (Rommel) was, and penetrate into the oil regions of the Near East.

The operational goals for 1942 were laid down in "*Fall Blau*" (case blue) and Directive Nr. 41 of 5 April 1942: Advance east into the Kalatsch area. Form a pocket in the Oskol area and smash the main Russian forces of the southern front. Then have the main German forces swing to the south into the Caucasus under an offensive screening operation at Stalingrad and the lower Volga.

The attack on Woronesh (first phase of "*Blau*") fell behind schedule due to strong Russian resistance and threw the operational plan into turmoil. The results from the pocket did not bring the hoped for results. Hitler and the *Oberbefehlshaber* of *Heeresgruppe Süd*, *Feldmarschall* von Bock, had increasing differences of opinion over operational control. On 7 July 1942 *Heeresgruppe Süd* was divided into *Heeresgruppe* A and *Heeresgruppe* B. *Feldmarschall* von Bock had to leave. *Feldmarschall* List took over *Heeresgruppe* A and *Generaloberst* von Weichs took over *Heeresgruppe* B.

The operational plan was changed on 13 July but, as was discovered later, it still did not enable the Germans to capture and smash the main Russian forces before their withdrawal to the east and south.

Hitler believed that the Russians were "finished" in the south and, instead of keeping it in the south, where he would need it desperately, sent the *11. Armee* from the Crimea to Leningrad. Hitler dictated his Directive Nr. 45 on 23 July 1942 at his "*Wehrwolf*" headquarters in the forests near Winniza. As the first task for *Heeresgruppe* A, the directive assigned it to surround the escaping Russian formations east and south of Rostov and to smash them. Under points 2. and 3. were listed the additional tasks for *Heeresgruppe* A:

> 2. After the destruction of the enemy forces south of the Don, the most important assignment for *Heeresgruppe* A is to occupy the whole east coast of the Black-Sea, and thereby eliminate the enemy Black Sea fleet and the Black Sea harbours...With an additional force, in which all remaining *Gebirgs* and *Jäger* Divisions are combined, a crossing is to be forced over the Kuban, and the mountainous areas of Maikop and Armawir are to be occupied...
>
> 3. At the same time, the area around Grosny is to be captured with an armed force to be created from mobile units, and partial forces are to block the Ossetian and Grusinian military road in the mountain passes. Subsequently, the area around Baku is to be occupied by advancing along the Caspian Sea...The *Heeresgruppe* can count on later being reinforced by the Italian Alpini corps (which was marching toward Stalingrad – comment by the author).
>
> These operations by *Heeresgruppe* A received the cover name '*Edelweiß*'.
>
> 4. In addition to building up the Don defences during the advance on Stalingrad, *Heeresgruppe* B is assigned the task, as ordered, to also smash the armed forces in the area, occupy the city itself, and block the land bridge between the Volga and the Don.

In conjunction with this, mobile forces are to advance along the Volga with the task of advancing to Astrakhan and there block the main arm of the Volga.

These operations by *Heeresgruppe* B received the cover name *'Fischreiher'* (heron)...

The basic premises of that fateful Directive Nr. 45 were soon challenged by the *Oberbefehlshaber* of *Heeresgruppe* A, *Feldmarschall* List. List, born in 1880 in Oberkirch, Baden, (already a first general staff officer during the First World War, at its end he was the *Wehrmachtsbefehlshaber Südost*, and then was briefly transferred to Scandinavia), was an experienced soldier and army commander. He did not understand many of Hitler's orders and soon recognized that his *Heeresgruppe* was given tasks and goals way beyond the ability of the troops of *1. Panzerarmee* and *17. Armee* to carry out.

The underestimation of the Russian enemy by Hitler, and the overestimation of German capabilities in dealing with two very far apart goals at right angles to one another (Stalingrad-Caucasus), led to the result that none of the large operational goals were achieved. The German *Ostheer* got into, up to then, its most severe crisis, which led to the beginning of the total military defeat of Germany.

The stormy advance led the *5. SS-Freiwilligen-Panzergrenadierdivision "Wiking"*, as part of *LVII. Panzerkorps* (*"Wiking"* and the mobile Slovakian division) of *General der Panzertruppen* Kirchner, through Rostov, to the gate of the Caucasus, through Kuban, Ladau and Bjelaja into the foothills of the Caucasus Mountains, the Greater Caucasus. There, natural limits applied to a *Panzergrenadierdivision* like *"Wiking"*. Armour and motorized vehicles can only operate in a limited fashion. Nonetheless, *Heeresgruppe* ordered *LVII. Panzerkorps*, with the *"Wiking"* at its head, to make the city of Tuapse on the Black Sea its goal. After a step-wise fighting retreat from river barrier to river barrier, the Russian resistance increased significantly in the Krasnodor-Maikop area. There, good defensive positions were available and the Russians knew how to use them. Resistance became even more effective when the Russians brought up rested and newly-established formations.

During a situation conference on 10 August 1942 in Kurtschewskaja, the commander of *XXXXIX. Gebirgskorps*, *General* Konrad, made the following suggestions to *Oberbefehlshaber* of *Heeresgruppe* A, *Feldmarschall* List:

To remain close on the heels of the enemy with *SS-Division "Wiking"* and to advance as far as possible on the mountain road to Tuapse to possibly capture the rail and road crossings over the Goitsch pass from the march, thereby making room for the following mountain troops before the enemy could establish a strong defence.

Following the directive, *SS-Division "Wiking"*, at the head of *LVII. Panzerkorps*, forced an entry into the Greater Caucasus on 11 August 1942 at Beloretschenskaja. Simultaneously, 30 kilometres farther southeast, the *13. Panzerdivision* (Herr) at the head of *III. Panzerkorps* (von Mackensen) penetrated into the Greater Caucasus at Maikop.

With that, *SS-Division "Wiking"* was on a broad mountainous front and was forced to use all of its resources to cover the flanks of a rough, unclear terrain. At that time *III. (finnisches)/SS-Freiwilligen-Panzergrenadier-Regiment "Nordland"* arrived at the division.

In the meantime, *III. (finnisches)/SS-Freiwilligen-Panzergrenadier-Regiment "Nordland"*, which had recently received its vehicles, and *SS-Regiment "Westland"* were brought up from the Mius area. The *III. (finnisches)/"Nordland"* departed Mokryj Jelantschik on 10 August 1942 at 0300 hours; practically along the same route that the rest of the division had taken before it. It was noon in Rostov. The pontoon bridge over the Don was crossed, as was the long dam through the meadows of Bataisk. The *Bataillon* reached Kagalnizkaja at 1730 hours and bivouaced there. The march was approximately 240 kilometres long.

The trip continued on 11 August. After an early start from Kagalnizkaja, the *Bataillon* passed through the granary of the Kuban region. With sweat-soaked dusty faces, in shimmering sun, heat and endless dust clouds, the troops marched through the vast region during a beautiful summer. In the evening, accommodations were taken up in Nowo Alexandrowka, north of Armawir. The distance covered that day was 240 kilometres.

On 11 August, its third day of marching, the *Bataillon* crossed the Kuban River over the military bridge built by *III. Panzerkorps* at Armawir. The Kuban flows broad and leisurely across a region that bears its name. It originates in the 5,600 metre high Elbrus massif of the Caucasus Mountains, flows for 907 kilometres, and empties into the Sea of Azov. The Kuban Cossacks lived on its banks.

The *Bataillon* reached the oil city of Maikop through Armawir and drove parallel to the Bjelaja River, through Chanskaja, to Beloretschenskaja. The march lasted 150 kilometres. The *Bataillon* made its quarters in a forested area near Beloretschenskaja, readied for battle, and waited for deployment orders from the division.

The planning of the attack across the passes of the Caucasus Mountains rested on the work done by the *Militär-Geographische Bearbeitung* works of the German *Hochgebirgsschule* (high mountain school) Fulpmes of the mountain troops, abbreviated: *Mil.Geo.-Bearbeitung*. The study described all of the mountain passes and identified them by number. Number 1 was the coastal road by the Black Sea from Noworossisk to Batum, number 2 was the Maikop-Tuapse road, number 3 was the Maikop-Kurdshinskaja-Tuby Pass, and number 4 was the Maikop-Dachowskaja-Adler road. The *Mil.Geo.-Bearbeitung* relied on Russian geographic literature, which in part stemmed from the Czar's time, from statements by those knowledgeable about the region, and prisoners. Regarding number 2, Maikop-Tuapse, we read the following:

> Approximately 190 kilometres. In good condition, is constantly maintained. Uniform descent to Tuapse. At some places a gradient of over 10%. Good cover. Few curves up to Apscheronskaja. Fuel station nine kilometres southwest of Tuapse and in Apscheronskaja. Many curves 90 kilometres southwest of Tuapse. Construction material available (forest).

The use of roads number 3 and 4 appeared problematic right from the beginning, according to *Mil.Geo.-Bearbeitung*. In spite of that, the *XXXXIV. Jägerkorps* (de Angelis), after closing up to *III. Panzerkorps* in the Maikop area, was directed there. Each division received "its pass". That meant scattering of the German forces.

On 12 August, the day during which the Finnish *Bataillon* closed up to "*Wiking*" at Beloretschenskaja, the division strove with two assault groups, one in the Pschisch valley and one in the Pschecha valley, toward Chadyschenskaja and Apscheronskaja.

As well, one *kampfgruppe* from *16. Infanterie-Division* (motorized) was advancing on road number 2 from Maikop to Chadyschenskaja. *Regiment "Nordland"* advanced along the Pschisch valley as far south as

Twerskaja. *Regiment* "*Germania*" reached the area south of Kubanskaja in the Pschecha valley. The *16. Infanterie-Division* (mot.) was also unable to advance as far as Chadyschenskaja; due to heavy fighting, it remained hung up in the oil region of Neftegorsk.

It then became obvious that the enemy and the fighting conditions for our own troops had been underestimated. For combat purposes, the terrain there, with forested mountains and narrow valleys, poor, curving roads and impenetrable rhododendron bushes, did not justify the deployment of a *Panzergrenadierdivision*.

Nonetheless, the corps demanded the continued advance of "*Wiking*", with the initial goal being Chadyschenskaja and the oil wells in the Neftegorsk-Neftjanaja area. Following on foot, were the oil specialists. They were to get the oil wells functioning again immediately, as part of the overall plan. The terrible fighting terrain and the long open flank placed impossible tasks in front of "*Wiking*" that, as it turned out later, could not be solved by bringing up regiment "*Westland*" and the *III. (finnisches)/"Nordland"*.

The *Bataillon* commander, Collani, sent his *1. Ordonnanzoffizier*, *Untersturmführer* Ertel, ahead to the division command post to report the approach of the Finnish *Bataillon*. He arrived just as the command staff was moving, and was ordered by *General* Steiner to bring up the Finnish *Bataillon* immediately.

During the evening of 12 August 1942, in Beloretschenskaja the *III. (finnisches)/"Nordland"* received its deployment orders for 13 August: the *Bataillon* is to move to Komsomolzkaja and defend the division command post. The *Bataillon* is attached to *Regiment* "*Westland*" for that purpose…

On 13 August, the *III. (finnisches)/"Nordland"* arrived in Komsomolzkaja already at 0700 hours, and immediately set up defences. Komsomolzkaja, basically a group of houses on the Beloretschenskaja-Chadyschenskaja rail line clustered around a railroad station of the same name, was an important rail node because the rail line from the Neftegorsk-Neftjanaja (Neft=oil) oil region entered the main rail line there. Strong enemy artillery and mortar fire was landing on Komsomolzkaja. The *Chef* of *10./"Nordland"*, *Obersturmführer* Gilker, and the *Chef* of *11. Kompanie*, *Hauptsturmführer* Schnabel, were killed during one of those sudden barrages. It was a painful loss for the Finnish *Bataillon*. The *10. Kompanie* was taken over by *Obersturmführer* Porsch, the eleventh by *Untersturmführer* Lüttgens.

In the meantime, *I.* and *II./"Nordland"* continued to advance farther south in the Pschisch Valley. The *III. Bataillon* was brought up. During the evening it reached the village of Twerskaja, which it defended together with *I. Bataillon*. The Finns brought in 46 prisoners after some local skirmishes.

One day later, at 0515 hours on 14 August, *III. (finnisches)/"Nordland"* also took over the sector of *I. Bataillon*. For the defence of Twerskaja, the *Bataillon* was given the support of one 21 cm *Mörser* battery and one cannon battery of a *Korps-Artillerie-Abteilung* under *Oberst* Roßmann.

In the meantime, *I.* and *II./"Nordland"* continued to advance farther south in the Pschisch Valley. After capturing Kabardinskaja, the lead elements reached the oil region of Muk, where the oil fields and refineries were burning. *Regiment "Germania"*, as the most easterly group of *"Wiking"*, reached Apscheronskaja in the Pschecha Valley. With that, the *"Wiking"* was in two places next to road number 2, the build-up Maikop-Tuapse mountain road. The flanks had become even longer and more open. *Regiment "Westland"* was brought up to cover the left flank of *Regiment "Germania"* and deployed itself. By noon the long right flank of *Regiment "Nordland"* in the Sacharow area was covered toward Lineinaja by *11./"Nordland"*. More forces were not available there. The right flank of *"Wiking"* and that of *Regiment "Nordland"* were especially threatened because the 17th Kuban Cossack Cavalry Corps was assembling in the Lineinaja area. This corps, a number of times the enemy of *"Wiking"*, most recently at the Bjelaja crossing and during the attack on Pschechskaja, had been renamed the IV Kuban Cossack Guards Cavalry Corps as appreciation for its good defensive fighting while covering the main Russian forces during their withdrawal from the Jeja sector to the area west of Maikop. Its two cavalry divisions were correspondingly renamed. In consideration of the situation, and the previous assignment to penetrate to road number 2 in the direction of Tuapse, the leadership of *"Wiking"* hoped for *XXXXIV. Jägerkorps* to close up. It was still two days of marching distant. The *101. Jägerdivision* of *Generalmajor* Diestel closed up to *"Wiking"* while *97. Jägerdivision* of *Generalleutnant* Rupp closed up to *13. Panzerdivision* in the area south of Maikop. The two *Jägerdivisionen*, equipped and trained for mountain warfare, each one somewhat in the middle between a mountain and an infantry division, consisted of two *Jägerregiments* and one artillery regiment as well as divisional formations, were to be deployed in the expected *schwerpunkt* sectors at the Goitsch and Tuby passes.

On 15 August, *Regiment "Nordland"* prepared for the attack on Chadyschenskaja, *Regiment "Germania"* for an attack on Apscheronskaja and the oil region of Neftjanaja.

For the *"Nordland"* to attack Chadyschenskaja, it first had to capture the mountain ridge west of Muk and the railroad tunnel below it to eliminate the threat from the right flank by an identified Russian armoured train, which could advance at any time and threaten the supply line of the regiment. The attack on the railroad tunnel, on the Beloretschenskaja-Tuapse section of the rail line, was to be carried out by *III. (finnisches)/"Nordland"*. Southwest of Muk, the company commanders were briefed by *Sturmbannführer* Collani on their sectors and the attack plans.

On 15 August *III. (finnisches)/"Nordland"* was in defensive sectors near Sacharow and Kabardinskaja, the *9. Kompanie* at Muk. On that day it was determined that the threat from the right flank, the Lineinaja area, had to be eliminated first before the attack by *Regiment "Nordland"* could continue. In the left divisional sector, cleaning up actions by *"Germania"* and *"Westland"* against dispersed enemy forces were unavoidable. The front of the *"Wiking"* was expanding even more. Fortunately, the *Jägerdivisionen* of *XXXXIV. Jägerkorps* arrived on that day.

From the Württemberg *101. Jägerdivision* (a drawn bow and arrow as its divisional insignia), *Jägerregiment 228* moved into *"Nordland"* sector and *Jägerregiment 229* into the *"Germania"* sector. The *97. Jägerdivision* (the partridge cock feather division) moved into the sector of *13. Panzerdivision.*

The Slovakian mobile division on the right of *"Wiking"* was closing up too slowly. *Generalmajor der Waffen-SS* Steiner and his 1st General Staff officer, *Sturmbannführer* Reichel, no longer counted on the Slovaks. Farther to the right the *V. Armeekorps* (Wetzel) had already advanced as far as Gorjatschij-Klutsch with its *198. Infanterie-Division*, and was sending flank security elements in the direction of *"Wiking"*. Between the two divisions was the battle-capable IVth Kuban Cossack Guards Cavalry Corps.

The farther advance of *"Wiking"* to the south was cancelled. The *XXXXIV. Jägerkorps* was to continue. In corps order No. 108, which had the addition "to advance to the Black Sea coast", it stated:

> *XXXXIV. Jägerkorps*, departing from the Beloretschenskaja-Maikop area, is to advance through the line Kabardinskaja-Chadyschenskaja-Ssamurskaja-Dachowskaja, and capture the Tuapse-Adler coastal sector.

The defence of the flank, and the mountainous forested area in between, was assigned to *SS-Division "Wiking"*. Division ordered the cleaning up of the Lineinaja crisis area as part of the operation. On 15 August 1942, at 2300 hours, the regimental order from "*Nordland*" arrived for *III. (finnisches)*/"*Nordland*" to attack Lineinaja on the next day. The *Bataillon* was to line up directly behind the *Panzerabteilung* of *Sturmbannführer* Mühlenkamp.

16 August 1942, 0330 hours: A new day arose from the dark of the forested mountain and from the foggy river valleys. Far in the east the sun was rising with red, blazing rays from dark clouds over the snow covered, glistening mountains of the mountain ridge. In a motorized march, *Bataillon Collani* travelled from Muk and Kabardinskaja, back along its arrival route, and turned off between Kabardinskaja and Twerskaja to the west. There, after a discussion of the attack plan, it assumed its attack position, along with *Panzerabteilung "Wiking"* coming from Twerskaja. The *9. Kompanie* coming from Muk mounted the tanks at 0710 hours: "*Panzer marsch*!"

The tanks, with their mounted *Panzergrenadiere*, drove in combat formation along a forest road toward Lineinaja; securing, halting, observing, onward. The *10. Kompanie* was also brought up at 0730 hours to provide march security.

Suddenly, the appearance of a large clearing gave a clear view of Lineinaja, which lies on the western edge of the open plain. Mühlenkamp's tanks lined up in battle formation. Then the tank attack broke over enemy occupied Lineinaja like a sudden thunderstorm. On the tanks, and between the rapidly moving tanks, ran the Finnish volunteers from *Obersturmführer* Hoy's *9. Kompanie*. *Panzerjäger* and the light infantry howitzer platoon of *12. Kompanie* moved up quickly. In the process, *Obersturmführer* Reus, platoon leader of *lIG-Zug* and simultaneously commander of the heavy company, was killed. Further casualties from the Finnish assault group included two *Unterscharführer* killed, and seven wounded. Enemy resistance was broken by 1030 hours and Lineinaja was in our hands. The Russian cavalry corps withdrew into the forests toward the southwest. *Sturmbannführer* Collani arrived in Lineinaja with his *Adjutant*, *Obersturmführer* Hirt, and the *1. Ordonnanzoffizier*, *Untersturmführer* Ertel. The *9. Kompanie* sent out security elements. *Obersturmführer* Hirt interrogated Russian prisoners. The regimental commander, *Oberführer* von Scholz, arrived already by noon in Lineinaja to congratulate *Sturmbannführer* Collani on his successful attack.

General Steiner wrote the following about the attack on Lineinaja:

> The Finns attack with unbelievable élan, supported by two companies of tanks. Lying flat on the tanks, they tackle an enemy cavalry brigade in the Lineinaja village and throw themselves on them with machine pistols and Puukkos (Finnish knife in a leather sheath), just as they did in their Finnish forests. The enemy flees in panic toward the west.[4]

The *11. Kompanie* was brought up at 1130 hours and combed the woods southwest of Lineinaja, whereby a number of prisoners were brought in. However, that strip of woods remained an insecure sector.

At 1500 hours the woods were combed again. Skirmishes with dispersed enemy soldiers took place. *Untersturmführer* Lüttgens, the commander of *11. Kompanie*, was killed in the process. More Russian prisoners were brought in. *Obersturmführer* Mühlinghaus took over *11. Kompanie.*

During the battle for Lineinaja the Finns captured the following: Two Russian 4.7 cm *Pak*, two *Ratch-Bumm* 7.62 cm, five mortars, two trucks, numerous hand-held weapons, and a large number of horses. It turned out that the bulk of the Russian cavalry corps was able to withdraw into the dense wooded area to the southwest. That was confirmed by an air reconnaissance report during the evening; according to it, approximately one hundred vehicles and numerous riders escaped to the southwest.

At 1700 hours *Oberführer* von Scholz briefed the *Bataillon* and company commanders in Lineinaja on *Regiment "Nordland's"* situation and on the general situation at large. With the attack on Lineinaja the attacks by "*Wiking*" in the central Caucasus stopped for the time being. The *XXXXIV. Jägerkorps* continued its advance. The advance of *Generaloberst*

4. Steiner, Felix "Die Freiwilligen", Plesse-Verlag Göttingen 1958; page 158.

von Kleist's *1. Panzerarmee* in the eastern Caucasus oil region of Grosny had come to a halt. The *III. Panzerkorps* was transferred from the Maikop area to the Terek to get the offensive moving again. As part of that process "*Wiking*" had to take over the greatest part of *13. Panzerdivision's* sector south of Maikop. As a result, it had a 60 kilometre-wide sector to cover. Due to a lack of personnel, that long frontage could only be covered in a strong-point fashion; mainly the river valleys, the road intersections, and the villages. The phrases "all around defence" and "*Igel*" (hedgehog) were starting to make their appearance in directives and orders.

Before the mobile Slovakian division could close up, *Regiment "Nordland"*, on the right wing of "*Wiking*", had to master some crises. The Finnish *Bataillon* was positioned on the open flank at Lineinaja. The *11. Kompanie*, securing the left wing of the *Bataillon*, was given the assignment of making contact with *II./"Nordland"* (Stoffers), which was stationed west of Kabardinskaja. The contact reconnaissance troops of *11. Kompanie* passed through dense mountain forests, across mountains, and dark valleys. Orientation was difficult. The Finns proved themselves to be woodsmen, hunters and stalkers, like at home in their Finnish forests. Contact was made on 17 August, but the three kilometre-wide gap to *II./"Nordland"* still remained to the enemy like a wide open barn door.

On 18 August, on the outermost left wing of the Finnish *Bataillon*, near Kura Zize, 41 Red Army soldiers from the 15th Rifle Division (regiments 25, 33, and 43) defected; a day later they were followed by another 43.

The Slovaks finally arrived on 19 August. At approximately 1300 hours, a Finnish reconnaissance troop established contact with the 20th Slovakian Infantry Regiment in Apschaskaja. At 1400 hours, a reconnaissance troop reconnoitering Suchaja Zize (northwest of Kura Zize) found that it was occupied by the enemy. Until evening 13 Red Army soldiers from the 11th Rifle Division and the 15th Rifle Division defected to the Finnish defenders; on the following day it was another 24. With that, the number of prisoners and defectors rose to 150 since the attack on Lineinaja.

A contact reconnaissance troop, leaving in the morning of 22 August from Lineinaja to the mobile Slovakian division, determined that the western part of Suchaja Zize was occupied by the Slovaks and the eastern part by the Russians.

On 24 August 1942 a *Bataillon* of the mobile Slovakian division took over the defensive sector of *III. (finnisches)/"Nordland"*. The *9.* and *11. Kompanie* left their positions. *Obersturmführer* Porsch remained with his *10. Kompanie* in Lineinaja as security. The company reorganized and occupied with strong defences mainly the roads leading into Lineinaja from the west. Lineinaja provided additional security to the road system that went in a southerly direction in the Pschisch Valley. With the Slovaks closing up, the right flank of "*Wiking*" became shorter, but by no means any safer.

On the morning of 25 August, *III. (finnisches)/"Nordland"* transferred to Kabardinskaja and relieved the *I. Bataillon* (Polewacz) positioned on the eastern flank of the regiment in the defence.

Both sides checked on each other daily with reconnaissance patrols. On 29 August a Finnish reconnaissance patrol determined that the Wjeselij farm, approximately five kilometres southwest of Kabardinskaja, was occupied by the enemy, and in the process two prisoners were brought back. During the day 10 Red Army soldiers defected to the Finns. A detailed enemy picture emerged from the interrogations. The Russian 32nd Infantry Division (regiments 80, 82, and 85) had been in front of the Kabardinskaja defensive sector for the previous five days. There was an assembly position in Tuapse, which collected the dispersed soldiers, created new formations from them, and immediately sent them to the front.

The Russians had overcome the shock of the sudden withdrawal from the Rostov area through the Kuban Steppe to the forested Caucasus. With the entering of the forested Caucasus, good defensive possibilities became available. They were utilized by small but determined units willing to fight under the command of energetic and spirited commissars and officers. STAWKA, the Russian supreme command, the Central Committee of the communist party of the Soviet Union, and local party leaders intervened vigorously and combated withdrawal moods and war weariness with drastic measures. The Caucasus defence was reorganized; from 1 September on, command was tightened and reorganized through the creation of the "Transcaucasian Front" with the "North Group" on the Terek and the "Black Sea Group" at Maikop and Noworossisk. The "Black Sea Group" of the "Transcaucasian Front" was commanded by General I. J. Petrow, who had defended the Crimea. Forward of Tuapse,

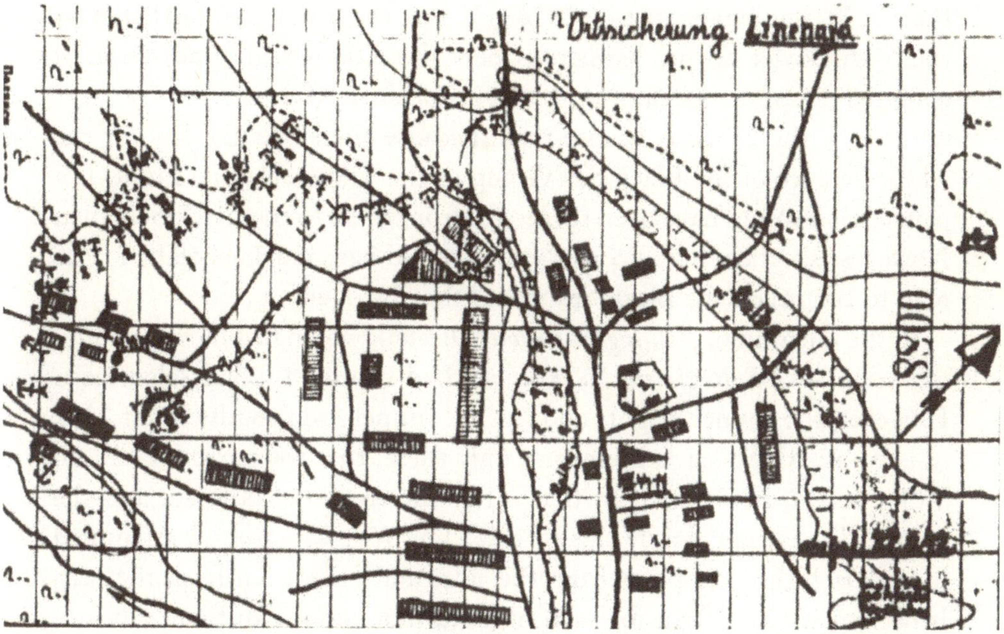

Defence of the village of Lineinaja after the battle of 16 August 1942 Sketch from the war diary.

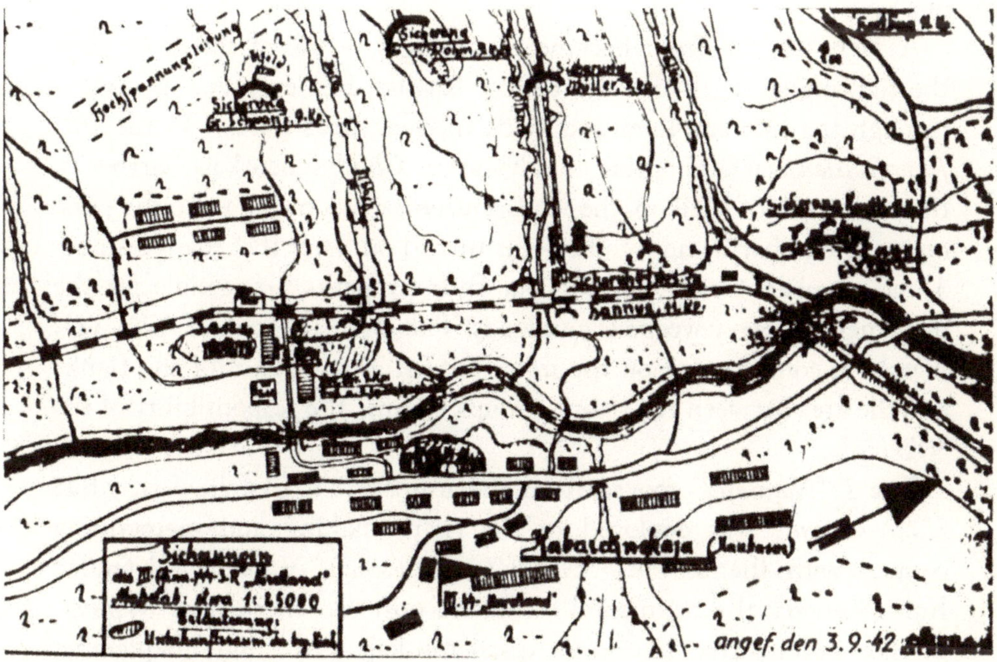

Position sketch from the war diary of the defences near Kabardinskaja.

that is, in the battle area of "*Wiking*", was the 18th, and farther west the 56th Soviet Army. Numerous new formations had appeared as if conjured out of the ground. Both sides concentrated their efforts on road number 2, the Maikop-Tuapse road, because there was the key for the whole defence of the Black Sea Group of the Transcaucasian Front. If a penetration would have been successful from there to the Black Sea, then Noworossisk, the western corner stone, would have inevitably fallen. The road to Batum on the Black Sea would then be open.

In the meantime, *101. Jägerdivision* (Diestel), which had moved up into the sector of *SS-Regiment "Nordland"*, had captured Chadyschenskaja. However, the tunnel heights and the rail tunnel itself southwest of Muk resisted all attacks. It is there, and only there, that the narrow Pschisch Valley had to be entered. In that valley the river, the railroad, and the road to Tuapse ran closely side by side. The *101. Jägerdivision* attempted to approach that key point from the sides and take it out from the rear. It became a bitter fight for each hill and mountain, a difficult advance over mountains and through valleys, through swampy river meadows and tangled mountain forests. In small groups, the Wurttemberg *Jäger* chewed their way into the Russian-dominated areas like the front teeth of a saw.

As a result, the front became even longer, while at the same time the fighting strength was decreasing. Russian battle groups infiltrated through the German lines and made the rear areas unsafe. While *101. Jägerdivision* was attempting to advance at Chadyschenskaja, farther to the east, south of Maikop, the *97. Jägerdivision* was trying to do the same on roads number 3 and number 4. It turned out later that roads number 3 and number 4 were nothing but swampy paths, impossible for the movement of heavy weapons and loads! The *Jägerdivisionen* of *XXXXIV. Jägerkorps* concentrated on the *schwerpunkte*. The defence of the flanks and the area between the assault groups became the responsibility of the "*Wiking*".

The *I./"Nordland"* moved from Kabardinskaja to Asfaltowaja, while *II./"Nordland"* was deployed to the right, making and maintaining contact with the Slovaks. The *III. (finnisches)/"Nordland"* defended Kabardinskaja; the regimental command post was there. The "*Wiking*" division headquarters moved to Apscheronskaja. On 7 and 8 September *SS-Regiment "Germania"* relieved parts of *97. Jägerdivision* in the

Neftjanaja-Neftegorsk area. The *97. Jägerdivision* moved closer to road number 2 while *SS-Regiment "Westland"* took over its left sector at Kmennomostkaja.

The front could only be defended in strong-point fashion. The *schwerpunkte* were more heavily defended. Supplies had to be brought forward under escort because ambushes took place all the time in the overgrown, forested mountains. Battle-capable units, many times in company strength, had to establish contact daily because motorcycle troops in *Gruppen* strength had been massacred. The fighting in that area was cunning and treacherous.

As part of the increased vigilance, in addition to defending Kabardinskaja, *III. (finnisches)/"Nordland"* also had to block the western entrances into the mountain village. The *9. Kompanie* (Hoy) was employed for that task.

On 1 September, in addition to the defences of *11. Kompanie* (Mühlinghaus) next to the northwestern edge of Kabardinskaja, the three rifle platoons from *9. Kompanie* were pushed far to the west for added security. *Blocking Group Müller*, reinforced by sMGs, defended the Wjeselij-Kabardinskaja road into the river valley.

The blocking group of *Untersturmführer* Dohm occupied Hill 226 on the mountain ridge between the two brooks (oil brooks) which flowed into the Pschisch near Kabardinskaja. A heavy mortar group from the heavy platoon of the company was also there. *Blocking Group Schwarz* occupied the high ridge left of *Gruppe Dohm* and secured the supply route running along there for *I.*/"Nordland". There was radio contact with the advanced blocking groups.

The men from the blocking groups fulfilled a very important task. Observing and being constantly battle-ready was standard routine. Having free time and long hours of guard duty, as well as maintaining weapons and improving the position, were the norm.

The Russians became more active during the first days of September. Reorganization and tighter command control under the newly-created "Black Sea Group of the Transcaucasian Front" became more noticeable. A Russian reconnaissance troop showed up at *Blocking Group Müller*; four Red Army men from the 68th Brigade were captured.

The *10. Kompanie* defending Lineinaja reported the supply route to the Slovakian division becoming unsafe, as well as an attack on *II./"Nordland"* defending to the southwest of there. The Russians approached to within 100 metres of the Slovakian division west of Lineinaja and dug in.

The Russian air force also became active again. There were two air raids on Kabardinskaja and one on Lineinaja on 5 September. Bombs were dropped and four men were wounded at the Finnish command post at Kabardinskaja. The German supply routes were made unsafe by bombing attacks and partisans.

On 9 September a contact reconnaissance troop from *10. Kompanie*, which had remained for the defence of Lineinaja when the *Bataillon* withdrew, made it to the left neighbour, *II./"Nordland"*, while another reconnoitred toward Apschaskaja. The *11. Kompanie* marched to Apscheronskaja to be at the disposal of the division commander.

Following thorough artillery and Stuka preparations, the *101. Jägerdivision* repeatedly attacked the railroad tunnel and the hill above it. It was impossible to crack the Russian key position, neither on 18 nor on 28 August. From now on, the tunnel height is only referred to as "hell height". It fell to renewed, reorganized German *Jäger* formations on 28 September.

During September 1942, it became clear that the decisive breakthrough along the Pschisch Valley to Tuapse was not going to be accomplished by *XXXXIV. Jägerkorps* without reinforcements. The *XXXXIX. Gebirgskorps*, positioned at the high mountain passes of the Caucasus, had to give up half of *1. Gebirgsdivision* as well as half of *4. Gebirgsdivision*. After reorganization and the formation of a new *schwerpunkt*, these forces, combined as *Division Lanz*, renewed the attack on Tuapse with the support from *XXXXIV. Jägerkorps* . After the onset of winter the high mountain passes were held by weak forces of the *Gebirgsjäger-Korps*.

There was also no advance on the Terek. The river, together with the bare mountain region behind it, form a mighty barrier, which protects the Grosny oil region. There too, the dispersed, retreating Russian troops were reorganized and placed under the new, tighter command of the "Northern Group of the Transcaucasian Front". *General* Ott's *LII. Armeekorps* had come to a halt at Mosdok. It is there that *SS-Division "Wiking"* was to get the attack on Grosny going again. The hours that *"Wiking"* had left in the western Caucasus were numbered. The eastern Caucasus was waiting.

On 15 September, at 1200 hours, the defensive positions of *9./"Nordland"* were taken over by *Bau-Bataillon 503*, while those of the *10. Kompanie* were taken over at 1300 hours by a Cossack squadron. The companies remained in Lineinaja and Kabardinskaja until the time for departure, *11. Kompanie* in Apscheronskaja.

Regimental orders regulated the withdrawal on 16 September of the *bataillone* from their previous sectors, and the relief by *Korps* formations from *LVII. Panzerkorps* and from units of *101. Jägerdivision*, whose sector became substantially smaller by the arrival of *97. Jägerdivision*.

The Finnish volunteers said farewell to a strip of land blessed with beauty, but which also hid treacherous fighting. The silent mountain forests of the forested Caucasus still rustled in their ears for some time, which were then suddenly ripped out of their silent beauty by the sound of weapons. They still had the peculiar odour of oil in their noses, that brown, cloudy brew, of which the ownership was so bitterly contested.

March to the Terek

After reaching the Caucasus mountain range, new assignments were given to the *Armeen* of *Heeresgruppe A*, the *17. Armee* on the western wing, and *1. Panzerarmee* on the eastern wing. The *17. Armee*, consisting mainly of foot soldiers, advanced on Tuapse and Noworossisk, and with *XXXXIX. Gebirgskorps* across the high mountain passes toward Adler and Suchumi. In the meantime, *1. Panzerarmee* with the *III.* and *XXXX. Panzerkorps* advanced along the mountains to the east. Its first goal was the Grosny oil region. Then a continued advance to Machatschkala and along the Caspian Sea to the south until Baku, the distant goal of the German offensive. Simultaneously, the *XXXXIX. Gebirgskorps* was to penetrate across the high mountain passes into the Trans-Caucasus.

Russian resistance increased soon again and brought the advance of *1. Panzerarmee* to a halt at the river barrier of the Terek. *General* Ott's *LII. Armeekorps*, which initially marched eastward on the southern side of the Manytsch River, to act as the union between the diverging directions of advance between *Heeresgruppe* A and *Heeresgruppe* B (Caucasus and Stalingrad), was turned sharply to the south after reaching Elista in the Kalmyk Steppe, to create a *schwerpunkt* as part of *1. Panzerarmee*. The *16. Infanterie-Division* (*mot.*) was inserted in the Kalmyk Steppe as a contact group between the two *Heeresgruppen*, and had to guard that area, which was as large as Belgium.

While *III. Panzerkorps* under the command of *General* von Mackensen attacked along the mountains to Ordshonikidse, the starting point of the Krestowyj (cross) military road to Tiflis, *General* von Schweppenburg and his *XXXX. Panzerkorps* attempted to cross the Terek River at the great Terek bend, behind which lay the Grosny oil region. In the meantime, on 2 September 1942, the first division from *LII. Armeekorps*, *111. Infanterie-Division*, arriving from the Kalmyk Steppe, built a bridgehead from the *XXXX. Panzerkorps* base at Mosdok. The *370. Infanterie-Division* was able to expand it, but then the strength of *LII. Armeekorps* was exhausted. To get the attack moving again, the *5. SS-Freiwilligen-Panzergrenadierdivision "Wiking"* was brought up from the western Caucasus, and was attached to *LII. Armeekorps*.

The *III. Panzerkorps* was transferred to the eastern Caucasus after the arrival of *XXXXIV. Jägerkorps* from the Maikop area. The "*Wiking*" then also left *LVII. Panzerkorps* and rolled toward the Terek.

On 17 September 1942 at 0600 hours, *III. (finnisches)/"Nordland"*, which had been relieved the day before, marched from Kabardinskaja as part of the process of transferring "*Wiking*". The march took place along road number 2 to Maikop.

There, still seen on both sides of the road, were kilometre-long fallen tree road barriers that the Russians, retreating into the mountains, had quickly created in the forested areas of Chadyschenskaja and Apscheronskaja. The Russians had cut down trees so that they fell across the road. The *pioniere* cut them up with chain saws and moved them to the sides.

After a 145 kilometre-long march, *III. (finnisches)/"Nordland"* arrived in Labinskaja (east of Maikop) at approximately 1530 hours and bivouacked there. It departed for Labinskaja on 18 September, at 0600 hours. The *Bataillon* marched through Armawir toward Olginskaja, where it arrived at 1530 hours and took up quarters. The march was 135 kilometres long. On 19 September, it started out at 0600 hours and marched through Newinnomyskaja to Lissogorskij, entering the village at 1230 hours. The length of that leg was 100 kilometres. The *Bataillon* left Lissogorskij at 0800 hours on 20 September, with its march goal being Stara Pawlowskaja, between the Kuma and Terek rivers.

Summer was once more showing its best side. The sun burned in the sky. Mighty dust clouds accompanied the march of "*Wiking*". To the right was the chain of mountains. Mountains and valleys glowed in autumn gold. Behind them appeared the bizarre and mighty ridges and mountains of the high mountain chain, the Elbrus peak with its snow cap, and then farther east, the Kasbek, the second highest peak in the Caucasus Mountains.

The march took the unit past Mineralnyje Wody, a spa for Russian notables, and a pearl on the northern edges of the mountains with mineral springs and a mild climate. There was an abundance of fruit and vine grapes in the region. Georgiewsk was passed and then the vehicles turned to the northeast. The mountains remained behind. At 1430 hours, after a 110 kilometre-long march, *III. (finnisches)/"Nordland"* reached Stara Pawlowskaja and rested there overnight. The other battalions of *SS-Regiment "Nordland"* reached the same area.

The commanders started early on 21 September with a small escort. The deployment of *SS-Regiment "Nordland"* was to take place in the sector of *111. Infanterie-Division* (Recknagel). At 1000 hours, in the Mosdok bridgehead, the regimental commander, *Oberführer* von Scholz, and *bataillon* commanders, Polewacz, Stoffers, and Collani were briefed by the commanding general of *LII. Armeekorps* and the troop leaders of *111. Infanterie-Division*. At 1435 hours, in a 110 kilometre-long march, *III. (finnisches)/"Nordland"* was brought up from Stara Pawlowskaja through Sowjetskaja to Stokijaneff.

On 22 September, following the usual start to the march, after a few kilometres on the road the Finnish *Bataillon* was ordered back to its quarters. The attack plans had been changed. *SS-Regiment "Nordland"* was to attack Malgobek from Nish Kurp, with *Panzerabteilung "Wiking"* and *SS-Regiment "Westland"* assaulting from the positions of the *370. Infanterie-Division* (Becker).

In the morning of 23 September, *Sturmbannführer* Collani and a small staff drove ahead to be briefed on the new assignment and to reconnoitre the terrain. The *Bataillon* was brought up at 1200 hours from Stokijaneff to Pawlodolskij and took up quarters there. Pawlodolskij is situated on the Terek River. A pontoon bridge built by German *pioniere* connected Pawlodolskij with Gnadenburg, which lies on the other side of the river. At 1700 hours the order arrived for the Finnish *Bataillon*:

> Get ready to continue the march. Positions will be occupied during the evening!

The *Bataillon* departed Pawlodolskij at 1735 hours. The pontoon bridge over the Terek was crossed. The many wheels of the vehicles rumbled monotonously across the bridge beams. On the other side was a steep river bank, high and mighty like a wall. After a short drive, the *Bataillon* cut through the valley to Gnadenburg. During the evening twilight the drive continued along field roads over bare hills to Nish Kurp, where the men dismounted from their vehicles. Soon thereafter, the *Bataillon* relieved parts of *370. Infanterie-Division* northeast of Nish Kurp. The relief process continued until the morning of 24 September. The *Bataillon* had the reinforced *10. Kompanie* on the left, and the reinforced *9. Kompanie* on the right, in the foremost frontline.

Russian mortar fire landed on the German positions on 25 September. Snipers also made their presence felt in an uncomfortable way. German artillery fire descended on Malgobek. The day was filled with assault preparations. Malgobek, a small oil town, was to be attacked on 26 September after *I.* and *II./"Nordland"* were brought up. The bare, hilly terrain overgrown with withered steppe grasses in the large Terek bend, would become the focus of the fighting in the eastern Caucasus during the following weeks and months, and the focus of the battle for the Malgobek and Grosny oil region. The Terek and the Terek sector were mentioned nearly daily in the German *Wehrmachtsbericht*; initially offensive successes, then defensive successes. The Terek became the place where German defences were worn down. *Generaloberst* von Kleist's *1. Panzerarmee* burned itself down to slag.

The Terek is 616 kilometres long. Its source is in the glaciers of the Kabek and it flows 150 kilometres north of Machatschkala into the Caspian Sea. The untamed, wild river flows from the valleys of the mountain ranges initially to the north and then bends at Prochladny, where it is already "tamer", sharply to the east and then rushes through the Nogay Steppe. The Terek is a natural protective barrier in front of the Grosny oil region.

The very high, hilly south and eastern banks in the great Terek bend offer good defensive possibilities, which had already been identified before "*Wiking*" arrived. Even the undulating, hilly steppe terrain behind it, upon which only steppe grass and the odd corn field grew, offered the defender greater advantages than the attacker. And the Soviets knew how to use the advantages well. The Finnish volunteers soon began to notice that the fighting became increasingly more deadly.

Attack on Malgobek and Ssagopschin

German offensive planning gave *Heeresgruppe* B the task of reaching Stalingrad during the rapid advance to the Volga, building up a northern screen along the Don, and bringing the lower Volga up to Astrakhan under control. Then, *4. Panzerarmee* was to be transferred from *Heeresgruppe* B to *Heeresgruppe* A in the eastern Caucasus. But *4. Panzerarmee* (Hoth) did not become free due to the difficult fighting in Stalingrad and so it became the task of *1. Panzerarmee* (von Kleist) to attain the far-reaching goals in the eastern Caucasus on its own. Those exceeded its strength. Initially, *1. Panzerarmee* tried to advance along the Terek, block the Grusinian military road at Ordshonikidse, capture the Grosny oil fields, and then advance to Machatschkaja on the Caspian Sea, by reorganizing and bringing up all possible reserves. With that, the roads used by the Allies to supply aid by way of Iran would be blocked.

With the attack by *III. Panzerkorps* (von Mackensen) on Ordshonikidse, the *LII. Armeekorps* (Ott) was to simultaneously attack along the northern slope of the Mussakai mountain range in the valley basin south of Malgobek and capture Ssagopschin. With that Mussakai would be surrounded on two sides, the exit of the Grusinian military road at Ordshonikidse blocked, and the road for an advance toward the Grosny oil region open.

The road to Grosny passes over the bare, mountain ridges of Malgobek, a small, widely-dispersed oil city 12 kilometres south of Mosdok. The *LII. Armeekorps*, worn out and situated east of the Terek and south of Mosdok, became the new spearhead of the army and was given *Division "Wiking"* coming from the western Caucasus. Initially *"Wiking"* had only infantry regiments *SS-Regiment "Nordland"* and *SS-Regiment "Westland"*, because *SS-Regiment "Germania"* was still tied up in the western Caucasus.

Division commander Steiner, as well as the regimental and *Bataillon* commanders of *"Nordland"* and *"Westland"*, the *Panzerabteilung*, and the artillery, were in advance of their units to make the necessary reconnaissance and briefings for the attack on Malgobek and Ssagopschin. The plan was for *SS-Regiment "Nordland"* to attack Malgobek from the mountain ridge north of the Ssagopschin valley and thereby eliminate the threat to the flank of the, somewhat echeloned to the rear, attacking forces of the *Panzerabteilung* and *"Westland"*.

The *III. (finnisches)/"Nordland"* relieved parts of the grenadier regiments of *370. Infanterie-Division* (Becker) northeast of Nish Kurp during the night of 23/24 September 1942.

On 25 September, *II.* and *III./SS-Artillerieregiment 5* arrived from the western Caucasus and took up firing positions near Nish Kurp. The *Panzerabteilung* (Mühlenkamp), which had also arrived, took up positions in the many balkas at Nish Kurp.

There was a final conference with all commanders at the command post of *III./SS-Artillerieregiment 5* (Bühler) regarding the deployment, which *Korpsartillerieführer*, *Oberst* Lukasch, also attended. The attack plan was as follows:

> *I./"Nordland"* was to attack Malgobek from along the southern slope (looking into the valley) of the Malgobek mountain range.
>
> *III./"Nordland"* to the left, on a higher range, was to simultaneously attack, with the assignment of eliminating enemy fire from above on *I./"Nordland"*.
>
> *II./"Nordland"* was to attack Kesskem from south of Nish Kurp on the northern slopes of Mussakai and, simultaneously with the assignment, interrupt flanking enemy fire into the valley.
>
> *Panzerabteilung* and *SS-Regiment "Westland"* were to attack, after a sufficient advance by *SS-Regiment "Nordland"*, in the lengthy valley between the mountain ranges and capture Ssagopschin.

The *Oberbefehlshaber* of *1. Panzerarmee*, *Generaloberst* von Kleist, pointed out once more in a teletype message to *Generalleutnant der Waffen-SS*, Felix Steiner, the special importance of Ssagopschin as the key point for the continuation of the attack on Grosny.

The last units of *I./"Nordland"* arrived at their assembly areas in Nish Kurp during the night of 26 September.

On 26 September 1942, at 0445 hours: German artillery bellowed and opened the attack on Malgobek and Ssagopschin. The field howitzers of *Abteilung Bühler*, in the balkas and by the field road near Nish Kurp, fired without interruption, the echoes rolling like a thunderstorm across the mountains and the valleys.

On the enemy side, the impacts of the shells rose like bright mushrooms out of the ground. In their departure positions, the storm troops hugged the night-cool earth, checked their weapons and equipment once more, and pushed hand grenades under their belts. In the balkas at Nish Kurp, Mühlenkamp's tank crews filled their tanks with fuel and stowed amour piercing and high explosive shells into the bellies of their steel warriors.

As it turned out later, the Russians did not notice the introduction of *SS-Regiment "Nordland"*. They prepared to attack, as did the Germans, with four battalions on Nish Kurp to relieve their forces under pressure at Elchotowo (Caucasus gate) from the attack by the *13. Panzerdivision* (Herr). However, the Russian attack was slated for half an hour later than the German attack. Approximately equal forces were opposing each other, but the defender, sitting in prepared positions, had the advantage. The Russians were forced into the role of defenders by necessity.

The *Panzergrenadiere* were lying, ready to jump, on the reverse slope from the enemy. The shells howled non-stop over their heads toward the enemy. The new day was still grey, blurred. Milky morning fog hung in the valleys. The *III. (finnisches)/"Nordland"* was in the position taken over from *370. Infanterie-Division*, with its *10. Kompanie* under *Obersturmführer* Porsch and the *9. Kompanie* under *Hauptsturmführer* Troiker to the right. *Obersturmführer* Mühlinghaus' *11. Kompanie*, as the spearhead, was ready to attack behind *9. Kompanie*. *Obersturmführer* Mühlinghaus and his platoon leaders, *Obersturmführer* Hannus and *Untersturmführer* Sartio, looked out over the attack area from the position of the *9th*. It was going to be difficult!

At exactly 0500 hours the artillery preparatory fire ceased; only individual batteries fired on targets farther back. "*Auf – marsch*!" The *Bataillone* of *SS-Regiment "Nordland"* attacked.

Obersturmführer Mühlinghaus' *11. Kompanie* stormed across its own position against the enemy-occupied hill. Platoon leaders Hannus, Hortling, and Sartio stormed in the very front, carrying their Finnish countrymen with them. The first hill was reached in a violent storm assault. Machine pistols and machineguns rattled, hand grenade detonations echoed through the valley. At 0630 hours the *11. Kompanie* reported to *Bataillon*:

"First attack goal reached!"

The platoon leaders gathered their platoons again, organized them and gave the *Gruppen* new tasks. The company's objective was the next hill.

And again: "*Vorwärts-Angriff*!" Initially things went well, but then the assaulting platoons ran into flanking fire from the southeast and frontal fire from a corn field that extended to the top of the hill. The corn field was full of positions and bunkers, which the attackers had difficulty in identifying. Heavy defensive enemy fire was hitting the attacking Finns. The *11. Kompanie* had four dead and eight wounded during the first assault. The attack bogged down.

At 0730 hours, as the *11. Kompanie* was forced to go to ground, enemy fire was shifted onto the *10. Kompanie*, which was also attacking. Quickly, the company had three wounded.

To try and get the attack going again, the German artillery and the heavy weapons of the *Bataillon* laid down a heavy barrage on the hill before the small village of Stary Sowetskij. The attack on that hill was also of critical importance to *I. Bataillon* attacking from the south. Once more, there was a boxing match, involving heavy losses, across hilly steppes and corn fields. The Russian positions were masterfully arranged; the narrow trenches and positions provided safety, and only direct hits by the artillery could eliminate them. Russian snipers had a rich harvest amongst the Germans and Finns. Each Russian position had to be taken out of the defensive system separately, which involved hand-to-hand fighting with machine pistols and hand grenades. Platoon leader *Obersturmführer* Hannus was killed. The *11. Kompanie* had another eight killed and thirty wounded during the second attack, which, after gaining some ground, also bogged down. At 0900 hours the exhausted *11. Kompanie* dug in along the line where it was stopped.

In the meantime, *I./"Nordland"*, attacking on the right, was also unable to advance. Numerous losses and exhaustion brought the entire attack plan of "*Wiking*" into disarray. Only *II./"Nordland"* gained ground to the east along the northern slopes of the Mussakai. Since it became evident that the artillery at Nish Kurp had a poor firing angle and was unable to intervene effectively in front of *III. Bataillon* and *I. Bataillon*, the deployed *sIG* of the thirteenth changed firing positions and fired right across the valley into the Russian positions in front of the two *bataillone*.

Time was pressing. The main objective for the far-reaching attack remained Ssagopschin. In spite of insecure flanks due to flanking fire, Mühlenkamp's *Panzerabteilung* and *SS-Regiment "Westland"* attacked in the valley between the mountain ridges, crossed the antitank ditch cutting through the valley, and advanced a good distance before they too were forced to break off the attack due to flanking fire from the mountains.

The demands by *III. Bataillon* and *I. Bataillon* for the elimination of the flanking fire from the mountains near Malgobek was becoming louder and louder. At 1000 hours the *bataillone* reorganized and brought up reinforcements from their own ranks to the assault companies. At 1130 hours, a rifle platoon, a heavy machinegun and a mortar *gruppe* from the *9. Kompanie* were inserted into the lines of the tied down *11. Kompanie*, which also brought with them a re-supply of ammunition and hand grenades. The *lIG* and a half-platoon of *Pak* from the *12. Kompanie* went into position directly behind the *11. Kompanie.*

The attack was re-started at 1500 hours. Once more, heavy defensive fire greeted the courageous Finns, especially from the southeast into the flanks. The second attack goal, the drawn-out hill in front of Stary Sowjetskij, and the corn field positioned in front, were a single defensive system. Each metre required selfless effort from the Finns. By 1700 hours the reinforced, but again weakened by losses, *11. Kompanie* had approached the top of the hill to within 20 metres. However, once more, completely exhausted, it had to remain just in front of the attack goal. It was feared that the gained position could not be held against Russian counterattacks. The Finnish losses had increased to 25 dead and 54 wounded; amongst them the severely wounded *Untersturmführer* Müller, platoon leader of *9. Kompanie.*

It did not look any better at *I./"Nordland"*. It was becoming certain that *III.* and *I./"Nordland"* would not be able to advance against Malgobek.

The regimental commander, *Oberführer* von Scholz, had followed the assault of the two *bataillone* with concern and had established through a personal inspection at the foremost frontline that there was no advancing under those circumstances. He pushed for a change of the attack with the division commander. From him, he received the assignment to halt the attacks by *III.* and *I./"Nordland"* and defend the line that had been reached.

At 1745 hours, it was already twilight, the *11./"Nordland"* withdrew as ordered from the enemy hill and went into position on the initially-captured hill.

So much for the general report on the first day of attack on Malgobek. How that difficult day looked from the perspective of the assaulting soldier, the nondescript frontline fighter, who only saw his *Gruppe*, his *Zug*, at the best his *Kompanie*, but above all his comrades, is obtained from the diary entries written down by Eero Tulonen of the *11./"Nordland"* during the evening of 26 September 1942:

> 26 September 1942: A dark day. We attacked at about 0600 hours in the morning. Everything went well in the beginning. Then we ran into Russian machinegun fire in a fog. We could not see the enemy. It hailed so many bullets that we could only advance by crawling. Hannus (died later of his wounds), Nisula, and Siimestö were wounded and Alaja killed. Then Rahtu, Lusa, Muilu, Saarela, and Voutilainen were killed. The remainder dug themselves in. After a while we crawled back. Only Tuokko, Penttilä, Salonen, and I remained from our Platoon Hannus.
>
> We attacked again in the afternoon and then surprisingly penetrated into the Russian position; escaping Russians fell under the hail of our bullets. Penttilä was wounded slightly in the head; I took his machine pistol and, together with Nieminen, captured a pair of Russian prisoners. Teräväinen received two holes in his leg and in the afternoon an additional bullet through the hand. Peltovuori played around with a Russian explosive until it exploded in his hands and threw him five metres out of his foxhole. His upper part was shredded to the shoulders, the one leg right to the upper thigh. Initially we didn't know who it was. After we found his *Soldbuch* we recognized with dismay that it was Peltovuori, one of our best comrades.
>
> One time I was storming beside Turunen. He called out to me: How is it going with you?"
>
> I had answered: "Good!"
>
> Immediately after that I heard a shout that Turunen had been killed.
>
> Another time Jätinmäki stormed less than five metres beside me. Suddenly I heard some moaning. I called to Jätinmäki but received no answer.
>
> Pirttiniemi received a bullet through the chest. I showed him the direction toward the rear. He crawled back and made it through.

The attack ground to a halt. I dug myself in beside Jätinmäki. Here I recalled everything that I had learned at Groß Born: While head, chest, and elbows remained close to the ground, the hand shoved earth out from under the chest with the spade, and in this way a protective wall was created in front of the head. The heels remained pressed to the ground. Once we had completed our foxholes and hollowed out an area we determined through calls who had been killed and who was still alive.

In the morning our platoon had consisted of 34 men, by evening only 9 men. We had 8 men killed and 17 wounded.[5]

Now to the *Luftwaffe*.

The Russians dominated the air space during the attack on 26 September. Repeatedly, Russian ground-attack aircraft, of the IL 2 type, intervened in the ground battle. The German *Flak* shot down a few enemy aircraft. *Jagdgeschwader 52*, commanded by *Major* Gollob, was available for support to *1. Panzerarmee*. *Jagdgeschwader* was an inflated term for that unit because it had to give up one *Gruppe* to Stalingrad, leaving it with only the *III. Gruppe* and the *Geschwader* staff. Its initial jumping off airfield was at Mineralnyje Wody.

Major Gollob reconnoitred a new field aerodrome on 26 September to save on fuel and to get to the battle area faster. He found a large suitable meadow approximately ten flying minutes west of the Mosdok-Malgobek fighting area.

The ordinary soldier in the trenches criticized the deployment of the *Luftwaffe* during the fighting at the Terek. Very few German fighters appeared during the time of the oppressing Russian air superiority, and then usually after the Soviets had left. But the reality was different.

The *Me-109* fighters suffered from a chronic lack of fuel and only took off after enemy incursions had been reported. It was obvious that they would arrive late in many cases. The authorized strength of *III./JG 52* was 30 machines. The *Gruppe* had barely half that number of machines available in Armawir. There were barely four aircraft combat-ready on the Terek. There was a lack of replacement parts, of fuel, and of ammunition.

5. Mauno Jokipii, loc cit, page 530.

The *III./JG 52* intervened in the fighting on the Terek most of the time with only two Rotten (four aircraft) alternately, which made the true situation clear. Nonetheless, the pilots did what they could.

As happened often later on, two *Me 109* fighters swept the area clear of Russian fighters and ground-attack aircraft, sending numerous Russian machines to the ground trailing a blue-black trail of smoke. *Major* Gollob reached his 150th air victory on the Terek. It was also there that the *JG 52* shot down its 1,500th air enemy, *Hauptmann* Dickfeld his 120th. This should clear up the air situation on the Terek.

The *III.* and *I./"Nordland"* reorganized during the night of 26/27 September 1942. The *10. Kompanie* took over part of the sector of the *I. Bataillon*. The *schwerpunkt* was moved more to the right.

27 September 1942, 1030 hours: the *10. Kompanie*, commanded by *Obersturmführer* Porsch, attacked. The *9. Kompanie* was brought up so that it was readily available. The greatly-weakened *11. Kompanie* became the *Bataillon* reserve.

To all appearances the Russians had withdrawn part of their forces, with which they had planned to attack in the morning, to the Ssagopschin area. They assumed correctly that that is where the German *Schwerpunkt* would be. The attack by the *10. Kompanie* went well. By 1430 hours three hills had been captured, one after the other. The enemy 59th Brigade lost 15 prisoners and 30 dead were counted. Their booty included three heavy machineguns, five light machineguns, four antitank rifles, 10 machine pistols, and 50 rifles.

The *9. Kompanie* and *10. Kompanie* took up positions on the captured hills at 1530 hours. At 1730 hours the *9. Kompanie* pushed a security element to the north and blocked the Ossemyj road intersection. The *Pionier Zug* from the *12. Kompanie* lifted 140 Russian wooden mines. The *Bataillon* had three dead and eight wounded on that day.

The *I. Bataillon* had also advanced farther south, but Malgobek, the goal of both *Bataillone*, was still very far away. In spite of flanking fire, the *Panzerabteilung* and *SS-Regiment "Westland"* fought their way to Ssagopschin, but the village itself resisted all German attacks. Ssagopschin was the key to the far-reaching operational goals into the Grosny oil region; during the following few days the terraced village was fought over with unbelievable ferocity.

There was bitter fighting on 28 September for Ssagopschin. Heavy flanking fire, and heavy artillery, from the Malgobek area, interfered greatly with the *Panzerabteilung* and *SS-Regiment* "*Westland*". From the Malgobek hills, the Russian cannons had direct fire possibilities on the German movements in the Ssagopschin Valley. If there was to be any progress at Ssagopschin, Malgobek had to fall.

Malgobek was still the objective for the *III.* and *I./"Nordland"*. Both *Bataillone*, as well as the adjacent *Grenadierregiment 70* of the *111. Infanterie-Division*, reorganized for a new attack on Malgobek. Russian artillery and fighter-bombers interfered with the reorganization. Already at 0600 hours a series of salvoes from "*Stalinorgel*" landed on *10. Kompanie* positioned on the left wing of *III. (finnisches)/"Nordland"*, and continued thereafter. The beginning of the attack was postponed. At 1430 hours a reconnaissance troop determined that the hill in front of *10. Kompanie* had been evacuated.

At 1630 hours the *11. Kompanie* (previously *Bataillon* reserve) relieved the *2. Kompanie,* taking over part of *I. Bataillon's* sector. The *11. Kompanie* simultaneously defended the position change and the new positions of the batteries of the *SS-Artillerieregiment* in a valley of the Malgobek hills exiting to the south.

The *10. Kompanie* was to be attached to *Grenadierregiment 70* (Tronnier) for the attack on Malgobek and was withdrawn to the line of the *9. Kompanie*. There were new considerations and new plans by the German command staffs. First Malgobek had to fall and only then would it be possible to take Ssagopschin. At 2310 hours *10./"Nordland"* was withdrawn from its positions and attached to *Grenadierregiment 70*.

There was bitter fighting on 28 September for Ssagopschin. The *I./"Westland"*, brought from the west Caucasus the day before and immediately thrown into the battle, had heavy casualties. The losses at *Panzerabteilung "Wiking"*, through enemy activity and materiel damage, rose quickly. The attack begun during the morning fog (one relied on it) on Ssagopschin came to a halt after the sudden disappearance of the fog. Then, a heavy enemy battery from the Malgobek area (by the white house) was able to effectively intervene with direct fire into the German attacking forces, forcing them to go to ground. To all that bad luck during the attack on Ssagopschin was added a Russian counterattack with armoured forces, which was to advance along the Mussakai up to the antitank ditch by Nish Kurp and block the valley there. It was a clever Soviet plan: solidify the rear and then smash the German forces in the valley through concentrated fire from the positions on the hills. But it did not come to that. Mühlenkamp's tanks faced the Russians. There were tank duels from the closest of distances. Finally the Russians gave up their intentions.

There were severe disagreements between the *LII. Armeekorps* and the leadership of "*Wiking*". The commanding general, *General* Ott, ws not diverted from his intentions: direct attack in the valley against Ssagopschin. The division commander, Steiner, wanted to withdraw the attacking group somewhat in the valley, eliminate the flanks on both sides on the hills, and then renew the attack on Ssagopschin. *General* Ott insisted on an immediate and direct attack on Ssagopschin, probably based on the overall situation, in consideration of reaching the designated goals before winter, and the pressure from the *Panzerarmee.* On the evening of 28 September, the commander of *SS-Regiment* "*Westland*", *Oberführer* von Scholz, was designated sector commander of the valley in front of Ssagopschin. The regimental commander of *SS-Regiment* "*Westland*", *Obersturmbannführer* Geißler, was thereby placed under his command.

In the morning of 29 September, *10./"Nordland"*, attached to *Grenadierregiment 70*, was brought to the assembly area for the attack on San Lonoj. The company already had heavy losses during the move from Russian artillery, presumably guided by a forward observer who noticed the movement. The company withdrew into a covering valley and was to move into the assembly area during the night. However, the attack was cancelled during the night. The *10./"Nordland"* returned to *III. (finnisches)/"Nordland"*, which had in the meantime taken over the sector from *I. Bataillon* east of Nish Kurp. The *I./"Nordland"* transferred to the valley in front of Ssagopschin. On 30 September *I./"Nordland"* and *II./"Westland"* attacked Ssagopschin; again without success. The losses were great. During the evening, *Oberführer* von von Scholz (sector commander), Gille (commander of *SS-Artilerie-Regiment 5*), and *Obersturmbannführer* Geißler (regimental commander of "*Westland*"), drove to division to protest against the senseless attack with insufficient resources. Steiner, who was always against the attack in the valley, passed the protests on by telephone to *General* Ott. However, Ott claimed to be bound by orders from "above". He suggested that all less-exposed frontal

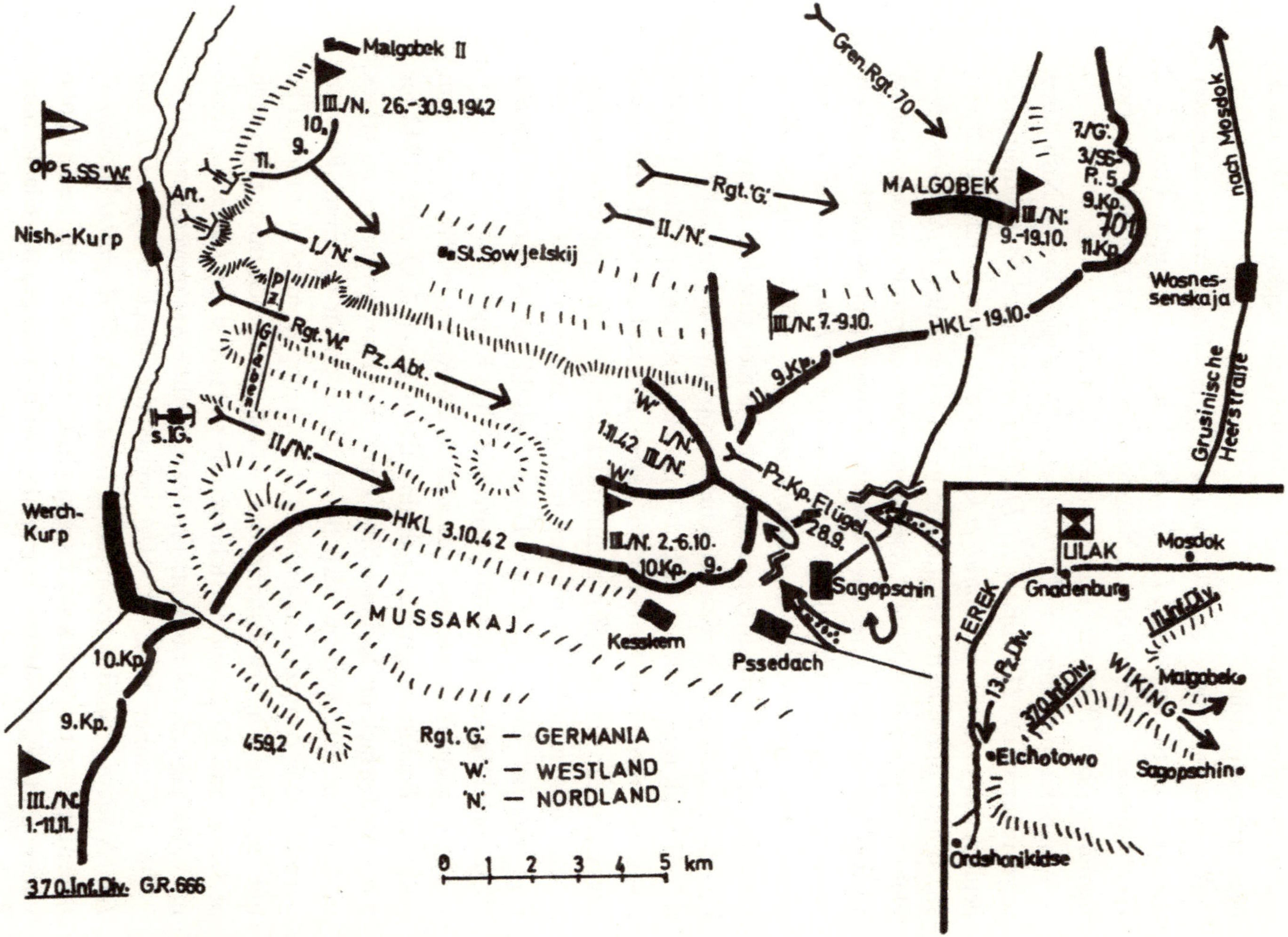

Fighting on the Terek, September – November 1942.

sectors be lightened and that the freed-up forces be deployed in the attack against Ssagopschin.

A new order arrived at 1800 hours: *III./"Nordland"* was to take over the sector of the weakened *II./"Westland"* during the night. The *I.* and *III./"Nordland"* were to attack Ssagopschin the next day and the two *Bataillone* from "*Westland*" were to screen the flanks.

While the companies of *III. (finnisches)/"Nordland"* east of Nish Kurp were relieved by *111. Infanterie-Division* and marched to their new deployment area, *Sturmbannführer* Collani and a small staff had driven ahead to reconnoitre the terrain and to brief the units. *Untersturmführer* Dohm, the platoon leader of *9. Kompanie*, was to carry out a reconnaissance against Ssagopschin after the company arrived, and establish the best approach routes to the village. Because the *9. Kompanie* had not yet arrived by darkness, the *1. Ordonnanzoffizier* (*001*) of the *Bataillon*, *Untersturmführer* Ertel, went ahead with the men that had arrived from the *10. Kompanie*. The reconnaissance troop advanced carefully through a corn field, made contact with its own *Pak* position, and then had the open, flat terrain of Ssagopschin before it. Ertel reported and made suggestions to the *Bataillon* commander and his company commanders for the subsequent deployment of the shock troops. Only then did Ertel find out that *Untersturmführer* Dohm was killed by shrapnel from a "Stalinorgel" as he left his old position at Nish Kurp.

The *I.* and *III./"Nordland"*, as well as *SS-Regiment "Westland"* with only two *Bataillone*, got ready during the night of 1 October 1942 for a renewed attack on Ssagopschin. That time there would be an attack in depth on Ssagopschin, with the shock troops at the front. For that purpose, each company organized a shock troop from its best men. The line-up in the Finnish *Bataillon* was as follows: Shock troop from each of *11.*, *9.*, and *10. Kompanie*, followed by the rest of *10. Kompanie*. Once more, the fog was counted on. The starting time was moved forward.

On 1 October 1942, at 0415 hours, the shock troops of *I.* and *III./"Nordland"* lined up from left to right, with *SS-Regiment "Westland"* screening, for the attack on Ssagopschin. They were the best platoon leaders and NCOs of the companies, with courageous, reliable men. Each shock troop had a heavy machinegun crew, somewhat farther back. Everything had been thought through and agreed upon. The shock troops of *I./"Nordland"* were moving silently forward on the right; brave

15 October 1941: Swearing in of the Finnish *SS-Freiwilligen-Bataillon* on German soil – troop training area Groß Born – handing over of the flag by the Finnish military attaché, Oberst Horn, and the Finnish liaison officer, Major Levälathi. Right, *SS-Hauptsturmführer* Collani (killed) as *Bataillon* commander.

December 1941: On the march to the front through Winniza, Uman, Kirowograd, and Dnjepropetrowsk.

Dismounting and pushing. Everything struggles laboriously forward.

The *2. Kompanie* marches in a snowstorm to Rutschenkowo; at the front is *SS-Untersturmführer* (*Leutnant*) Pohjanlehto.

Before the frontline cinema in January 1942: From the left: *Scharführer* Koschmieder, Vaaramo, *SS-Untersturmführer* Pohjanlehto and *Obersturmführer* Pallesche.

In the most-forward frontline trench (winter 1941/42).

SS-Untersturmführer Ertel and *SS- Unterscharführer* Winkler in front of the command post of *I/2. Kompanie.*

Position of *2. Kompanie* on the Mius River, near Steljanski-Bachmutzkij (large Mius bend).

The Caucasus. Air reconnaissance missions were flown constantly.

Pionier group of the *Bataillon* near Malgobek.

Crossing the Kuban at Grigoripolinskaja.

SS-Oberführer Fritz von Scholz interrogates Russian prisoners after the battle for Linejnaja. *SS-Untersturmführer* Hirt, the *Bataillon Adjutant*, has to translate with a bare upper body because he was surprised during his morning clean-up.

The commanding general of *LII. Armeekorps*, Eugen Ott, at the command post of the Finnish *Bataillon*.

5 cm *Pak* (*Panzerabwehrkanone*)

…and heavy machinegun during training (summer 1942, Demidowka).

SS-Untersturmführer Karl Heinz Ertel, after the battle at Linejnaja (16 August 1942), beside a *Panzer IV* from "*Wiking*".

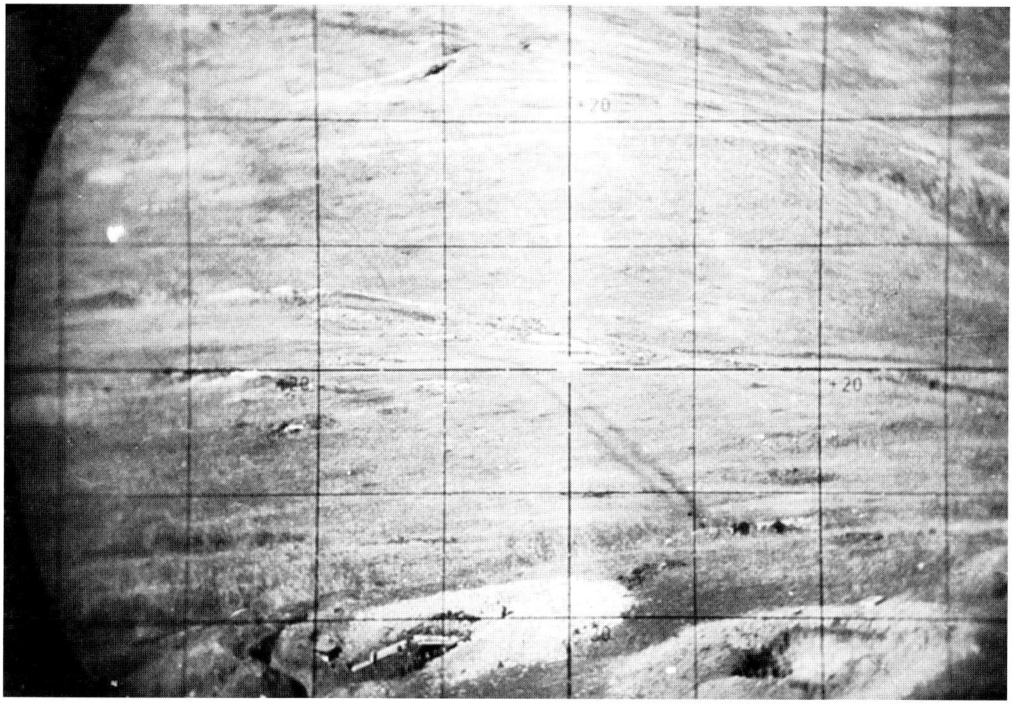

Near Malgobek (October 1942) and Alagir, after the *Bataillon* captured Hill 701.

Military bridge across the Terek at Chamidija. The entire division "*Wiking*" crossed here for the attack on Ordschonnikidse.

A motorcycle platoon brings in a camel-drawn cannon as booty, as well as captured Russian prisoners at Metschiniskaja.

Farewell in Ruhpolding, parade formation.

The *Bataillon* departs and goes back to its homeland.

Hännikäinen and Elmgren on 1 January 1943: withdrawal from the Caucasus.

On 14 January 1943 – ready for the counterattack.

Unterscharführer Taisto Kuuri, a daring *Gruppenführer*, on the march to the Kalmyk steppe on 9 January 1943.

Sturmmann Torrinen in the foremost frontline.

Rottenführer Pyyhtia was mentioned in the Ehrenblatt of the German army because of outstanding bravery.

Alf Silfverberg with the Tank Destruction Badge.

Light machinegun in the defence.

Left is Spieß Oberscharführer Pape. On the right, Oberscharführer Spock hands out leave papers in Tampere.

Fighting for Krasnoje Snamja.

Company commander Ertel and *Kompanie-Truppenführer* Pape from *9. Kompanie*.

SS-Gruppenführer und *Generalleutnant* Felix Steiner, commander of *5. SS-Freiwilligen-Panzergrenadierdivision "Wiking"* with *Obersturmbannführer* Collani (killed) on 2 June 1943 in Hanko (Finland) during the handing over of the *Bataillon* to the Finnish Armed Forces.

Festive farewell formation on Finnish soil, and marching past the courageous and honoured Collani, *SS-Gruppenführer und Generalleutnant der Waffen-SS* Felix Steiner, Finnish General Finnish *Freiwilligen-Bataillon*. From the left: *Bataillon* commander and *SS-Obersturmbannführer* Malmberg, commander of home troops.

War blind Finnish *SS-Unterscharführer (Unteroffizier)* Matti Alonen is greeted specially by Finnish General Malmberg (Tampere 1943).

During the departure of the troop transport, German comrades *SS-Obersturmführer* Deck (*11. Kompanie*), *SS-Obersturmführer* Hirt (*Bataillon Adjutant*), and *SS-Untersturmführer* Scholz (*Ordonnanzoffizier*) salute their Finnish brothers-in-arms one last time.

Tampere, 3 June 1943: *General* Steiner with Finnish officers.

Finnish General Talvela and *Generalleutnant der Waffen-SS* Felix Steiner in Aleandrowka.

11 July 1943, Hanko. In the uniforms of the Finnish army, one hour after leaving the *Waffen-SS* – and again in battle!

men, Germans, Danes, and Norwegians. To the left, brave and battle experienced Finns. Behind them, ready to assault, were the companies. No artillery preparation whatsoever was carried out to keep the moment of surprise.

At first the shock troops make good progress, but then they ran into the first Russian defenders who raised the alarm and withdrew. Barrier fire set in. Nonetheless, the shock troops fought their way forward. Ssagopschin was getting closer. The sun broke through the fog just when the first shock troops were within 50 metres of the main Russian position before Ssagopschin. With that, a murderous defensive fire set in, nailing the troops to the ground.

Additional attempts to continue moving forward were nipped in the bud by Russian artillery and mortars. The shock troops in the valley were sitting ducks and dug themselves into the ground to get some protection from the devastating flanking fire, especially from Malgobek. Only at dark were they able to move back to their starting positions. The Finnish *Bataillon* had two dead and nine wounded, which came mainly from the shock troop of the *11. Kompanie*. Amongst the dead was *Obersturmführer* and platoon leader Erkki Rafael Lautia from Rauma, Finland.

During the night of 2 October, anew *HKL* was built-up three kilometres west of Ssagopschin. As part of the reorganization, the Finnish *Bataillon* went into position before Pssedach and Kesskem, with the *10. Kompanie* on the left (adjacent to *I./"Nordland"*) and the *9. Kompanie* on the right. The *11. Kompanie* was *Bataillon* reserve.

Eero Tulonen described that day of fighting from his point of view as a member of *Shock Troop Lautia* of the *11. Kompanie*:

> 1 October 1942: We started out at midnight, an *Abteilung* of about 180 men, shock troops from *I.* and *III. Bataillon* at the front. We managed to approach the Russian positions undetected as morning arrived by moving along a long hollow. We waited for the attack signal. I was totally tired out and fell asleep beside a foxhole.
>
> In the meantime, it became light and the Russians recognized us. Suddenly, heavy fire set in. I woke up and threw myself into a foxhole, which had been dug during the battles of the previous days. A rain of bullets greeted you from 100 metres distance from machine pistols as soon as you raised your head a little. There were

three platoons from our *Bataillon* in the long hollow, but I did not see our other *Gruppe. Obersturmführer* Lautia was killed right at the beginning and *Unterscharführer* Jalkonen died after receiving a severe wound.

Saari was also wounded. He was able to find cover in a foxhole. Penttilä wanted to help him but got several bullets in his head when he rose from his foxhole. After that, his lifeless body jerked every time a new bullet hit it.

Finally Kiviluoto and I managed to get near Saari. He had five entry wounds, the worst through the right shoulder, which had gone through the lung and was stuck in his chest. In addition, he had a grazing shot on the left wrist and on the underarm, and an additional wound in the right lower leg.

The recovery of the severely wounded was very difficult. We dragged Saari about 1.5 kilometres along the ground with leather straps. Nettles reddened his face. No sound of complaint passed his lips. He only cursed his fate and constantly encouraged us to go on: 'Pull boys pull, get going!' He suffered a lot but did not complain a single time. His calm demeanour, and his modest behaviour were still dominant, even during the greatest crisis. After the doctor had seen his wounds and bandaged him he said to us; 'He is going to make it!'

I saw how Valle was shooting, how he was hit, how the sparks flew from his helmet. The helmet had a dent. Naumann experienced the same thing.

We slowly withdrew during the morning and occupied a new position about 500 metres away from the enemy. Here we remained the whole day under the burning sun, hungry and thirsty.

Some attempted to bring back the dead Lautia to recover his golden watch for his relatives, but it was not possible. The dead Lautia and Penttilä remained in front of us. We returned to the company under the cover of twilight; the platoons Ingerö and Sartio. We devoured our food since we had had nothing to eat for 24 hours.

The regimental commander (Fritz von Scholz), who had observed the attack from some distance, was of the same opinion as we; that a new assault without the support of tanks and heavy weapons would be impossible."[6]

---

6. Mauno Jokipii, loc cit, page 541.

Heavy artillery and mortar fire lay on the positions at Pssedach during the next few days. Our own reconnaissance patrols alternated with enemy advances. The Russian air force was as active as before and then rained down phosphorous. An attempt to attack Ssagopschin along the northern slope of Mussakai with *II./"Nordland"* (Stoffers) also failed.

After several attempts, *Division "Wiking"* was unable to capture Ssagopschin. *General* Ott, commanding general of *LII. Armeekorps*, demanded a new plan from *Generalleutnant der Waffen-SS* Steiner for the continuation of the attack on Grosny. The *III. Panzerkorps* also could not advance; the front before Ordshonikidse solidified. Steiner pointed out that Malgobek was the key for the attack on Grosny and that without capturing the dominating hill city even the forward *HKL* in the valley before Ssagopschin could not be held. *General* Ott agreed to an attack on Malgobek, which was to take place after the arrival of *SS-Regiment "Germania"* and *I./SS-Artillerie-Regiment 5* from the western Caucasus.

Malgobek and Hill 701

It was clear to all troop leaders: The road to Grosny, the goal of *1. Panzerarmee*, was through Malgobek.

It is on 5 October 1942 that the formations from *I.* and *II. Bataillon "Germania"*, *I./SS-Artillerie-Regiment 5*, and other parts of *Division "Wiking"* finally arrived from the western Caucasus, where they had been relieved by mountain troops. Only *III./"Germania"* at Maikop could not be relieved. With the new forces from *"Wiking"*, Malgobek was to be taken out of the Russian defence system and the road to Grosny was to be opened.

Already on 4 October, as the assault force, *Regiment "Germania"* attacked with *I. Bataillon* on the right and *II. Bataillon* on the left. Parts of *Panzerabteilung "Wiking"* supported the attack. To the right of *I./"Germania"*, somewhat back, was *II./"Nordland"*, and left of *II./"Germania"* were parts of *Grenadierregiment 70* from *111. Infanterie-Division*. The attack started from the mountains approximately six kilometres west of Malgobek. At 1100 hours *Regiment "Germania"* was 500 metres in front of Malgobek and stayed there. At exactly 1120 hours, German *Stukas* dropped bombs on the city. Then *"Germania"* attacked again and, at approximately 1400 hours, Malgobek-West was in German hands. Worn out, the companies went over to the defence. Only then did it become obvious that the stretched-out city, with a number of interlinking housing areas, could not be taken in one stroke. Resistance flared up in each housing sector anew, and the artillery, which had been silent during the *Stuka* attack, also intervened strongly again.

The attack was continued on 6 October during the morning fog. The German forces, screening the flanks, closed up. By 1500 hours Malgobek-East and the large oil storage tanks were in German hands. The next objective was the village of Wosnessensskaja on the Grusinian military road. The assault spearheads had to be reinforced for that assault. That could only happen through a reorganization because neither *Armeekorps* nor *1. Panzerarmee* had any operational reserves. As part of the reorganization, *I./"Nordland"* took over the positions of *III./"Nordland"* in front of Kesskem by extending its frontline.

On 6 October 1942, a group under *Sturmbannführer* Collani, reconnoitred the area south of Malgobek for approach routes, and for assembly areas for *III. (finnisches)/"Nordland"*.

The Finnish *Bataillon* was relieved in the Kesskem area during the night of 7 October. The *Bataillon* departed for the new assembly area in a loose formation and arrived in driblets with its last units during the morning of 7 October.

In the morning of 7 October *SS-Regiment "Germania"* was again on the attack toward the east. Then, powerful Russian reserves entered the battle from the Ordshonikidse and Elchotowo area, and the German attack progressed only with great difficulty. Every German movement of forces was countered by Russian force movements with the force ratio being neutralized by the enemy. A battle of attrition began for each hill. *SS-Regiment "Germania"*, which already had 250 casualties during the attack on Malgobek, shrunk even more. At 1300 hours, the *III. (finnisches)/"Nordland"* entered the fighting on the southern wing of the assault wedge. It was only able to advance slowly due to strong *Pak* and artillery flanking fire from Ssagopschin. At 1645 hours, it finally dug in on a captured hill.

The *Bataillon* command post was located on the reverse slope of the mountain with the "white house". The "white house" of Malgobek will always remain in the memories of the soldiers that fought there.

During the morning of 8 October, *III. (finnisches)/"Nordland"* again entered the fighting as part of the overall operation. The *Bataillon's* attack sector was in a line with Ssagopschin. At 0900 hours, shortly after the beginning of the attack, the assaulting *III.* (*finnisches*)/"*Nordland*" received strong flanking fire from a corn field to the southeast and from Russian artillery in Ssagopschin. While *11. Kompanie* captured a hill, the attacking *9. Kompanie* and *10. Kompanie* advanced only slowly due to the flanking fire from the corn field. At the same time, these companies had to repel an enemy counterattack supported by four tanks. By the onset of twilight, they were in line with *11. Kompanie*. The *Bataillon* dug in. Its daily report noted three dead and 23 wounded; amongst them *Chef* of *10. Kompanie*, *Obersturmführer* Porsch, who was killed.

Even the attack by *SS-Regiment* "*Germania*" brought only small territorial gains. Bare hills and heights, covered with dried steppe grass and corn fields, cut through with deep balkas, offered the defender great advantages.

Oberführer Wagner, commander of *SS-Regiment* "*Germania*", was forced to again reorganize his attacking forces after he received the smallest of units that the division managed to somehow free up. As the flanks became longer, the need for more forces grew constantly. As part of that reorganization process, the *III.* (*finnisches*)/"*Nordland*" had to give up its captured terrain and the old departure position secured by other elements. The Finnish *Bataillon*, as part of *SS-Regiment* "*Germania*", was to attack on the next day the dominating Hill 701. Situated between Malgobek and Wosnessensskaja, it had a view over the Grusinian military road. Hill 701 and the defensive area around Wosnessensskaja were the last bulwarks before the 60 kilometre-distant, and fervently desired German objective, Grosny oil region to the east.

On 9 October, at approximately 0415 hours, the *III.* (*finnisches*)/"*Nordland*" was attached to *SS-Regiment* "*Germania*" and marched into its new assembly area two kilometres east of Malgobek. At approximately 0700 hours, the assembly was completed on a reverse slope in front of Hill 701. After the Chef of *10. Kompanie*, *Obersturmführer* Porsch, was killed, the weak *10. Kompanie* and *11. Kompanie* were combined and commanded by the *Chef* of *11. Kompanie*, *Obersturmführer* Mühlinghaus. At 0845 hours the company and platoon leaders were briefed by *Sturmbannführer* Collani and the attack was discussed. A reconnaissance troop was to be sent ahead because the enemy situation was not clear.

A reconnaissance troop under *Obersturmführer* Pohjanlehto departed. At 0930 hours Pohjanlehto reported as follows to the commander: it was a 300 metre-long slope descending to the east without any cover in the direction of the attack. The reconnaissance troop already received both strong frontal and flanking infantry fire on the coverless slope, resulting in four men of the reconnaissance troop being wounded.

Collani held a council with his company and platoon leaders. The *Bataillon* reported the conclusions of this discussion to *SS-Regiment* "*Germania*": The attack could not be successful under these flanking conditions; initially the flanking situation on the right, from Dieckmann's Hill and from the left in the battle area of *II./* "*Germania*", had to be eliminated. The *I./* "*Germania*" and *II./* "*Germania*" had been fighting for these heights since early morning.

The telephones were ringing at headquarters. The wires were busy. There was a discussion as to what to do. Heavy weapons were brought up and became active. German artillery had been pounding Hill 701 since noon. *SS-Regiment* "*Germania*" did not make a decisive breakthrough. At 1300 hours *Oberführer* Wagner insisted on bringing up *III. (finnisches)/"Nordland"* because he was of the opinion that only a fight, hill by hill, promised any chances of an advance.

German artillery covered Hill 701 with smoke grenades just before the attack by the Finnish *Bataillon*. The Mühlinghaus assault group (*10. Kompanie* and *11. Kompanie*) attacked at 1350 hours. The Russians laid down barrier fire with artillery and mortars and their tanks fired from the Dieckmann's height area (from the right). By 1500 hours the Finns had advanced 400 to 500 metres, but then the enemy fire became impenetrable. At 1545 hours *SS-Regiment* "*Germania*" ordered its assault *bataillone*: Transition and reorganize for defence. The Finns also dug in. The casualties for *III. (finnisches)/"Nordland"* on that day were three dead and 24 wounded. A *Pionierzug* (24 men) from *Grenadierregiment 70* (*111. Infanterie-Division*) was attached to the *Bataillon* during the following night. Its mission was to blow up obstacles and to combat enemy tanks.

On 10 October, just as the Finnish volunteers were getting ready for a renewed attack on Hill 701, a heavy Russian artillery barrage at 0855 hours on the assembly area, resulted in eleven casualties (amongst them two leaders). Six Russian tanks had been observed on the right, the Dieckmann heights, which could have substantially disrupted the *Bataillon* attack. Two enemy tanks were on Hill 701. The Russians expected the German attack and had brought up reserves; their artillery

Affix
stamp
here

Pen and Sword Books
c/o Casemate Publishers
1950 Lawrence Road
Havertown, PA 19083

was firing nervously. At 1000 hours the two *VB* (*vorgeschobener Beobachter* – forward artillery observer) from *1. SS-Artillerieregiment 5* and from *Heeres-Artillerie-Abteilung 607*, who were to control the fire of their batteries during the attack, became casualties through direct hits.

The I./"Germania" and *II./"Germania"* were attacking again to the left and right of the Finnish *Bataillon*. Collani received the order to get ready to also attack. The Finns began their assault at 0950 hours; they again did not get very far. At 1000 hours the fresh Soviet 9th Rifle Brigade, supported by 12 tanks, attacked from the east and southeast. Dangerous situations arose. The Germans and Finns were forced to go over to the defensive from the attack. The thin German front threatened to tear apart at several places. *Gruppe Mühlinghaus* had to be inserted on the left wing of the *Bataillon*, its front facing to the north and northeast, to support the *II./"Germania"*, which was being attacked, and to prevent the threatened penetration of the *HKL*. The *pioniere* from *111. Infanterie-Division* were deployed to defend the route that led to Malgobek between the hills defended by *II./"Germania"* and *III./"Nordland"*. The staff from *III./"Nordland"* prepared for close-in defence. The battle swayed to and fro the entire day. By 1700 hours the Russian attacking force was finally broken. That day of fighting indicated clearly that *SS-Regiment "Germania"* had powerful enemy forces in front of it. They were in a deeply-echeloned defensive system with strong support, from which they were also able to attack. On 10 October the Finnish *Bataillon* had four dead and 24 wounded.

11 October was spent defending against Russian attacks. At 0810 hours the Russians attacked *Gruppe Mühlinghaus* from the east (remainder of *10. Kompanie* and *11. Kompanie*) and at 0900 hours *Gruppe Troiker* (*9. Kompanie*). Strong enemy *Pak* and mortar fire kept the Finns pinned down. By 0930 hours the Russian counterattacks had been repelled. *Untersturmführer* Walgenbach, an NCO and three men were killed.

The *9. Kompanie* under *Hauptsturmführer* Troiker, which was defending the sector of *III. (finnisches)/"Nordland"* nearly all by itself, also repelled all enemy attacks on12 October. Only in the right sector did weak enemy forces penetrate into the group of houses at the kolhoz. Our own reconnaissance troop sent out in the afternoon toward the house grouping brought back six prisoners with weapons. According to their statements, the Russians were planning a night attack. On that basis, the German artillery fired on the suspected assembly areas.

On 13 October, supported by three tanks, the Russians renewed their attacks. German artillery, by then well-coordinated with the infantry, smashed the attacking waves with barrier curtains of fire. But the Finnish casualties also left gaps in the Finnish *Bataillon*. They could only be closed with the last reserves from the *Pionierzug* of the *12. Kompanie* and one *Zug* from the *11. Kompanie* (16 men). There was a crisis situation on the right wing of the *Bataillon*, at the *9. Kompanie*. The Russians were able to dig themselves in 50 metres in front of the kolhoz on the right wing of *9. Kompanie*. One combat reconnaissance troop sent out during the evening to the kolhoz chased the Russians out of the houses and brought back two prisoners, one sMG, two lMG, and two machine pistols. The *9. Kompanie* closed up a bit to the right. At 1900 hours the remainder of *10. Kompanie* and *11. Kompanie* (*Gruppe Mühlinghaus*) were deployed on the left wing of the Finnish *Bataillon*. The sick *Hauptsturmführer* Troiker, *Chef* of *9. Kompanie*, was replaced by *Obersturmführer* Pallesche. The *Bataillon* casualties for 13 October were two dead and four wounded.

The German *HKL* near Hill 701 was like a finger that pushed far to the east, where the military objective of Grosny lay. There, amongst the mountains and ridges, with its steppe-like character, the god of war tested the combatants of both sides. Technology and materiel did not play the decisive role there. There counted the infantryman, the *pionier* and the lone fighter who, with courage and total disregard for death, with the strength of his heart, brought about decisions; decisions that, in the final analyses, depended upon the law of numbers. To relieve some of the offensive pressure on that jutting finger, a *Kampfgruppe* from *111. Infanterie-Division* attacked farther north with the support of tanks from *13. Panzerdivision*, and pushed that frontal sector a number of hills farther east. On that 14 October, the fighting near Hill 701 was restricted by both sides to the deployment of artillery, mortars, and *Pak*. But already during the next night, Hill 701 became part of the planning of German staffs. The attacking groups Dieckmann (*I./"Germania"*) and Nickel (*Grenadier-Regiment 70* from *111. Infanterie-Division*), with the support of *Sturmgeschütze*, were to get the German attack on Wosnessensskaja-Grosny moving again on 15 October. The *I./"Germania"* got ready for the attack against Dieckmann's hill and *Bataillon Nickel* against Hill 701. *Bataillon Nickel* had *9./"Germania"* attached to it. The *III./"Germania"*, the last *"Wiking"* unit that had arrived from the western Caucasus, was inserted in company form into the gaps of *SS-Regiment "Germania"*.

On 15 October 1942 the German attack groups began the assault at 0700 hours. The fighting continued all day long without any decisive success. At 1615 hours *Oberführer* Wagner ordered *Sturmbannführer* Collani to take up position with *III. (finnisches)/"Nordland"* near the kolhoz on the right wing of the *Bataillon*. *Obersturmführer* Pallesche's *9. Kompanie* attacked from its positions but was soon forced to go to ground due to enemy blocking and flanking fire. Then, strong enemy forces attacked from the flank and, when the encirclement of *9. Kompanie* became apparent, Pallesche ordered a withdrawal to the starting positions. The Finnish *Bataillon* suffered 13 dead and 16 wounded on 15 October.

Hill 701 occupied the minds of the military commanders. The commander of "*Wiking*", *Generalleutnant der Waffen-SS* Felix Steiner, wrote about that:

> The commanding general (Ott) demanded the capture of Hill 701, which blocked the line of sight to the Grusinian military road at one place. To the question from the division commander (Steiner) as to 'why', he answered, 'indispensable for artillery observation and continuation of the operation'. There was no answer to the question 'with what is the attack to continue?' There were great differences, into which the *Armee* also intervened and demanded the deployment of the last reserves...Responsible soldiers will make every effort to carry out assignments when orders and conscience are in agreement. For the first time, that was not possible at Malgobek.[7]

The *LII. Armeekorps* once more demanded the capture of Hill 701. The division had to use the previous *bataillone* because no others were available. *Sturmbannführer* Collani went into the positions of his *bataillone* on 15 October to explain to his men the renewed orders. That meeting and the subsequent attack on the following day were recorded by Tauno Pohjanlehto, and their context was given here:

On 15 October, when Collani arrived, at the foot of Hill 701, directly under the Russians in one of their abandoned bunkers, was

7. Steiner, loc cit, page 172.

Obersturmführer Pohjanlehto's platoon from *9. Kompanie*. Collani explained the deployment for the next day. Pohjanlehto's platoon was to open a breach as the spearhead on the next day. Time of attack: During the evening hours of 16 October, an unusual time for an attack. They relied on surprise. To maintain the moment of surprise, the artillery did not open the attack. In a surprise move, *I./"Germania"* on the right and *II./"Germania"* on the left were to attack simultaneously with the Finnish *Bataillon*, which was to also send out shock troops. That is it from Collani.

The men had listened attentively. They were determined to fight and were willing to once more attack Hill 701; that time at great speed, with surprise. Someone in the bunker hummed the devil's song; the "ha-hah-haaah" was shouted so loudly that the Russians must have heard it. That fired up the enthusiasm of Mühlinghaus, *Chef* of the *11. Kompanie*, who also happened to be in the bunker, so that he did his best with the "trumpet of Vionville" in French. Collani left the bunker late.

On the morning of 16 October 1942, the mountains and valleys near Malgobek were covered in fog. Five tanks from *1./Panzerregiment "Wiking"* were brought up to support *III. (finnisches)/"Nordland"*. Once more, the staffs of the attacking *bataillone* tried to delay the attack, or even get it cancelled by the superior commands. But the decision remained the same: *Attack!* And then, as planned, a surprise attack during the evening hours without any preparatory fire by the heavy weapons, which were only to intervene during the second phase.

The Finns prepared carefully for the attack. Shock troop leader Pohjanlehto briefed his squad leaders. They prepared a plan. The Russians had expected advances in the morning; they were on guard particularly during the fog. And when nothing happened during the day, they obviously let their vigilance slip a little toward evening. That was the exact time that the Finns chose for their attack.

At 1700 hours the shock troops from both *bataillone* of "*Germania*" and the Pohjanlehto shock troop from the Finnish *Bataillon* were ready in their departure positions for the attack. The men readied their weapons, and stuck hand grenades under their belts. *Obersturmführer* Pohjanlehto looked at his watch. Slowly, too slowly, did the hand move forward. Feverish tension was everywhere.

The watches moved to 1730 hours. A hand signal was given, not a word was spoken. Like tigers leaping toward their prey, the men of the shock troops jumped up and ran toward Hill 701. In no time at all, the Finns were at the Russian positions on the ridge. They fired bursts from machine pistol into the first Russian foxholes from the shortest of distances. In a state of battle intoxication, the Finns totally surprised the Russians. Before the Russians really knew what was going on, the Finns were in the centre of their positions.

Only then did the Finns recognize the deeply-echeloned Russian defensive system. The deeper they penetrated, and the higher they got, the more intense was the awakened Russian defensive fire. To isolate the shock troops and to prevent the arrival of reinforcements, the Russian barrier fire from the heavy weapons became a thick curtain behind Pohjanlehto's men. German artillery then fired onto the Russian defensive system and the mountain ridge in front of the shock troops. Everywhere, there was the chattering of machineguns and machine pistols, and the detonations of hand grenades.

Pohjanlehto's shock troop was in the centre of the Russian mountain position. The German tanks had penetrated through the Russian barrier fire and were rolling up Hill 701. However, they soon received heavy *Pak* fire from the mountain top and had to drive under cover. Pohjanlehto's men fought like lions. Hand-to-hand fighting raged everywhere. A heavy Russian shell exploded among the storming *Gruppe Pyyhtiä* and *Sturmmann* Kesti was literally torn to pieces. To the left of the storming shock troop leader, a hand grenade flew toward *Unterscharführer* Metz, who attempted to catch it. He was not successful. The hand grenade detonated between Metz's legs and killed him.

Unterscharführer Miettinen received a stomach wound from a short distance as he was charging ahead; he fired an entire magazine from his machine pistol into a Russian foxhole as he fell. *Obersturmführer* Pohjanlehto and his messenger Sakari Miettinen jumped into a Russian foxhole but did not find enough room for two; so they lay firmly pressed on the ground with MG bursts just sweeping over their heads. Nearby, they recognized a Russian under full cover in his foxhole with his MPi lying at its edge. It was a question of: *Either you or me*. Pohjanlehto pushed his MPi forward, aimed, and waited. A few metres away, a Russian hat came into view, then a head. Pohjanlehto pulled the trigger and the Russian received an MPi burst to the head. Onward!

The Finns then raced toward the last part of the mountain ridge. In the process, three Russian *Pak* were eliminated by hand grenades. Dead

Russians lay everywhere and others began to flee. Once the *Pak* had been eliminated the German tanks drove up the mountain. With them arrived *Obersturmführer* Mühlinghaus, and the men from the *10. Kompanie* and the *11. Kompanie*, which formed *Gruppe Mühlinghaus*. They brought more hand grenades and magazines to the shock troops. The mountain ridge was cleaned up. Approximately a company of Russians were taken prisoner. In addition, there was a lot of booty in the form of numerous antitank rifles and machineguns, two heavy infantry howitzers, and a large number of hand-held weapons. By 1800 hours Hill 701 was in the hands of the Finns. The battle had lasted thirty minutes. What had been attempted during many days of assault with great losses was accomplished on 16 October 1942 within half an hour. What nobody believed would happen, had happened.

The last six men from *Shock Troop Pohjanlehto* sat on the hill and took a breather. Just getting to the top of the mountain on the run was quite an achievement. They had removed their steel helmets from their heads. Sweat ran down their dirt covered faces. They held the first cigarettes in their shaking fingers. Only slowly did the excitement ease off. Then it was onward once more. The Russians were forming up for a counterattack. German artillery, guided by *VB* in the foremost line, fired into them. Quiet set in as it got dark. Hill 701 was firmly in the hands of the Finns.

That was the gist of Pohjanlehto's report.

The war diary of *III. (finnisches)/"Nordland"* added that enemy counterattacks were repelled by the Finns with the support of tanks from *1./Panzerabteilung "Wiking"*. Eighty prisoners were captured, as well as 5 *Pak*, 2 antitank rifles, 6 lMGs, 4 sMGs, 30 MPi, and numerous other war materiel. The attack cost the *Bataillon* two dead and 16 wounded.

Hill 701 towers above the other hills. From there is a view of the Wosnessensskaja area, where the Grusinian military road ran. Along that Transcaucasian road was delivered Allied aid to the farthest corners of the Russian Terek sector. However, an effective barrier could only be created where that road exited the mountains near Ordshonikidse. The *III. Panzerkorps* of *General* von Mackensen was advancing along the mountains to the east to create such a barrier.

The loss of Hill 701 meant restricted movements for the Russians and they would do everything possible to recapture Hill 701. That was also quite obvious to the German commands. As they had no reserves worth mentioning, they looked with trepidation to the coming days. The German artillery had to pick up the slack because the infantry had been severely weakened. New barrier fire areas were established and sufficient ammunition made ready.

During the night of 17 October 25 replacements, having arrived at the trains, were brought forward to the Finnish *Bataillon*.

The Russians had given themselves the goal for recapturing Hill 701 on 17 October. The assaults started in the early morning, initially with Russian artillery. At 0500 hours began the continuous, company-strong, enemy attacks, aided by thick fog. The Russians made them from directly in front of the Finnish positions. Machineguns and machine pistols started to rattle. There were shadowy movements in the morning fog; an eerie war. If one could only see!

The *9. Kompanie* lay to the left on Hill 701, the *10. Kompanie* and the *11. Kompanie* (combined into *Gruppe Mühlinghaus*) to the right.

The *9. Kompanie* had only 15 men in the position. The heart and soul of the defence were Elmgren and Kuuri, two daring Finns. The *HKL* was occupied thinly, too thinly, and the Russians could infiltrate everywhere in the fog. But the company had five lMGs and one sMG in position. Every second man operated a machinegun. The Finns were going to sell their skins as dearly as possible. A Russian group penetrated into the Finnish lines due to the lack of visibility in the fog. At the company command post, a hole directly behind the peak, the company commander of the *9. Kompanie*, *Obersturmführer* Pallesche, was severely wounded. The Russians were thrown back. Over the intact telephone line to the *Bataillon*, the company troop leader reported the situation and the wounding of the *Chef*. There, the bad news reports came thick and fast; some also arrived from *Gruppe Mühlinghaus*. *Sturmbannführer* Collani ordered his *1. Ordonnanzoffizier*, *Untersturmführer* Ertel, to take over command of the *9. Kompanie*. Ertel was given 12-man replacements to take with him and as much ammunition and hand grenades as the men could carry.

It was still twilight when Ertel moved forward with the new men. Right after that, at 0515 hours, the news of Pallesche becoming a casualty, arrived at *Bataillon*. The path was still visible, the blurred outline of Hill 701 showed up against the morning sky. Red and white flares indicated the boundaries of the Finnish *HKL*, as well as the situation. At the company command post, a miserable hole, Ertel was briefed by the company troop leader, but there was not much to be briefed on; the Russians were attacking and the situation was constantly changing. At the front, Elmgren and Kuuri were keeping the Russians at some distance. The weapons were making a racket. There were muffled explosions of hand grenades. The replacement men jumped into the gaps. *Obersturmführer* Pallesche lay beside the company command post with a thick bandage around his head. He still moaned as the men carried him away; when he arrived at the first aid post he was dead.

To the right, a similar confused situation existed at *Gruppe Mühlinghaus*. There, the Russians were attacking even more vigorously. One group of Russians had passed through the thin frontline and reached the company command post, the same Russian bunker in which *Shock Troop Pohjanlehto* had assembled on the evening of 15 October. *Obersturmführer* Mühlinghaus, just in the process of going to the front, was killed at 0515 hours. *Unterscharführer* Sahlmann and his messengers chased the Russians back. Sahlmann temporarily took over command and reported the situation to *Bataillon*. From there came the order for *Obersturmführer* Pohjanlehto to take over the remnants of *10. Kompanie*, *11. Kompanie*, and *Gruppe Mühlinghaus*. Pohjanlehto, the last officer from that group, was in position at the very front and guided the defensive battle, insofar as there was something to guide in tha situation. *Unterscharführer* Sahlmann, the company troop leader, was killed. *Obersturmführer* Pohjanlehto, a forester by profession, was the heart and soul of the defensive battle in the right sector of the Finnish *Bataillon*.

At 0530 hours the *VB* from *11./SS-Artillerie-Regiment 5* was wounded. The *VB* from *3./SS-Artillerie-Regiment 5* had no contact with the firing position. Need makes for inventiveness: The lines from Hill 701 to *Bataillon* command post were still intact, and telephone lines ran from the *Bataillon* command post to the command posts of the artillery. In such a roundabout way, contact was made with the firing positions. The barrier fire was activated at the right time and was guided onto the correct positions.

Close combat with machine pistols and hand grenades continued. The Finns defended themselves with the courage of desperation. They exceeded themselves during that hour. Comradeship, where one supports the other, showed itself in its highest form. They helped each other, and warned each other by shouting. Everywhere, machineguns rattled, machine pistols chattered and hand grenades exploded with dull echoes that resounded through the valley. The mountain crest seethed from the battle. The Finns held their ground.

The enemy launched a new attack on Pohjanlehto's company, on the right wing of the *Bataillon* sector. Under the cover of the fog, by 0700 hours the Russians had worked themselves forward to within 20 metres of the Finnish positions. Pohjanlehto rushed to the threatened wing, had hand grenades brought forward, and sent a messenger to the tanks positioned on the reverse slope. He requested them to advance and support his men because he expected a penetration in his thin, outermost right wing. Then two tanks arrived. Supported by the Finns, they chased the Russians back in a counterattack. The tanks returned to their assembly area because they were not safe from close-in antitank attacks in the fog.

The Russians moved up again and put pressure on the right wing of the *Bataillon*, where Pohjanlehto was with his men. The infantry howitzers and heavy mortars of the *Bataillon* began firing again at 0730 hours and kept the Russians pinned down, preventing them from making that final jump into the Finnish position. They fired continuously. At 0735 Pohjanlehto received 25 replacements, young Finns from *Ersatz-Bataillon Graz*, and filled his gaps with them. The young Finns received the most difficult possible baptism of fire. They looked upon the veterans and copied them, and by 0800 hours that attack also collapsed in a hail of hand grenades. Then the fog also dissipated and the view improved.

Russian artillery fire rained down on Hill 701 all morning. The Finns dug deeper into the ground and improved their positions.

At noon a call came from *Bataillon* to the command post of the *9. Kompanie*. *Sturmbannführer* Collani was on the telephone and asked for *Untersturmführer* Ertel.

Collani:

> It is being reported that the enemy is attacking in front of you, is that correct?

Ertel:

> Nothing has been reported to me but I will go immediately to the front and then inform you.

Ertel crawled to the front, to *Gruppe Kuuri. Unterscharführer* Kuuri stared intensely and did not let Ertel's arrival interrupt him. Ertel also stared but did not see anything unusual. Or were his "*Ordonnanzoffizier's*" eyes not yet attuned to that of a front line officer?

Then Kuuri spoke a single word: "There!" and pointed with his hand toward his front. Then he said once more:"There, there they come!" And then Ertel could also see the brown figures 200 metres in front of him. He quickly crawled back, reported to Collani what he had seen, and requested artillery barrier fire. The fire control, as mentioned before, was somewhat elaborate. Ertel personally guided the fire of a heavy 15 cm sFH 18 battery of a *Heeres-Artillerie-Abteilung.* Shortly after, the heavy packages were rushing over their heads. The barrier areas had been determined. Ertel corrected a little. The barrier fire lay directly in front of their positions. The heavy packages had a relatively slow trajectory and, when one looked carefully, they were visible as they flew over. One could also hear how they literally drilled themselves into the ground and then exploded with a dull roar.

Then the machineguns also replied at the front. Ertel heard Kuuri call out: "Oikealle, vasemalle!" (To the right, to the left!). That is how he corrected the MG fire. Although the enemy attack was already smashed in its infancy, the situation remained tricky in front of *Gruppe Kuuri.* One of the German tanks, under the command of the south Tirolean *Untersturmführer* Nicolussi-Leck, drove to the front shortly after noon and fired into the Russians with its MGs and cannon. After a brief presence on the ridge, the tank remained in readiness on the reverse slope, in the vicinity of the command post of *9. Kompanie.* The effect that such a tank had was tremendous! Confidence grew in the ranks of the *9. Kompanie.* A powerful "brother" was then with them.

At approximaetly 1400 hours the enemy artillery fire increased again. Hill 701 shook under the impacts of shells. Then, 300 Red Army men, supported by four tanks, struck again at Pohjanlehto's position. Barrier fire by the German heavy weapons was initiated immediately after the identification of the attack at 1402 hours. The Russians ran under the fire and many got through. Once more, there was a danger of an enemy penetration on the right wing of the *Bataillon.* At 1430 hours, five German tanks rolled up, spread out on Hill 701, and fired all that the barrels would allow. When two Russian tanks were immobilized by fire the Russians broke off the attack and withdrew to their starting positions.

At 1445 hours, once more heavy enemy artillery, *Pak*, and mortar fire landed on Hill 701. The Finns expected the attack and got ready, but nothing happened. The 337th Rifle Division had lost its appetite for attack. At 1515 hours loud shouts by officers and commissars attempted to drive the Russians forward, but the "*Muschiks*" no longer wanted to do that.

On 17 October 1942, in spite of heavy Russian counterattacks, Hill 701, strongly fortified by the Russians with positions and bunkers, (some constructed of concrete) remained in the hands of the courageous Finns. In true brothers-in-arms form, the Finns and Germans had gained a great defensive victory. The ranks of the Finnish volunteer *Bataillon* had been decimated by 11 dead and 36 wounded on that day. A total of 22 prisoners from regiments 1127 and 1129 were brought in. The dead could not be counted.

As evening twilight set in, *Untersturmführer* Ertel went to the right to establish contact with *Gruppe Pohjanlehto* (remnants of *10.* and *11. Kompanie*). That is where the *schwerpunkt* was all day long. Ertel passed one of our own *Pak*. The crew showed him the way. Then Ertel met *Obersturmführer* Pohjanlehto at the company command post.

Ertel and Pohjanlehto were friends. They were once *Zugführer* with the *10. Kompanie*. Ertel called Pohjanlehto by his nickname "Poku". "Poku" reported the situation to Ertel. The Russians were attempting to regain Hill 701 by any and all means. Beside the command post, a shot-up Russian bunker was situated a burned-out motorized vehicle, a Russian *Pak* prime mover. Ertel portrayed the situation at his company and could not miss the deep folds in his friend's face. The previous few days of fighting had left their mark on Pohjanlehto's face.

The friends wanted to tune out and squeeze in some remembrances during a cigarette break. They brought up the lazy hours in Kirowograd, where they had carried out a ring blowing competition with cigarette smoke in their accommodations.

But already the seriousness of the situation of that hour had returned to them again. They discussed defence possibilities and had the feeling that they could rely on one another. They knew that they were the only officers of the Finnish volunteer *Bataillon* on Hill 701 and held it as ordered. The German *Untersturmführer* Karl-Heinz Ertel and the Finnish *Obersturmführer* Tauno Pohjanlehto were friends who symbolically showed their friendship within the *Bataillon*, yes even between two countries. And only when night covered the tortured earth did they part in silence.

As a result of the blood letting, only weak enemy advances took place against Hill 701 on 18 October; they were repelled effortlessly.

On 19 October, initially it was even relatively quiet. The morning fog rose and visibility improved. Around noon a violent artillery surprise barrage shook Hill 701. The defenders prepared for more enemy attacks. At 1200 hours approximately 300–400 Red Army soldiers launched a frontal attack on Hill 701. The defensive measures started with precision. At 1203 hours the barrier fire of all heavy weapons began. A thick curtain of fire lay in front of Hill 701. Nonetheless, by 1235 hours some enemy groups had advanced to within 50 metres of *Kompanie Ertel*. There, they remained in the defensive fire of the Finns. One more, the Finnish *Unterscharführer* Elmgren and *Unterscharführer* Kuuri controlled the defence with stoic calmness. At 1250 the *VB* of *SS-Artillerie-Regiment 5* was wounded and was replaced later. Heavy enemy artillery fire came down on Hill 701. The Russians were also able to close up to *Kompanie Pohjanlehto*. At 1315 hours three German tanks come onto the hill and provided some breathing space in two counterattacks. The Russians were pinned down 100 metres in front of the *HKL* of the Finnish *Bataillon*.

At 1535 some brave Russian officers and commissars tried to get the attack going again. In some places the Russians got to within hand grenade range of the Finnish position, resulting in hand grenade duels. The Russians did not succeed in accomplishing that last push. At approximately 1630 hours their attacking power slackened off noticeably. They withdrew as quick as a flash, leaving 19 Russian prisoners. Those were led to the rear and interrogated at the command post of *III. (finnisches)/"Nordland"*, and then transported farther to the rear.

Toward evening *Obersturmführer* Heder, *Chef* of *3. Kompanie* of *"Wiking's" Pionier Bataillon*, which was in position on the north slope of Hill 701, came to see *Untersturmführer* Ertel to establish contact. Upon Heder's question about the situation, Ertel replied: "Come, let's first have a drink of Schnaps!" They sat on the edge of a foxhole, let their legs hang inside, and drank a Schnaps that a messenger had brought. Then Ertel explained the situation quite calmly and soberly. Ertel's demeanour so impressed Heder that he has not forgotten it to this day.

During battle there is very little time to worry about the neighbour because one has so much to do. But one knows when one can rely on his neighbour. That, Heder the *Pionier-Kompaniechef*, found out once more on that evening.

The relief of the Finnish *Bataillon*, still during the same evening, came as a surprise. At 2215 hours the *III. (finnisches)/"Nordland"* on Hill 701 was relieved by *I./"Germania"* so that it could get some rest in the valley before Ssagopschin; a quiet frontal sector. The men from the Finnish *Bataillon* had earned that rest after such hard battles; all who were there will never forget Hill 701. There, Finnish fighting spirit came to the fore.

Quiet Front Sectors

On 19 October, when it became evident that the attack by *LII. Armeekorps* at the great Terek bend toward Grosny would have no operative success, the *III. Panzerkorps* was tasked by *Oberbefehlshaber* of *1. Panzerarmee*, von Kleist, with an attack to the east, along the mountains, against Ordshonikidse. As part of the process of regrouping to a new *schwerpunkt* in the Baksan-Terek triangle, the front at Malgobek and Ssagopschin was thinned out. That resulted in the shifting of sector boundaries of the corps and divisions.

The regrouping within "*Wiking*" was related to the new offensive of *General* von Mackensen's *III. Panzerkorps*. The *370. Infanterie-Division* (Becker) to the right of "*Wiking*" at Werch Kurp, moved to the right and took over the sector of *13. Panzerdivision* (Herr) at Elchotowo on the southern slopes of the Mussakai. In addition to defending its own sector, the "*Wiking*" took over the previous sector of *370. Infanterie-Division* south of Werch Kurp.

20 October 1942, 1600 hours: The two companies of *III. (finnisches)/"Nordland"* were to relieve, as they arrived, the *3. Kompani*e and *4.* of *Regiment "Westland"* in the valley before Ssagopschin. During a drive to the new frontal sector, *Obersturmführer* Hirt, *Adjutant* to Collani, drove accidentally with his car into no-mans land and onto a mine. Hirt was wounded and his driver was killed.

At 2300 hours *Sturmbannführer* Collani reported to *Regiment "Nordland"* the taking over of the new sector. Attached to the *Bataillon* were *1./SS-Pionier-Bataillon 5*, and a 2 cm *Flakzug* from *Flak-Abteilung "Wiking"*. The *8./SS-Artillerie-Regiment 5* was assigned as support.

The new front sector was quiet. Both sides tested each other through small advances. The Russian positions were 500 metres back leaning against the positional system of Ssagopschin. Only during the night did the Russians have listening posts pushed to directly in front of the Finnish position.

Sturmbannführer Collani had to be brought to the hospital with a high fever. Initially *Obersturmbannführer* Weitzdörfer, then *Hauptsturmführer* Hoy, commanded *III./"Nordland"* on a temporary basis.

A divisional order went out to all units. After that the trains within the *Bataillon* were kept under stricter control. The strength of a company train was not to exceed 25 men. The missing personnel were to be filled by Russian *Hilfswillige* (*Hiwis*) (literal translation: willing to help). All personnel freed from the trains by that action were used to fill up the fighting strengths of the companies.

On 21 October 1942, Generalleutnant Talvela, the Finnish liaison officer at the *Führerhauptquartier* (previously Generalleutnant Östermann), visited division "*Wiking*" in the Malgobek area. Of course, he was particularly interested in his Finnish countrymen. Talvela handed out many Finnish awards, and also some to Germans. Amongst them, *Untersturmführer* Ertel, commander of *9./"Nordland"*, received the Finnish Cross of Freedom, IV. Grade.

On 22 October 1942, Generalleutnant Talvela sent a report of his visit to the Finnish volunteer *Bataillon der Waffen-SS* [*III. (finnisches)/"Nordland"*] to Marshal Mannerheim, his superior commander, which is provided in the appendix.

The *III. Panzerkorps* Offensive against Ordshonikidse

The *III. Panzerkorps* offensive against Naltchik and Ordshonikidse started on 25 October1942. Each action on one side results in a counteraction from the other side. To defend against the attack by *III. Panzerkorps* with the *13. Panzerdivision* and *23. Panzerdivision* against Ordshonikidse, the Soviets were forced to denude other quiet sectors, especially in the Ssagopschin valley and by Werch Kurp, and to throw those obtained reserves into the threatened sector at Ordshonikidse. Russian resistance stiffened at the Ardon and Fiagdon rivers. The last division was always missing to force a decision. On the German side the Berlin-Brandenburg *50. Infanterie-Division* was in the process of arriving from the Crimea.

As part of new reorganizations the *III. (finnisches)/"Nordland"* was relieved in the valley before Ssagopschin. The sector of the *9. Kompanie*, and that of the combined *10.* and *11./"Nordland"*, was taken over by *II./"Nordland"* with its *5. Kompanie*. The sector of the attached *1./SS-Pionier-Bataillon 5* was taken over by *I./"Nordland"*. By stretching the rest of *Regiment "Nordland"* it was possible to free the *III. Bataillon*, which then marched into the sector south of Werch Kurp.

In the morning hours of 1 November 1942, the *III. (finnisches)/"Nordland"*, again under the command of *Sturmbannführer* Collani, relieved *I./"Westland"* in an approximately eight kilometre-wide sector south of Werch Kurp. The *Bataillon* had placed all its men in the front line but it was still only thinly-occupied. But the Russians also had to withdraw their combat-capable units to Ordshonikidse to counter the new German offensive. The Finnish *Bataillon* faced formations composed of Caucasus peoples of very little fighting value. On a nearly daily basis, defectors from the Russian 19th Brigade crossed over and immediately found employment as *Hiwis*. The enemy artillery and mortar fire was somewhat disturbing, as were the activities of well-camouflaged snipers, who waited for "notches" on the western slopes of the Mussakai.

It became obvious that the *"Wiking"* was urgently needed in front of Ordshonikidse. The *50. Infanterie-Division* (Friedrich Schmidt) raced on foot, on horse and by train, so that it could take over the sector from *"Wiking"*.

On the evening of 8 November 1942, the Finnish *Bataillon* was given a construction battalion from the *Heer*, which was inserted in groups throughout the wide sector of the *Bataillon*. Was the construction battalion to take over the sector of *III. (finnisches)/"Nordland"* until the *50. Infanterie-Division* arrived? Was it that critical to have the *"Wiking"* at Ordshonikidse? The *Bau-Bataillon* consisted of elderly men that could build bridges and positions well but had never been in the *HKL* during that war. Their conduct corresponded to that reality. Two days later the groups from the *Bau-Bataillon* were again withdrawn from the front of the Finnish *Bataillon*.

A crisis arose at Ordshonikidse before the *50. Infanterie-Division* arrived to relieve "*Wiking*" in the Werch Kurp-Malgobek sector. Again, the success and the failure of a German operation were positioned on a knife's edge. It was a matter of hours. As so often happened before, missing was the last *Bataillon* that could have tilted the scales.

Because of the crisis situation of the *III. Panzerkorps* at Ordshonikidse, the *III. (finnisches)/"Nordland"* was relieved by *II./"Westland"* in the area south of Werch Kurp during the night of 12 November, so that it could be transferred to the endangered frontal sector.

Personnel changes at "*Wiking*"

From the end of October to the beginning of November 1942, personnel changes took place at the "*Wiking*". The commander of *SS-Regiment "Nordland"*, *Oberführer* von Scholz, was transferred to the northern front. *Obersturmbannführer* Joerchel, who previously commanded *II./"Germania"*, became the new commander of *SS-Regiment "Nordland"*. The commander of *I./"Nordland"*, *Sturmbannführer* Polewacz, handed over his *Bataillon* to *Sturmbannführer* Lohmann and took over the command of *SS-Regiment "Westland"*.

When *Oberführer* Fritz von Scholz left, *SS-Regiment "Nordland"* lost an experienced and well-liked commander. He understood how to win the hearts of the Finnish volunteers with warmth and kindness. Fritz von Scholz was simultaneously a commander and a father figure to them. He never pushed his superior rank to the front, or demanded more from his men than he demanded from himself. Fritz von Scholz was always to be found where the situation was most critical and he always led from the front. He was a comrade amongst comrades, to whom his Finnish volunteers have shown respect and honour to this day.

In the shadow of Kasbek

One of the most important mountain pass roads across the Caucasus Mountains was the Grusinian military road. It linked Ordshonikidse (the old Wladikawskas) to Tiflis, the capitol city of Georgia. The

Grusinian military road had been important from ancient times. It was an important traffic artery of the Turkish Empire, which at one time included all of the Caucasus. Many mountain tribes were and still are adherents to the prophet Mohammed. Only after the Turkish Empire collapsed did the Russians penetrate into the Caucasus from the north, subjugate the mountain tribes after many battles and make them into Christians. The annexation of the Caucasus followed in 1801. At the end of the Christianization a large cross was erected at the peak of the pass, after which it is named.

However, the Russians were unable to completely quell the desire of the Caucasian tribes for freedom. Insurrections arose repeatedly, even in Stalin's time. One of Stalin's co-workers was the Grusinian labour leader and creator of Soviet heavy industry, Grigori Ordshonikidse. To honour him, Wladikawskas was renamed as Ordshonikidse. Ordshonikidse was the northern exit route of the Grusinian military road across which Allied aid had been flowing since the summer of 1941 through Persia to the Russian southern front. Ordshonikidse and the Grusinian military road also took on a great importance in the German operational planning. To get a measure of the importance of the military road, the works by the *Mil. Geo.-Bearbeitung* of the *Hochgebirgsschule* Fulpmes are repeated here. It relied on prisoner statements, descriptions by people who knew the region, Russian literature, and statements by agents. All mountain passes were numbered to hide their identity. Under number 17 of the study we read:

> Ordshonikidse through Kreuz-(Krestowyj-) Pass-Tiflis (Grusinian military road), 214 km: Suitable for all kinds of traffic, with the exception during January and February, due to snow blockage at the pass.

There follows a detailed description of the pass road.

The Anhalt-Altmark *13. Panzerdivision* had made it to Ordshonikidse as part of the new operation. The division and the screening *23. Panzerdivision* had to use all their reserves due to the long flank. The Soviets continued to throw new forces into the battle to deny the *III. Panzerkorps* success at the last minute. Division "*Wiking*", which was desperately needed there, could not be withdrawn from Malgobek and

Ssagopschin because the *50. Infanterie-Division*, which was to relieve it, had not yet arrived from the Crimea.

The Soviets were the dominating power at Ordshonikidse on 7 November 1942 and dictated the terms of battle. The *13. Panzerdivision* (commanded by Crisolli after Herr) was surrounded in the Gisel (west of Ordshonikidse) area. The *23. Panzerdivision* (von Boineburg-Lengsfeld), which had to cover long flanks, was not in a position to free the *13. Panzerdivision*.

When a negative development appeared imminent at Ordshonikidse, forces of "*Wiking*" in the valley before Ssagopschin were withdrawn and replaced by battle-inexperienced construction units, so that they could be available to *III. Panzerkorps* (von Mackensen) in a crisis situation.

The situation at Gisel became critical. The first units from "*Wiking*" were sent to the hot spot. During the night of 12 November 1942 the *II./"Nordland"* established contact with the surrounded *13. Panzerdivision* at Gisel and led the formation back to a blocking position created by other parts of "*Wiking*" on the Fiagdon. The true brothers-in-arms relationship between "*Wiking*" and *13. Panzerdivision* bore fruit once more. After it sustained heavy losses, the *13. Panzerdivision* was temporarily withdrawn from the front line. That, and strengthened Russian counterattacks made necessary the deployment of additional formations from "*Wiking*".

Because of the crisis, and the resulting re-grouping and necessary strengthening of the defence of the flank, the *III. (finnisches)/"Nordland"*, in position south of Werch Kurp, was relieved on 12 November by *II./"Westland"*. On the same day it was transferred by motorized march to Digora (100 kilometres away), where it arrived during the afternoon and bivouaced overnight. The *Bataillon* was attached to *SS-Regiment "Westland"* on the next day and brought into the area east of Chataldon, where it bivouaced.

On 14 November, at 0330 hours, the *III. (finnisches)/"Nordland"* relieved *I./Panzer-Grenadier-Regiment 126* (*23. Panzerdivision*) in position at the southeastern corner post of the front, near Chataldon-Dsuarikau.

The new position was well-constructed and reasonably quiet. It covered the main position on the Fiagdon against flank attacks from the mountains. The Finnish volunteers lay in the shadow of the Kasbek, which, with its 5,047 metre height, was the third highest mountain in the Caucasus. The Kasbek is a mighty mountain peak which glitters in the sun with its snow cap like a precious jewel and constantly draws the eyes of men. There, at the foot of the Kasbek, the Finnish volunteers had reached the farthest point of their march through Russia. Other standards had to be applied in the Caucasus. There, the oriental influence on all aspects of life was unmistakeable and there the day begins two hours earlier than in Germany and Finland. Winter was already waiting on the slopes of the Kasbek and would in time influence also the good climatic regions of Mineralnyje Wody, Pjatigorsk, and Kislowodsk. There, if not for the daily Russian artillery and mortar fire on the positions of the Finnish volunteers, they could have forgotten the war.

The quiet, positional war was also soon over. The *Bataillon* staff left on the afternoon of 21 November and drove to Karman-Ssindsikau, where it reconnoitred the defensive possibilities of the place and defined them in a plan. In the meantime, the companies remaining in position were attached to *I./"Nordland"*.

On 23 November the *Ersatz- und Ausbildungskompanie* (replacement and training company) of the Finnish *Bataillon,* commanded by *Hauptsturmführer* Ladau, arrived in Karman-Ssindsikau and took over the defence of the locality as outlined by the *Bataillon* staff. The *Ersatz- und Ausbildungskompanie* consisted of Finnish convalescents and replacements from Graz.

From 21 November on, the frontal bulge in front of Ordshonikidse was evacuated in stages. On the basis of that, the defence of the mountain flank was also shifted to the northwest.

The positional companies of the Finnish *Bataillon* in the Chataldon area were relieved by parts of *SS-Regiment "Germania"*. Under the guidance of *Obersturmführer* Deck, due to lack of officers transferred from division to *Bataillon,* they were brought to Karman-Ssindsikau, and there, integrated into the village defence.

On 25 November, as part of the withdrawal, *III. (finnisches)/"Nordland"* ended up in Tschikola by going through Digora. It was the village's defence until 28 November. *Sturmbannführer* Collani was the village *Kommandant.*

In the morning of 29 November the Finnish *Bataillon* was transported in a motorized march to Digora and became *Korps* reserve for the *III. Panzerkorps.* There was a constant alert status for the *Bataillon.* The *Ersatz- und Ausbildungskompanie* remained in Tschikola.

In the meantime the overall situation had changed in favour of the Russians. The *6. Armee* (Paulus) had been encircled at Stalingrad. The German *4. Panzerarmee* (Hoth) departed from the Kotelnikowo (Kalmyk Steppe) area for a relief attack on Stalingrad; it was given the *23. Panzerdivision* from the eastern Caucasus to do that. The *1. Panzerarmee* (von Kleist) was still in the eastern Caucasus, as a forward guard; the *XXXX. Panzerkorps* (Heinrici) north of the Terek with *Gruppe* Felmy, local Cossack units, and the *3. Panzerdivision*; by the bend in the Terek was the *LII. Armeekorps* (Ott) with *111. Infanterie-Division*, *50. Infanterie-Division*, and *370. Infanterie-Division*; in the sack by Ordshonikidse was the *III. Panzerkorps* (von Mackensen) with *13. Panzerdivision*, *SS-Division "Wiking"*, the Romanian 2nd Mountain Division, and local units.

After repelling the German offensive against Grosny and Ordshonikidse, the "Northern Group" of the "Transcaucasian Front" went over to the counterattack before Ordshonikidse with the 9th Army and 37th Army. Under the benefit of the developing situation at Stalingrad the Soviet soldiers overcame their low morale and saw everywhere an opportunity to pay the Germans back for their many defeats. The initiative for action passed over to them.

On the morning of 4 December 1942, forces from the Russian 37th Army attacked from the valley at Tschikola toward the northeast, initially capturing Tschikola. Then, in a further advance, they blocked the only supply route of *III. Panzerkorps* in the Uruch area. That was to create great difficulties for the *III. Panzerkorps*.

A thrown-together group under the command of *Oberstleutnant* Emsmann, commander of *Werfer-Regiment 52*, blocked the Tschikola area. *Gruppe Emsmann* consisted of *Werfer-Regiment 52* and *Werfer-Regiment 54* and the *Ersatz- und Ausbildungskompanie* of the Finnish *Bataillon*. The line was thin and only defended in a strongpoint fashion.

It was there at Tschikola that many men from the *Ersatzkompanie* of the Finnish *Bataillon* received their baptism of fire. The progress of the battle can be reliably reconstructed from the war diary of the *Bataillon* and from the writings of the Finns Pertteli Yli-Harja and Eero Tulonen.[8]

The Russian forces attacking on 4 December easily gained ground in the direction of Tschikola through the gaps in the German front. Only

8. Mauno Jokipii, "Panttipaljona", Weilin + Göös, Helsinki 1968, pages 579–582

Hill 710.5 south of Tschikola caused them any difficulties. A platoon from the Finnish *Ersatzkompanie* under the command of *Untersturmführer* Kuutti was in position there. They were 26 men. Hill 710.5 was quickly bypassed on both sides and *Zug Kuutti* was surrounded.

In the meantime, contact between *Zug Kuutti* and Tschikola was completely broken. Powerful Russian forces had inserted themselves between Hill 710.5 and Tschikola. *Untersturmführer* Kuutti recognized the hopelessness of his situation. He saw only one possibility of getting out of that trap. That was by advancing with his platoon in the direction of the enemy, toward a small wood by the mountain, and then returning to his own lines by a circuitous route through the densely-wooded terrain. Kuutti's order to assemble unobtrusively at a hill in the direction of the enemy was passed from foxhole to foxhole by the Finns on Hill 710.5.

Rottenführer Kalevi Könönen from Hiitola, riflemen Hauska from Viipuri, and Valtakari from Mikkeli, as well as the Germans Hellberg and Matuszewki lay in an MG position. Hellberg and Hauska were killed in an effort to reach the assembly point designated by Kuutti; Matuszewki and Valtakari were wounded.

It seemed impossible to leave the MG position. Each new attempt was extinguished by heavy enemy fire. Könönen and Pyyhtiä, the two Finns not wounded, saw no other possibility but to fight to the last and sell their skins as dearly as possible. And that is what they did. In the meantime, *Untersturmführer* Kaarlo Börje Kuuti from Porvoo and 17 men of his platoon broke out to the south and disappeared into the wooded terrain behind the Russians.

Immediately after recognizing the attack by the Russians on Tschikola as an attack on the important supply artery of *III. Panzerkorps*, *Oberstleutnant* Emsmann, commander of the blocking detachments, requested reinforcements from corps. The Finnish *Hauptsturmführer* Ladau commanded the defence of Tschikola. He soon had to recognize that he had gotten into a desperate situation. The first Russians had reached the southern outskirts of Tschikola and there was no more news from *Zug Kuutti*.

At 0900 hours the corps reserve, the Finnish *Bataillon* in Digora, was alerted and ordered to march. The *Bataillon* and company commanders went ahead and were briefed on the situation by Emsmann and Ladau.

The *10. Kompanie* and *11. Kompanie* were still combined. *Obersturmführer* Deck, just recently transferred to the Finnish *Bataillon* from division, had gone ahead to Tschikola to be briefed, while *Obersturmführer* Pohjanlehto brought up the remainder of *10.* and *11. Kompanie*, each consisting of a strong platoon. Pertteli Yli-Harja reports about the alert and the march:

> There is no snow on the ground yet. Now and then the sun breaks through the cloud cover and feeds the hope of a new spring with the growing seed on the fields and the still green hills. Our volunteer *Bataillon* is enjoying the deserved rest in Digora. Only the *Ersatzkompanie*, just arrived a few days ago, is in position as flank security.
>
> We are just in the process of baking an egg cake when the alarm is given: 'Immediate preparation for departure – we are leaving in ten minutes!' It appears extremely urgent. We quickly collect our things and the *Bataillon* is actually ready in ten minutes. With motors already running we are given a broad outline of the situation: The Russians have broken through and have surrounded one of our strongpoints (Hill 710.5), occupied by *Jäger*, with strong forces. We are to launch a counterattack and free our comrades.
>
> There was a certain disquiet while on the personnel transport vehicles: the magazines of the machine pistols are checked, steel helmets placed on heads, hand grenades tucked under belts, the entrenching tools carefully tightened.
>
> The trucks start moving. Everyone looks determined to the front where the Russians have not only threatened our "new ones" but the whole frontal sector with its vitally important *Rollbahn*.[9]

By 1100 hours the German command had an exact overall view of the situation. It was as follows: Two enemy battalions were advancing along the Chasnidon-Nowo Uruch high road. Two enemy regiments advanced from southwest and the south on Tschikola and the *Rollbahn* north of there; initially against the line brickworks-factory-refrigeration plant. There was mortar, MG, and rifle fire on the outskirts of Tschikola. Russian artillery fired into the village from the southwest. The outskirts

9. Mauno Jokipii, loc cit, page 579 ff.

of Tschikola were in Finnish hands, with the exception of the house grouping between the brickworks and the refrigeration plant.

Sturmbannführer Collani issued the deployment orders quickly and succinctly: *9. Kompanie* was to screen the *Rollbahn*, *11. Kompanie* (and the remainder of *10. Kompanie*) were to assemble by the refrigeration plant and throw the Russians back to the south across Hill 710.5.

The company commanders took charge of the arriving companies and briefed them on their assembly areas and security deployments. *Untersturmführer* Ertel's *9. Kompanie* quickly took over screening of the *Rollbahn*. It was 1120 hours. The remainders of *10. Kompanie* and *11. Kompanie* arrived after the *9. Kompanie*. Pertteli Yli-Harja reports about that:

> Daring and at high speed, we entered Tschikola at 1100 hours. The enemy attacking from the southwest and south had already reached the outskirts of Tschikola and was firing on the racing vehicles on the *Rollbahn*. Quickly, we jumped off the vehicles and behind the protection of the houses, and did a weapons and equipment check. Then *Obersturmführer* Pohjanlehto arrived with the attack orders for the platoon of *10. Kompanie* and explained the situation and how to carry out the assault: The Russians were located in the drainage ditches outside the village. It was a powerful force but with few heavy weapons. The combined *10.* and *11. Kompanie* initially attacked the houses this side of the drainage ditches and then spread out as soon as the drainage ditches were overcome. The attack was supported by two of our tanks and two *Flak* half-tracks, as well as *Nebelwerfer* (rocket projectiles) and our mortars.

The men from *10.* and *11. Kompanie* got ready for the attack by the refrigeration plant. The *Werfer* batteries fired. Howling terribly and screaming, the rocket projectiles passed over our heads toward the enemy with a long, fiery tail. The attack began at 1205 hours!

Pertteli Yli-Harja wrote:

> As our *Flak* half-tracks and the artillery were firing, gun powder smoke and dust rose in the enemy positions. The Russians remained under cover. Our assault was quick, the quickest I had ever experienced.

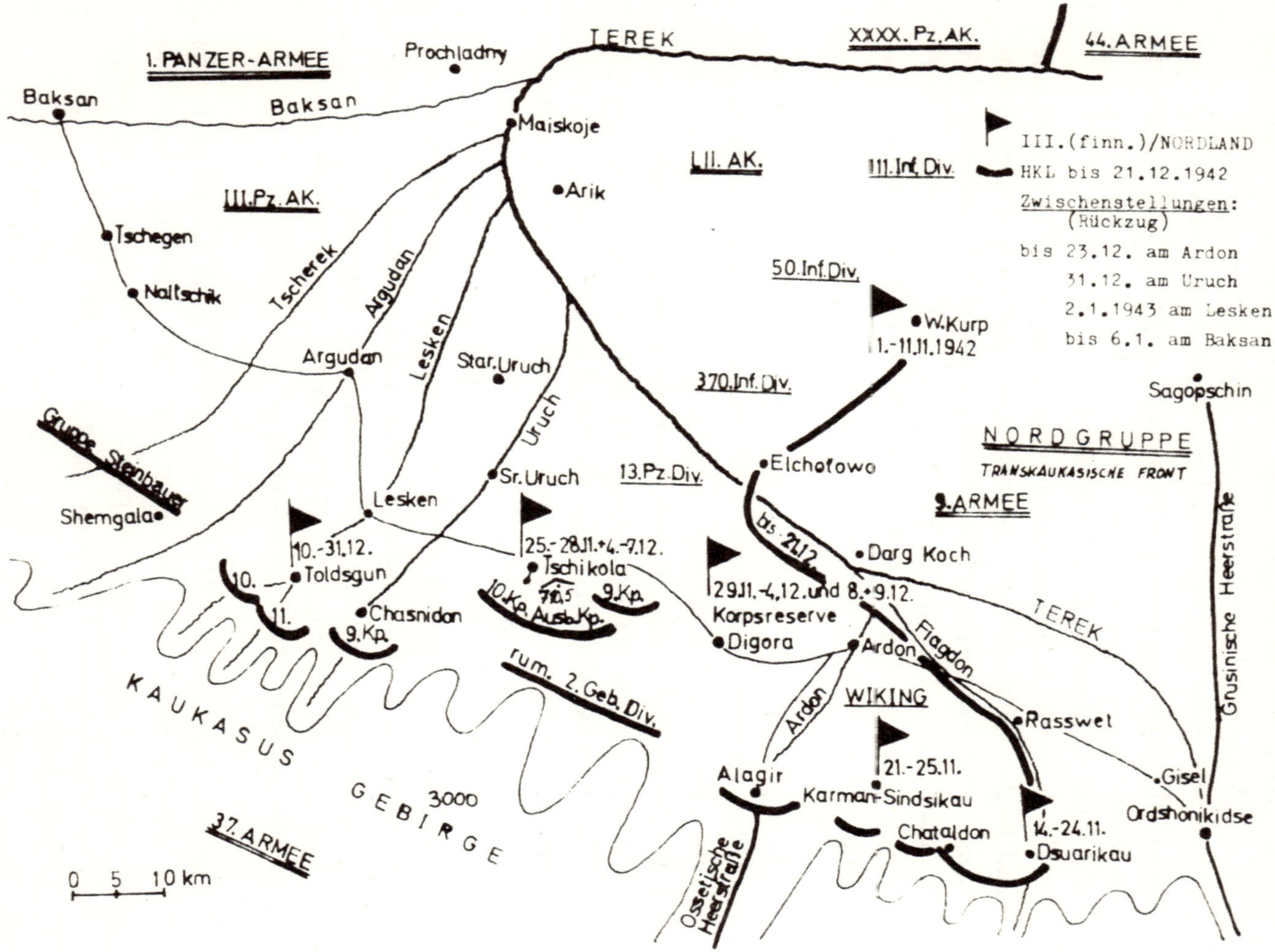

Fighting before Ordshonikidse on the mountain flank, November 1942–January 1943.

> Our heavy weapons supported us well. Soon, the first attack objective was reached. Onward! We waded through a watercourse, fanned out, and threw ourselves onto the enemy in the elongated hollow. After a few bursts from the machine pistol and a few hand grenades into the electricity building, 15 Russians came out and surrendered. Quickly onward! The enemy was firing from the hollow with machine pistols and machineguns. Bullets flew around our ears. Shells impacted in our vicinity. But our weapons also spoke. There, an MG gunner stormed forward, the Iron Cross on his chest, firing his MG from the hip. And over there, the Finnish machine pistol of our Finnish *Rottenführer* with the splendid full beard was singing. And there, by a fence, the German *Gruppenführer* was firing carefully aimed bursts into the enemy line. The first Russian positions were reached. An enemy machine pistol was pointed, but failed to fire. The Russian hurriedly grabbed his pistol and fired, missed, and was hit himself. Yelling, we lunged into the hollow. The enemy weakened. First one, then more took flight. And then it was chaos! The Russians fled. We went after them and fired on them. As I ran by I 'awakened' someone pretending to be dead.

Obersturmführer Deck was leading the attacking group consisting of *10. Kompanie* and *11. Kompanie. Obersturmführer* Hortling and *Obersturmführer* Pohjanlehto led the smaller groups. Weapons spoke everywhere. Initially the Russians defended themselves tenaciously, but then fled back into the mountain valley from which they came.

> Then enemy mortars fired barrier fire. The mortar rounds arrived at regular intervals. Nonetheless, *Zug Hortling* charged up the slope, toward our strongpoint, which was surrounded. The other groups continued the pursuit to the left and right. We took many prisoners, and many of those fleeing, trying to reach the wooded area, were killed by our fire.

Zug Hortling from the *11. Kompanie* stormed up Hill 710.5. There, too, the Russians retreated. The fearful question as to what had happened to *Zug Kuutti*, which had been in position on the hill, was answered. Eero Tulonen writes about that:

> We approached the foxholes of *Zug Kuutti* and were initially startled. Here was a German military coat, there a flask and mess kit. Up to then, no trace of our own. Then two men called out and waved to us, two of our own. We rushed forward, and found *Rottenführer* Könönen and rifleman Pyyhtiä alive in a foxhole, by a machinegun, with mountains of empty shell casings around them. We also found the wounded riflemen Matuszewki and Valtakari, and the dead Hellberg and Hauska. There was no trace of the other men of *Zug Kuutti*.
>
> Once we had reached Hill 710.5 the Russians unleashed murderous mortar fire upon it. We found cover in the foxholes. *Sturmmann* Järvi was killed on the edge of a foxhole by mortar splinters. A direct hit landed in the foxhole where *Obersturmführer* Hortling was and completely shredded his upper body. We had great concerns over *Zug Kuutti*. No trace of it. We assumed that they had been captured.[10]

By 1300 hours Hill 710.5 had been relieved. While *Zug Hortling* went into position there, the other assault forces of *10. Kompanie* and *11. Kompanie* continued. At 1400 hours they swung over to the west and attacked the southwestern part of Tschikola. Supported by a *Werfer* battery and a *Flak-Sfl-Zug*, the attack was swift. It quickly moved past the brickworks. By 1430 hours the southwestern part of Tschikola was reached. Consequently, the assault group was on the right flank of the enemy. Flanking fire also broke all resistance and the remaining cohesion of the Russian forces, which then tried to find safety in a hasty, disorganized retreat to the mountains. The Russian 295th Rifle Division lost 13 officers and 246 men as prisoners, as well as much war materiel. The victory by the assault group of *Obersturmführer* Deck with the remainder of *10. Kompanie* and *11. Kompanie* was built upon the courageous perseverance and behaviour of the Finnish *Ersatzkompanie* of the *Bataillon*. The Finns had six dead and seven wounded. Amongst the dead was *Obersturmführer* Kai William Hortling, born on 14 April 1916 in Iisalmi in Finland, and *Sturmmann* Joel Matti Järvi, born on 28 November 1921 in Ylihärmä in Finland. Both were killed on 4 December 1942 on Hill 710.5 at Tschikola in the Caucasus. Unending distances, childhood, youth, dreams and tears,

10. Mauno Jokipii, loc cit, page 580.

hopes and an unfulfilled short life in between – years of happiness and suffering, but only a brief moment to eternity.

According to statements by prisoners, the Russian 295th Rifle division was to capture Tschikola and continue in the direction of Darg Koch to block the supply road of *III. Panzerkorps* and bring about its destruction.

Pertteli Yli-Harja writes in conclusion:

> Soon everything was over. The enemy had withdrawn into a forest one kilometre distant. Many prisoners were taken in our sector and just as many enemy lay on the ground. Amongst the prisoners were two regimental commanders and, from one regiment, nearly the entire staff, which we had to get out of a basement. Amongst the prisoners also were a regimental adjutant and his wife. Another woman was amongst the dead. We received detailed information from the prisoners about the enemy and found out how bad his situation is. As food, one prisoner had a sheep's head. It was neither cooked nor roasted, nor even had the skin removed. No prisoner had bread with him. They received a soup from the field kitchen of some millet and grass seed. They were hungry. The enemy forces were five to six times superior to us. However, once their leadership had been taken prisoner, all of the Russian assault forces became helpless.

It was the men from *Zug Kuutti* who had a substantial part in the success of the *Bataillon* by holding Hill 710.5 and thereby slowing down the advance of the Russians. At the end, two dead, two wounded, and two men determined to fight were on Hill 710.5 and held it because they had no other choice. The God of war shoved two nondescript men into the deciding scales of battle, where they unexpectedly and unwillingly had to intervene and then, with their bravery, brought about the change. And how often does it happen that some nondescript men contribute substantially to victory!

The courageous Finns, *Rottenführer* Kalevi Könönen, born on 29 August 1918 in Hiitolä, and rifleman Yrjö Pyyhtiä, born on 20 July 1922 in Viitasaari, were mentioned on 27 August 1943 in the *"Ehrenblatt des Deutschen Heeres"* for their actions on Hill 710.5. They did not wear the associated "*Ehrenblattspange*" on their German field uniform because by August 1943 the *Bataillon* had already been disbanded.[11]

What happened to the men from *Zug Kuutti* who had retreated, under the command of *Untersturmführer* Kuutti, from Hill 710.5 in the direction of the enemy?

Untersturmführer Kuutti and the 17 men of his *Zug* were successful in breaking into the enemy hinterland. They had to choose that extraordinary route because the direct way to their own troops was blocked by strong Russian forces. The Kuutti group initially ran around confused in the enemy hinterland. It accidentally ran into Russian supply columns, reserves marching to the front, and even a field hospital. But it did not get involved in any fighting. *Untersturmführer* Kuutti led his men to the east because, according to his observations, that was the best direction to find a suitable crossing of the front-line. They proceed from one hiding place to another, all planned and safe. One move followed the other. It went better once it got dark because the danger of being discovered was less. The men already had 20 kilometres behind them and were becoming tired and apathetic. Kuutti motivated them time and again, and gave them courage and hope. They reached the front lines when it was completely dark. They listened and observed. Incomprehensible words convinced them that the front line was near – through it then! They were fired upon but without effect. They finally met German soldiers at Digora. There they found out that they had crossed the front line in the sector of the Romanian 2nd Mountain Division. What could have happened?

A vehicle from *III. Panzerkorps* took them from Digora to Tschikola. When *Untersturmführer* Kuutti reported his *Zug* to *Sturmbannführer* Collani as having returned, a heavy stone fell off the shoulders of everyone. *Untersturmführer* Börje Kaarlo Kuutti, born on 5 November 1918 in Porvoo, Finland, mastered an apparently hopeless situation with

---

11. Könönen and Pyyhtiä were ordered to an event in Helsinki by their front-line units in the spring of 1944 and were, in addition to other Finns, subsequently given the German awards during a ceremony. With the clasp came a document, which was signed by SS-Sturmbannführer Giese and had the date of 17 May 1944. One month later Könönen was killed on the Finnish front. The Finn Silfverberg, amongst others, was also awarded belatedly in the spring of 1944 the German Close Combat Clasp in Bronze by an office finalizing arrangements with the Finns. He only wore the clasp a few times because he was constantly asked by his comrades and superiors in the Finnish air force, in which he later served, from where he had obtained such a nice "Kalevalakoru" (decoration).

cold bloodedness and good sense. Two months later, on 2 February 1943, the courageous Kuutti was killed as an *Obersturmführer* at Kagalnizkaja. His surviving men will never forget their crazy 25 – 30 kilometre march behind the Russian lines.

While it was relatively quiet on the Tschikola sector, the Soviets attacked on 5 December from the Ossetian Pass road against Alagir. It is there that *I./Gebirgsjäger-Regiment 99* (*1. Gebirgsdivision*) and a *pionierkompanie* from *5. SS-Freiwilligen-Panzergrenadierdivision "Wiking"* repelled the attack of the Russian 251st Rifle Division. The attacks on Tschikola and Alagir were operationally joined.

On 7 December the defence sector of the Finnish *Bataillon* were taken over by the Romanian 2nd Mountain Division (Dumitrache). The *III. (finnisches)/"Nordland"* remained in Tschikola to finally undertake its long-delayed reorganization.

On 8 December 1942 a new *11. Kompanie* was formed from the *Ersatz- und Ausbildungskompanie* (158 men) and the old NCOs from the *11. Kompanie*. It was to be commanded by *Obersturmführer* Eugen Deck. All the other companies were also filled up with men from the *Ersatzkompanie* so that all were basically of equal strength. The *9. Kompanie* was commanded as before by *Untersturmführer* Karl-Heinz Ertel and the *10. Kompanie* (up to then combined with remnants from *11. Kompanie*) by *Obersturmführer* Tauno Pohjanlehto. The *12. Kompanie*, up to then commanded by the *Bataillon* staff since the death of *Hauptsturmführer* Brückner, because the platoons had been attached to other companies, was then taken over by the recuperated *Hauptsturmführer* Karl-Erik Ladau.

On 13 December *Obersturmführer* Hans-Joachim Porsch took command of *10. Kompanie*. On 9 December 1942 the Finnish *III. (finnisches)/"Nordland"* again became *Korps* reserve. While the *10.* and *11. Kompanie* initially remained in Tschikola, the *Bataillon* staff and *9.* and *12. Kompanie* transferred to Digora.

Already on 10 December, the *Bataillon* received new deployment orders:

> Move up and take over the Toldsgun sector from *Kampfgruppe* Dietrich (*Nebelwerfer* unit). Report to *Major* Dietrich.

The river valleys of Uruch and Lesken, exiting the mountains, provided many bases for the Russians to advance against the deep flanks of *III.*

Panzerkorps. The Soviet 2nd Guards Division and 11th Rifle Division debouched a number of times from those valleys.

The incursions increased and became stronger as the German situation in Stalingrad deteriorated and the *1. Panzerarmee* became weakened by having to give up units to the *4. Panzerarmee* (relief attack on Stalingrad). And so *Kampfgruppe* Dietrich also got into difficulties.

Untersturmführer Ertel's *9. Kompanie* was the first to reach the new deployment area and was attached to *Gruppe* Marchi on *Major* Dietrich's order. At Chasnidon, it defended the Uruch Valley exiting the mountains. The deployment of *9. Kompanie* at Chasnidon will be discussed in detail in the next section.

The *10. Kompanie* and *11. Kompanie* drove from Tschikola to Toldsgun. The *Bataillon* staff and the *12. Kompanie* arrived from Digora. During the following days, both sides increased their reconnaissance activity and harassing fire from heavy weapons. Two Russian battalions attacked during the early morning of 24 December from the Bol Kossolkun Valley, which was being blocked by *10. Kompanie*. When they were unable to advance there, they then attacked the defences of *11. Kompanie*, which was to the left of the *10. Kompanie*. The attacks were repelled. At 0930 hours and 1100 hours the Finns once again repelled attacks by the Soviet I./Rifle Regiment 875 and 70 paratroopers.

In the meantime, the first parts of "*Wiking*" had departed by rail in the direction of Stalingrad. During the Christmas holidays additional units from the division followed so that finally *III. (finnisches)/"Nordland"* was the last unit from "*Wiking*" defending the mountain flank of *III. Panzerkorps*. But the *Bataillon* was not left behind alone. *Generalleutnant der Waffen-SS* Felix Steiner had been commanding since 21 November 1942 the *Brandenburg III. Panzerkorps*. Since that time *Generaloberst* von Kleist had been commanding *Heeresgruppe* A, which Hitler had commanded "on the side" since the departure of *Generalfeldmarshall* List. Up to then, the *III. Panzerkorps* was commanded by *General* von Mackensen, who was then moved up to *Oberbefehlshaber* of *1. Panzerarmee*. The commander of *SS-Artillerie-Regiment 5*, *Oberführer* Gille, was given the command of Division "*Wiking*".

On 25 and 26 December, the *III. (finnisches)/"Nordland"* once more repelled Soviet advances from the Bol Kossolkun Valley with heavy losses for the enemy. A powerful enemy attack was launched on 27 December against the right *Bataillon* sector. West of Toldsgun, the

Russians approached extremely close to the positions of the *10. Kompanie* during the heavy fog. *Obersturmführer* Porsch had the situation in hand. Sometimes the Russians had to be repelled in hand-to-hand fighting.

There were more Russian attacks at 0700 and 0900 hours. However, the visibility had improved then. The enemy attacks collapsed in the fire of the Finns. When 300 Red Army men tried once more to destroy *Zug Zinnecker* they were annihilated in the open area in front of the position. As a result, 25 dead remained in front of the position while the others ran, or dragged themselves wounded, back.

An advance against the *10. Kompanie* in the Bol Kossolkun Valley took place on 28 December and on 29 December there were weaker advances from the Lesken Valley against the *11. Kompanie.* All attacks were repelled. Defectors stated that Rifle Regiment 1125 was brought up in double time from Karman-Ssindsikau to attack Toldsgun. In the meantime, the *III. Panzerkorps* had retaken the front bulge at Ordshonikidse and, in a number of moves, reached the Tschikola-Elchotowo line, where it made contact with the *LII. Armeekorps.*

The German catastrophe was playing out in Stalingrad. Nonetheless, Hitler hesitated to bring the *1. Panzerarmee* back to Rostov from its distant positions in the southeast, on the Terek. All military commanders could see what was coming toward *1. Panzerarmee*; only an immediate withdrawal through Rostov could save it from becoming a second Stalingrad. Rostov was the eye of the needle. It was toward Rostov that Russian units from the Don and from the Stalingrad area were already striving. In his headquarters in Pjatigorsk, the *Oberbefehlshaber* of *1. Panzerarmee, General* von Mackensen, briefed his commanding generals on 29 December, on the general situation. He based his future intentions on that by having his already-prepared withdrawal plan brought into immediate agreement with *Korps* and divisions. There were similar discussions on 30 December at *Korps* headquarters. The *Korps* and the divisions coordinated and designated all rear areas, so that only the button needed to be pushed.

Defensive Battle of the *9. Kompanie* at Chasnidon

Withdrawn from the *Bataillon* and attached to a totally foreign *kampfgruppe*, the *9. Kompanie* under *Untersturmführer* Ertel survived one of its most difficult, but also one of its most successful, deployments.

On 10 December 1942 the *III.* (*finnisches*)/*"Nordland"* (*Korpsreserve*) was alerted in Tschikola and Digora so that it could reinforce the threatened blocking group Dietrich in the Uruch and Lesken valleys. The Russians continually attacked the mountain flank of *III. Panzerkorps* from those valleys, to get behind it and destroy it. The defensive battles of the Finnish *Bataillon* in the Lesken and Bol Kossolkun valleys have already been described. Let us now turn to the *9. Kompanie*.

Untersturmführer Ertel's company was the first to arrive in the new sector and was attached to *Kampfgruppe Marchi* in Chasnidon. Chasnidon was located in a difficult-to-access mountain valley and could only be reached over a steep, unfinished mountain road with many serpentine turns. That was already the first problem because the *MTWs* of the company, with their powerful Klöckner-Deutz-Diesel, were unable to drive up the road, which was usually traversed only by donkey or horse carts. But there too, a solution was found: The all-terrain prime movers of Dietrich's *Nebelwerfer* unit, drove the *9. Kompanie* to Chasnidon. Ertel's company was expected with great anticipation.

In Chasnidon, a small, dreamy, mountain nest, was positioned *Kampfgruppe* Marchi, named after its leader. *Hauptmann* Marchi was a bony, mountain type, a police officer. He commanded a security *Bataillon* that consisted mainly of elderly, *g.v.F.* (fit for garrison duty in the field) men. Usually, such a unit carried out guard and field police duties. The *Bataillon* had bicycles. It also had a *Bau-Kompanie* (construction company) of Caucasian men, mainly Georgians.

Ertel reported to Marchi (pronounced as Marki). A good, trusting collaboration was established from the first minute between the two officers. Marchi, an experienced mountaineer, participated in an Andes expedition and wore a corresponding decoration. He briefly explained the situation: Enemy had been advancing from the mountains. One advance made it to the outskirts of the village. In the process, a few vehicles of the *Kampfgruppe* were plundered and destroyed.

Marchi also briefed Ertel on the terrain. Chasnidon is located on the western bank of the Uruch. The Uruch is a ragging mountain torrent from the Caucasus Mountains and rushes by the village in a deep gorge. Mountains surround the village. Toward the enemy, to the southwest, was a long slope that led into the mountains. The ideal defence would have been to occupy the hills around the village, but there were not enough forces available to do that. Additionally, the Georgian construction company could not be employed in a combat role because its combat value could not be gauged.

After extensive terrain reconnaissance the following decision was made: The security *Bataillon* was to defend the bank of the Uruch, reinforced by two sMGs (Russian) from the Georgians. The *9.* (*finnisches*)/"*Nordland*" was to form two *kampfgruppen*. *Obersturmführer* Sartio was to occupy the heights northwest of the village with *Zug Spöck* and two sMGs, with the firing *schwerpunkt* directly in front of the village. (That an *Untersturmführer* led a company in this company, and an *Obersturmführer* a platoon, was mainly due to language difficulties, as well as the different tactical methods of command. Ertel was designated to be in command of the *Bataillon* in this situation by order of Collani, and was in a better position to carry out his commands. This was not a unique case and does not indicate a denigration of the Finnish officer.) To that were added the two 88 mm mortars of the company (*Oberscharführer* Holmberg). *Oberscharführer* Grabow, *Zugführer* of the heavy platoon, was to control the employment of the sMGs and mortars.

The expected defensive *schwerpunkt* was thought to be directly in front of the village. Poor visibility, a limited field of fire, and a typical reverse slope position limited the defensive possibilities. Somewhat away from the village, the platoon of *Oberscharführer* Elmgren went into position. In addition, an sMG was in position in the foremost line with the *Gruppe* of *Unterscharführer* Kuuri.

Ertel and his *Zug* as well as *Grupppenführer* decide on each sMG position and foxhole. Finns and Georgians got to work. The Caucasians from the construction company were masters at constructing positions. The individual strongpoints and position were joined by communication trenches in two days. Trenches led from the individual strong points and foxholes to the *Gruppen* and *Zug* command posts, as well as trenches that led into the village.

First *Untersturmführer* Ertel clarified the enemy situation through reconnaissance patrols. No enemy contact; the Russian had retreated back into the mountains. In front of the village were some destroyed vehicles, horse- drawn wagons, and Russian booty vehicles, from the Marchi unit.

Because everything was quiet *Untersturmführer* Ertel drove on the next day in his *Kfz. 70* to the *Bataillon* command post in Toldsgun to brief the commander and get to know something about his right neighbour. The right neighbour was *Obersturmführer* Deck with his *11. (finnisches)/"Nordland"*; the company was blocking the Lesken valley. There was a large gap between the *9. Kompanie* and *11. Kompanie.*

Ertel had not been an hour at the command post when a call arrived from *Obersturmführer* Sartio: On the hill, which he had occupied with his *Kampfgruppe*, the Russian had occupied a bunker that had been build by the construction company but not occupied by his forces because it would have split the defensive force of *Kampfgruppe* Sartio. Ertel issued an order on the telephone to destroy the bunker with a combat patrol and immediately got on his way to Chasnidon. Sartio had already carried out the order by the time he arrived.

The command post of *9./"Nordland"* was situated behind a house in the southern part of Chasnidon, directly behind *Gruppe Kuuri*. A foxhole had been dug directly in front of the house. On the fence of the small yard in front of the house was a sign that could be seen from afar with the name "Ertel" on it.

Every German and every Finn knew what those few letters hid. The otherwise friendly and unassuming house started to come awake at dusk. Ration deliverers and messengers came and went. Peace and business were not disturbed by any enemy action, but was that going to remain so forever?

The close-in reconnaissance by *9. Kompanie* during the first few days did not meet any enemy forces, but all defenders felt that there was something in the air. A new reconnaissance patrol was to reconnoitre farther into no-mans land.

That assignment was taken on by *Unterscharführer* Kuuri and his *Gruppe*. Kuuri was a proven reconnaissance patrol leader, a hunter, a ranger, a reflection of his people; a man that was unafraid, and had confidence in his instinct. All members of *Gruppe Kuuri* were supplied with machine pistols; if not enough German ones were available, then Russian MPis were issued. *Gruppe Kuuri* departed silently.

They were already on their way for two hours. Nothing was stirring up front. In the positions of *Zug Elmgren* the men and company commander were waiting for the return of the reconnaissance patrol. Suddenly, the sound of heavy fighting came from the direction that Kuuri and his men took. What was going on? Thoughts and assumptions were expressed.

Time crawled and stressed the nerves of those waiting. Finally Kuuri showed up in the forefield, with all of his men. A sigh of relief. Then Kuuri and his men were back in their own position.

There was relief and joy in the glowing faces. Questions were answered. Here is Kuuri's report:

They were well defended and well camouflaged. They lived in bunkers in the forest that were barely identifiable. The reconnaissance patrol became aware of the bunkers and positions when it spotted a Russian cutting wood. As always, Kuuri wanted to know the details. A few signals and onward! As they were creeping forward, the reconnaissance patrol was surprised by a Soviet officer.

However, Kuuri was quicker and the Russian was cut down by a machine pistol burst. Kuuri quickly tore off the large Soviet star from the cap of the Russian as proof, which was usual with the Finnish soldiers. The surprised Russians then let loose with an unaimed barrage of fire, which the Finns returned with aimed machine pistol bursts; they fired to secure their retreat and all arrived back unhurt.

The defenders of Chasnidon were warned. Strong Russian forces had closed up and were in front of the village. One morning a machinegun burst from a Maxim passed through the wooden walls of the company command post. The boards tore apart like paper. Ertel and the men from the company troop, just eating breakfast, threw themselves at lightning speed to the floor. No one was wounded. Through a door facing away from the enemy, they left the unlucky place, which a sharp-eyed Russian observer had obviously identified as a command post. The company troop leader, *Oberscharführer* Pape, immediately looked for a new command post, which was established 100 metres farther back in a house cellar in the centre of the village.

On 22 December the special food supply for Christmas arrived at the front. In the face of the enemy threat, the company commander and company troop leader decided to issue the special rations immediately. What you have, you have! Ertel and Pape "played" Santa Claus. Olli Helaseppä was Ertel's assistant with the large sack on his back. The three went to the positions, spoke with the men, the *Gruppen* and *Zugführer*, and distributed the Christmas rations, cigarettes, alcohol, and Schoka-Kola.

The weather was and remained unsettled, with light frost during the night. The frozen ground gave more support. In the mornings there was heavy fog in the valley and on the heights of Chasnidon which make it easier for Russians to sneak up on the positions.

Suddenly, early on the morning of 24 December, the sound of fighting awakened the defenders of Chasnidon. There was continuous machinegun fire at *Gruppe Kuuri*. It was still dark, and foggy and damp. Machine pistols barked. Ertel sent a messenger to *Gruppe Kuuri*.

The battle noise was getting louder. Hand grenades exploded. Ertel no longer had any doubts: That was no minor reconnaissance patrol fighting, the Russians were attacking. The messenger returned and confirmed it: The Russians had crept up to *Gruppe Kuuri* under cover of the fog. Thanks to the alertness of the gunner at the sMG, who recognized the ghostly, earth-brown figures a few metres before his own position and fought them with annihilating fire from his sMG 34, the Finns were not overrun.

As it got light the fighting flared up again in front of *Zug Elmgren*. The Russians fired on the village of Chasnidon with heavy mortars and sent the odd isolated shot from a distant gun. The mortar group from *9./"Nordland"* fired barrier fire into the predetermined barrier zones. Company commander Ertel had complete oversight and did not have to do any regrouping or lead any counterattacks. There were no enemy penetrations anywhere. The Russians were repelled in front of the Finnish positions.

Around noon a *VB* from a Romanian mountain battery came to the front. He was briefed and established his observation post on the hill by *Kampfgruppe Sartio*. From there, there was a good view of the terrain, except for a hollow 200 metres in front of *Zug Elmgren*, into which he could not see. It is in that hollow that the Russians were assembling.

The Romanian battery's fire control proved to be insufficient. The Romanian *VB* seldom left his safe bunker. In addition, the Romanians seemed to have a shortage of artillery ammunition, and the battery supported the *Bataillon* in the Toldsgun area very infrequently. Most of the time it was *Obersturmführer* Sartio who controlled the fire of the Romanian battery. Even though only the odd shell landed in front of our positions, it still has a certain morale effect: To demonstrate strength to the enemy, give backing to our troops, and give the feeling that they were not all alone.

The fighting continued over the Christmas holidays. The Russians repeatedly worked their way forward to Elmgren's position, and there were some critical hours. The trains were stripped bare. All dispensable people, drivers, officials and cook's helpers, came under the command of the *Stabsscharführer*, the *Spieß*, *Oberscharführer* Heinkes, to the front to be the counterattack reserve, but were not required to intervene. *Zug Elmgren* held its position. Sven Elmgren always mastered the situation with unshakable calm. He and Kuuri were the outstanding fighters that prevented the Russians from getting a grip on Chasnidon. The men tried to emulate them, exceed themselves, and embody true Finnish soldierly values. They crouched in their foxholes and pricked up their ears. To remain alert meant: Survival! The machineguns repeatedly bellowed toward the enemy. Machine pistols and hand grenades joined the hellish din. Then there was quiet again, until the next time.

The defensive battle of *Zug Elmgren* was supported substantially by *Zug Sartio*. The sMG group on the heights was very effective with its flanking fire in front of *Zug Elmgren*. With predetermined height and side limits set on the mounts, the two machineguns could also fire "blindly", without the gunner seeing the target. That was also beneficial during the usual thick fog. From that position, it was easy to fire for barrier effect with the machineguns.

Naturally, the mortar group also lay down barrier fire. However, during those Christmas days the mortar people had problems with the just-delivered new ammunition. The 8 cm rounds were to bounce three metres into the air after hitting the ground and then explode, sending shrapnel, but only a few did that. Nonetheless, the mortar people kept up their fire. They knew their business but it was not their fault that not all shells exploded properly.

Hauptmann Marchi always breathed a little bit easier when *Untersturmführer* Ertel showed up at his command post. Ertel's 70 men in front of Chasnidon ensured that Marchi's 400 men would not be seriously tested. Never did Marchi's reserve, his peaceful bicyclists, have to intervene. Ertel, who always ran around with a ski cap with ear flaps made from cat's fur, which a "Pan" had made for him in Amwrosiewka for a pack of cigarettes, found it a little painful to always see men with steel helmets on grey heads at Marchi's command post. During the next visit he also put on a steel helmet so that he shone in his regulation service tunic.

On 26 December 1942 Ertel was informed by *Bataillon* that the major withdrawal was on. The company was given a *Nebelwerfer* (Dora), which was to fire off all of its ammunition during the night. You had to be a bit "lighter" during a withdrawal. As targets, the *Nebelwerfer* was given the hollow in front of *Zug* Elmgren and the terrain on the back of the slope in front of Kuuri. During the night, a rocket with a long fiery trail occasionally howled across the Finnish position. Its detonation created a thousand-fold echo amongst the gorges of the mountain that sounded like far away thunder.

In the early morning of 31 December 1942, ear-splitting battle sounds announced a renewed attack by the Soviets. The positions of Elmgren and Kuuri were under heavy fire. Even in the village, the shells were raining down at such a rate that it was difficult to move from house to house. Ertel's reserve was placed on alert. The company had the first dead and a number of wounded. At Elmgren's position the Finns were able to repel the enemy and hold their position. In the meantime Ertel had arrived with a reserve platoon from Marchi to reinforce Elmgren's positions. The situation had been cleaned up by 0800 hours. Quiet set in again. Nonetheless, the men felt as if they were sitting on hot coals because they knew that the withdrawal was proceeding. The withdrawal order finally arrived at noon. The vehicles were to be driven back to Toldsgun once darkness had set in. From there, they were to move with the *Bataillon* to Lesken. In Lesken the companies were picked up and then departed. The companies left behind in the positions were to remain there until midnight and then follow on foot.

The vehicles drove off in the evening twilight. Soon after the vehicles had left there was a fiery glow from the direction in which the vehicles had driven. What did the fiery glow mean? Riddles. Ertel sensed nothing good.

New Year's Eve. There would be no New Year's Eve fireworks. As the rearguard, *Kompanie Ertel* would be the last company to break contact with Chasnidon. The men left their positions silently. The last food was consumed. The last bottle of Schnaps was passed around at the company command post. And then the hands of the clock moved to the agreed-upon hour. The men left the position like silent shadows. Restrained hissing, a gas mask container banged gently, here and there was a suppressed curse. The *Gruppen* and *Züge* assembled and marched down to Chasnidon. The company commander received whispered reports of all being present and ordered: "*Marsch*!"

On 1 January 1943, at 0100 hours, began the retreat of *9./"Nordland"*. All was quiet. In the previous year, New Year's Eve was celebrated quite loudly on the Mius. It also remained quiet in the Russian lines. They did not notice the departure of the company. One after the other, the men stumbled along the stony mountain path. After some time they passed a burning truck that had driven off the mountain road and plunged into a gorge. It turned out later that it was the weapons truck of the *Kompanie*.

The withdrawal of *9./"Nordland"* was coordinated with the withdrawal of *III. (finnisches)/"Nordland"*. Beginning on the left wing, the *Bataillon* withdrew the Ertel company into an intermediate position near Bery Kessyn. There, *9. Kompanie*, released by *Kampfgruppe Marchi*, joined up with *Bataillon* again. That was the plan.

After a tiring night march, *9. Kompanie* reached the new intermediate position. Far behind the men lay Chasnidon, the little unassuming mountain town that would always remain in the memories of the men from *9. Kompanie* of the Finnish volunteer *Bataillon*. *Kompanie Ertel* had again returned to the soldierly family of the *Bataillon* but it would be tested and have to prove itself once more during the night of 1/2 January.

Untersturmführer Ertel and NCOs Elmgren and Kuuri were decorated with the EK I for their actions at Chasnidon while an additional 14 NCOs and men are awarded the EK II.

Retreat from the Caucasus

Hitler finally issued the order to *Heeresgruppe* A for the withdrawal from the Caucasus, which began at the Terek for *1. Panzerarmee*. *Korps Felmy* abandoned the strongpoints in the Nogay Steppe during New Year's Eve. The *XXXX. Panzerkorps* evacuated the lightly-manned positions north of Mosdok. The foot-marching units of *LII. Armeekorps* marched northwest from the Terek bend. The mountain flank of the *III. Panzerkorps* was evacuated in a number of stages. Hitler waited until the last minute before approving the retreat; the word "retreat" simply was not part of his vocabulary. Thank God that the far-sighted troop leaders and staffs of *1. Panzerarmee* had known for a long time that it had to come to that, and had secretly, and early enough, worked out the corresponding withdrawal plans.

The Russians exerted strong pressure in the direction of Rostov to catch the German troops there and prepare for them a second Stalingrad. The time lines of *1. Panzerarmee* could not be kept. It became a race against the clock, with the Russians at their back. Inconceivable demands were asked of people, horses, and machines. The *1. Panzerarmee* marched without interruption. The remaining motorized units halted at important terrain features and offered resistance to the enemy to provide more time for the foot-marching formations. Days later, the *17. Armee*, in position at the high passes of the Elbrus and by Maikop, also joined the retreat. What had to be accomplished during those January days by the soldiers of *Heeresgruppe* A was indescribable.

The wake of the retreat also sucked in *III. (finnisches)/"Nordland"* during New Year's Eve 1943. The *Bataillon*, defending at Toldsgun, received the order to withdraw into an intermediate position in the line Bery Kessyn, on 31 December 1942. Collani and his adjutant, *Obersturmführer* Hirt, prepared the withdrawal plans.

At the onset of darkness, the heavy weapons were moved back into the new intermediate position. The *MTW* and trains of the *Bataillon* drove to Lesken. The *9. Kompanie* disengaged first from Chasnidon during New Year's Eve and arrived in the morning of 1st January at the new intermediate position. One hour later, *11. Kompanie* gave up its position in the Lesken Valley and, somewhat later, the *10. Kompanie* left the Bol Kossolkun Valley. By morning both companies also reached the new intermediate position, a few kilometres farther west of the old position. There, all three companies closed up. The companies established contact with one another. There was a gap between *9. Kompanie* and *11. Kompanie*. The new position was located on an elongated height that permitted great observation during the day.

The men from the *9. Kompanie* spent the first few mornings of the New Year resting on a corn-covered hill east of the Lesken River. They prepared a cocoa drink from Schoka-Kola and water on an Esbit stove. The sun penetrated the morning mist early and warmed the soldiers. *Obersturmführer* Sartio led one more reconnaissance patrol against Chasnidon and reported that the Russians only entered Chasnidon hesitatingly at 0700 hours. *Untersturmführer* Ertel made contact with *11. Kompanie* and arranged with its commander, *Obersturmführer* Deck, that *11. Kompanie* would wait for the *9. Kompanie* when disengaging in the evening. They would then march together to Lesken because Ertel did not know either the road or the terrain.

After they noticed the withdrawal the Russians followed the Finnish *Bataillon* from Chasnidon to Toldsgun with one company; other enemy forces came from the Lesken and Bol Kossolkun valleys. At 0745 hours the heavy weapons of the *Bataillon* took an enemy assembly (approximately 600 men) in Toldsgun under fire. At 1300 hours the *10. Kompanie*, on the right wing of the *Bataillon*, repelled an enemy reconnaissance patrol; the enemy left behind eight dead.

The groups from the *Aufklärungs-Abteilung* of *13. Panzerdivision*, which were to form the rear guard from 1530 hours on, arrived at the companies of the Finnish *Bataillon*. At 1600 hours the companies from *III. (finnisches)/"Nordland"* left their positions as ordered to march on foot to Lesken. Whereas the withdrawal march of the *10. Kompanie* and *11. Kompanie* proceeded without friction or interruption, the march for *9. Kompanie* was a thorny one.

With the onset of darkness, the *9. Kompanie* marched to the agreed-upon rendezvous point, but *Obersturmführer* Deck and his eleventh were no longer there. There was no time to try and figure out what might have caused him to leave. It is difficult to determine whether that was the agreed-upon corner of the woods. Time was pressing, onward then. Ertel's company was supposed to be in Lesken at 2000 hours, after which the withdrawal was to take place by motorized march. Was Deck perhaps also having time problems?

For Ertel and his officers, as well as his NCOs, that was unknown territory. According to the map, there was supposed to be a road, in reality a field path, which made a wide turn to the southwest and then led over the only bridge across the Lesken River. Ertel felt that a march along that road was too risky because the Russians would then most surely pursue more closely. And he could not let himself get involved in a battle because that would throw off the whole withdrawal plan. Therefore, Ertel decided to lead his company back according to the compass.

The road to Lesken led through mountains and woods, and in between them was the Lesken River, which had to be crossed. It became a terrible march, with time breathing down their necks. Shouts and curses were heard continually. A dark mass, smelling of sweat, raced across mountains and through woods, stumbling through thick underbrush. Officers and NCOs closed both eyes as the mortar men emptied out the heavy cases.

Arriving in Lesken on time was more important, and they could only move forward fast if they did not have to carry a heavy load.

Finally, the woods became less dense. The night sky had become noticeably brighter. The watches showed 1915 hours. Far down below in the valley was heard the gentle roaring of diesel motors; the vehicles of the *Bataillon* had already been started.

The *9. Kompanie* had arrived at a steep river bank. The sound of motors was distinct and, way down in the valley, a blurred village could be seen. Was it Lesken? It could only be Lesken! The objective of the march was near but in front of the men was a yawning abyss. Far below, the water rushed; it could only be the Lesken. For the first time Ertel had some doubts as to whether the *Bataillon* could be reached in time. Would it wait? Those were gnawing questions. It would not have been the first time that a unit was left behind because of misunderstandings and a chain of unlucky circumstances!

It took only one minute to consider all the remaining possibilities. Ertel issued *Oberscharführer* Spöck, a mountain experienced man from the Steyr, the assignment to find a way down the gorge as quickly as possible. After some nerve wracking minutes Spöck returned to report that he had found a way down.

Spöck took over the lead. Let's go! *Panzergrenadiere* were turned into *Gebirgsjäger.* Curses were accompanied by warning shouts and directions. They felt their way forward step by step. An MG gunner fell down five metres; he was at the bottom, unhurt, but the shock made him temporarily blind. Finally, all the men from the company were down, on the bank of the wild mountain river.

Then the motors could be heard more clearly, they were idling. That provided new impetus. But between the company and the *Bataillon*, ready to march, was the 30 metre-wide Lesken River.

Ertel directed *Obersturmführer* Sartio to bring up the company. He himself rushed forward with the company troop to find a way across the river and to hold the *Bataillon* until the company had arrived. Nowhere was there a bridge or a gangplank in sight. Where was there a ford? There was no more time for searching, into the river then. The river was not very deep but the strong current created difficulties for the men. The water was ice cold and they were happy when they were across. And that is how the entire company followed them.

Ertel continued moving ahead with his company troop, but then had to recognize that they were standing in front of a dammed mill ditch, which presented an insurmountable obstacle. Was the terrible march still not over?

The company closed up. They were looking for a way to go around. Then shouts:

> "We have found logs and thick planks!"
> "Here with them, over here!"

A makeshift gangplank was quickly put in place. Man after man, the company moved across the wobbly gangplank and finally they had the road to Lesken in front of them. There were still *Bataillon* outposts at the outskirts of the village. The "Pojat" (youth) quickly made themselves understood in Finnish and German. The security outposts were also happy that the company had arrived. They made it! The Finnish *Bataillon* could then also be inserted into the withdrawal movement of *1. Panzerarmee.*

Untersturmführer Ertel reached the *Bataillon* command post at 2030 hours. When he entered the room *Sturmbannführer* Collani stared at him as if he were a vision. Collani was ready to march, his coat and hat on. When Ertel reported the company returned, Collani came toward him and put his arms around him as a father would do to a lost son.

Cold and wet through and through, the men of the *9. Kompanie* climbed onto their vehicles. None remained awake for very long. During the night of 2 January 1943, the *III. (finnisches)/"Nordland"* rolled through Argudan-Naltschik to the northwest. It arrived at 0245 hours in Baksan. With that, the *Bataillon* was out of the immediate battle area and was removed from the attachment to *III. Panzerkorps.* Quarters were taken up in Baksan. Tired and wet, the men from the *9. Kompanie*, as well as those of the other companies, climbed down from the vehicles. Drying out their things, and carrying out the usual activities associated with a motorized march, filled the day; as did resting and sleeping, sleeping. It was there that *Untersturmführer* Ertel found out that the burning truck they saw on the way from Chasnidon to Todsgun was the weapons and equipment vehicle of *9. Kompanie. Unterscharführer* Brosette, the *WuG* (*Waffen und Gerät* – weapons and equipment), promised to replace all lost weapons and equipment. Ertel did not ask how. There were favourable opportunities during the retreat; as soon as the company was in its new deployment area, Brosette reported that all lost weapons and equipment had been replaced.

The *III. (finnisches)/"Nordland"* left Baksan in the morning of 3 January and arrived in Pjatigorsk at 1430 hours, where it spent the night. It arrived in the Kurssowka area on 4 January and made its quarters in Alexjewskoje, where it had to remain also on 5 January due to lack of fuel. The fuel tankers finally arrived on 6 January. After refuelling, the *Bataillon* left Alexjewskoje at 0800 hours and arrived in Newinnomyskaja at 1100 hours. Fuel was waiting for them there. After refuelling, at 1400 hours they departed for Woroschilowsk, where the *Bataillon* arrived at 2200 hours. Again, all their fuel was completely used up. As there was no other fuel available, they were forced to halt.

The *Bataillon* was stuck in Woroschilowsk from the evening of 6 January until noon on 9 January. Woroschilowsk, the former Stawropol, was a rear area town, as reports from World War One described it. The hectic activities of the retreat had not reached it yet. In the town were innumerable staffs, huge supply depots, a forward-directing centre for transiting troops, a soldiers home, a transit hospital, and a front cinema. There also were German Red Cross nurses, *Wehrmacht* female helpers, and also beautiful Russian women.

The peace and change were good for the men of the Finnish *Bataillon* and quite a few bonds of love were made. In the front line cinema the men saw the film "*Die große Liebe*", with Zarah Leander, who with her throaty voice sang the hit: "*Es geht alles vorüber…*" (Everything passes…). How true that was: Chasnidon and that terrible march to Lesken were over. The quiet rest days in Woroschilowsk also passed. Fuel finally arrived on 9 January 1943 and the drivers refuelled their vehicles.

Departure was at noon on 9 January from Woroschilowsk. By evening, quarters were set up at Bessopassnoje. The *Bataillon* was already in Rasvilnoje by noon of the next day. In Rasvilnoje the *Bataillon* was again attached to *Division "Wiking"*, which, as part of the *LVII. Panzerkorps* (Kirchner) and the *4. Panzerarmee* (Hoth), resisted the Russian rapid advance on Rostov in a fighting retreat. *Panzerkorps Kirchner* had the assignment to hold until the *1. Panzerarmee* had passed through the bolthole that was Rostov.

On 11 January 1943, on the orders of division, the companies of *III. (finnisches)/"Nordland"* were brought forward by motorized transport from Rasvilnoje to Nag Renitschansky, east of Proletarskaja, to be ready to act as the reserve for *SS-Division "Wiking"*.

The long motorized march of the Finnish *Bataillon* from the Terek to the Manytsch was finished. It was a difficult march through snow storms and cold, which required the utmost from the drivers and *I-Staffeln*. The trains of the companies drove from Nag Renitschansky to Salsk, where they made themselves at home.

Krasnoje Snamja and Proletarskaja

After the failed relief attack by *4. Panzerarmee* on Stalingrad the German assault forces were increasingly forced onto the defensive by Russian forces that were growing stronger. After Stalingrad, the Russian objective was the destruction of the *1. Panzerarmee*, still far away in the eastern Caucasus, and of the *17. Armee* of *Heeresgruppe* A in the western Caucasus. Stalin was constantly urging his forces on to greater speed; they were to arrive in Rostov before the Germans.

The *LVII. Panzerkorps* of General Kirchner, the nucleus of *Generaloberst* Hoth's *4. Panzerarmee*, had the task of halting the Russian advance and holding open the Rostov area for the retreating formations of the German Caucasus *Heeresgruppe*. All soldiers from the *LVII. Panzerkorps* knew what was at stake there.

After the termination of the relief attack on Stalingrad the formations of *SS-Division "Wiking"* were transported by high speed rail from the Terek into the Kalmyk Steppe up to Kotelnikowo-Remontnaja. They were to somewhat even out the developing inferiority of the *LVII. Panzerkorps*, which faced three Russian Armies. That was especially crucial after the complete disintegration of the Romanian 4th Army, which retreated demoralized, on foot and on empty trains, to the west.

There, the men from "*Wiking*" encountered completely new fighting methods. It was very cold and snow storms struck often. The wretched villages were 30 – 40 kilometres apart. In between, there was nothing but steppe, which, covered with snow, looked like a moonscape. The white, featureless waste, at times hilly, was criss-crossed with balkas (gorges), which could only be recognizes when from directly in front of them. There were no solid roads, trees or shrubs.

A cold, east wind swept over the steppe and its force was not weakened by either woods or ground cover. Only in the western part of the steppe were there planted wind breaks of trees throughout the wasteland. Because of the cold wind, the houses of the Kalmyks were built into the ground so that only the tips of the straw roofs stuck out of the ground.

The Kalmyks were Tartars, followers of Genghis Khan, who had penetrated for some time into central Europe. Some of them took root in the Crimea. The last tribes of the returning Tartars did not make it across the Volga River, which had in the meantime flooded, and remained in that part of the steppe, between the Don and the Volga, which was later named after them. Although the Kalmyks were nomads, they were forced to become sedentary under Soviet rule and became the regime's enemy, which had taken away their customary way of life. Many Kalmyks concluded friendships with the Germans.

The war in the steppe had its own laws. Icy snow storms and temperatures down to minus 50 degrees Celsius forced the defensive lines to be placed within villages, by rail lines, and protective tree lines. The guards and field outposts had to be relieved frequently because no one could survive for long outside in the cold. Many times lubricants froze, making the weapons inoperable. The engines of the vehicles had to run constantly, otherwise the drive trains quickly became solid blocks and could not be set in motion. The war in the steppe was over villages; they meant warmth.

In spite of the abnormal fighting conditions, for days the *LVII. Panzerkorps* resisted three Russian armies that were attacking westward between the Ssal and the Manytsch rivers. It is there that the "*Wiking*" survived its up-to-then most difficult test. Remontnaja, Simowniki, Kuberle, and Orlowskaja were stations of the fighting withdrawal for the comrades of the Caucasus formations. During ice and snow storms, they strove toward Rostov in forced marches, so as to reach that eye of the needle before the Russians.

On 14 January 1943 the *LVII. Panzerkorps* was in position 30 kilometres east of Proletarskaja in the line on both sides of Romanow. On the left wing of the *Korps* was the proven *17. Panzerdivision*, in the centre at Krasnoje Snamja and Romanow was "*Wiking*", and on the left wing, adjacent to the Manytsch, the *23. Panzerdivision*, which had been transferred from Ordshonikidse to the *LVII. Panzerkorps* before the "*Wiking*" was.

When it became apparent that the *17. Panzerdivision* would be bypassed on its northern wing by the Soviet 2nd Guards Army and the

51st Army, the *16. Infanterie-Division* (mot.) of *General* von Schwerin, which had previously fought in the low-lying areas of the Manytsch, was brought up to cover the northern flank of the *Korps*. The oppressive superiority of the Russians led to the temporary encirclement of parts of *17. Panzerdivision*, and finally to the withdrawal of the northern wing of the *Korps*. Soviet forces streamed past the *Korps* toward Sporny and Manytschkaja. The Manytsch crossing at Sporny was blocked at the last minute by a *kampfgruppe* from *16. Infanterie-Division* (mot.), ensuring that the rear of *LVII. Panzerkorps* was kept clear.

In the meantime, violent battles were raging over Romanow and Krasnoje Snamja. Romanow was being held by the "*Germania*" and "*Westland*" regiments. "*Nordland*" defended on both sides of Krasnoje Snamja, with the *I. Bataillon* fighting at the *schwerpunkt* of Krasnoje Snamja. The positions of *I. Bataillon* were adjacent to the village.

Heavy fighting raged for Krasnoje Snamja on 14 January 1943. *Sturmbannführer* Lohmann's *Bataillon* defended itself with the courage of despair against an oppressing superiority. A pattern soon developed: enemy attack, defence, penetrations, and counterattacks. The Russians had tanks. A battle fought was for each shack. The men from the *I. Bataillon* knew that they had to hold so that the withdrawal timetable would not be upset. They knew that they had to hold because of the many wounded in the village and because a withdrawal on the next day across the open steppe would mean the destruction of the *Bataillon*. They clawed themselves into the clay walls and ruins, and held Krasnoje Snamja as ordered.

Sturmbannführer Lohmann described the situation to the regimental commander over the still intact telephone line. *Obersturmbannführer* Joerchel promised help. The *III.* (*finnisches*)/"*Nordland*", positioned in Orlowskaja on 12 January 1943 and moved to Donskoje a day later, received an order from regiment at 1430 hours to immediately send one company to Krasnoje Snamja to support the *I. Bataillon*. *Obersturmführer* Deck left with his *11. Kompanie* at 1505 hours. Simultaneously, two companies of *II. Bataillon*, located in Grakow (south of Krasnoje Snamja), which were not attacked as intensely, were brought to Krasnoje Snamja.

In the meantime the battle for the wretched steppe village of Krasnoje Snamja was reaching a climax. Eight Russian tanks and 400 Red Army men had penetrated into the eastern section of the village. The *HKL*, as far as it could be called that, ran through the centre of the village. The *Bataillon* doctor, *Hauptsturmführer* Dr. Spitzi, and his medical staff, grabbed weapons and defended the first aid station, which was still filled with numerous wounded men.

Obersturmführer Deck arrived with his *11./"Nordland"* at 1615 hours. Deck was briefed by Lohmann. After a quick preparation a counterattack was launched with shouts of hurrah. The weapons spoke and the Soviets were forced out of the village. But they quickly returned, occupying house after house. The cold drove them forward. By midnight the two companies of the *II. Bataillon* had also arrived.

Preparations were made for a counterattack. At exactly 2400 hours, a white flare hissed into the clear winter sky signalling the counterattack, followed quickly by the noise of battle. One enemy tank was eliminated in close-combat. The exploding ammunition completed its destruction, causing the other tanks to lose courage; they rolled backward. By 0030 hours Krasnoje Snamja was once again completely in Finnish hands. The wounded were immediately transported away. The *11./"Nordland"* suffered two dead and thirteen wounded. Two hundred Russian dead were counted.

The schedule tied *I./"Nordland"* again to Krasnoje Snamja on 15 January. The Russians were then also advancing on Grakow; the two companies of *II. Bataillon* had to be transferred there. For that reason, *9./"Nordland"* set out at 0710 hours on 15 January to Krasnoje Snamja and was attached to *I. Bataillon*.

As anticipated, supported by tanks, the Russians once more penetrated into Krasnoje Snamja on the morning of 15 January. And once more, a cat and mouse game began with the Russian tanks. The eastern part of the village fell into Russian hands once more.

The *9. Kompanie* arrived at noon with four *Sturmgeschütze* from *Sturmgeschütz-Abteilung 203* (tactical sign, an elephant) at Krasnoje Snamja. The commander of the *Sturmgeschütze*, a *Hauptmann*, and *Untersturmführer* Ertel, commander of *9./"Nordland"*, were briefed on the situation by *Sturmbannführer* Lohmann. The mission: counterattack!

The *9./"Nordland"* still had 35 men and was organized into two platoons. On the left side of the village street, the 2nd platoon under *Oberscharführer* Spöck was attacking, while the 1st platoon under *Oberscharführer* Elmgren attacked on the right. Directly behind *Zug*

Elmgren were the company troop, the sMG group, and the mortar group. In between were the *Sturmgeschütze.* The first enemy tank was set on fire soon after the beginning of the attack. Nothing could stop the Finns then. House after house was stormed. Smoke columns from burning enemy tanks proclaimed the victory. None of the seven enemy tanks returned to their lines and remained behind as blackened wrecks between the houses of Krasnoje Snamja. The assault troops reached the outskirts of the village. The last Russians were fleeing over a hill. The *Sturmgeschütze* pursued and guided back the encircled outposts in front of the village to *Oberscharführer* Stock and the *I. Bataillon*.

New Russian forces approached Krasnoje Snamja during the evening hours of 15 January. Just as *Bataillon Lohmann*, and its attached units, started to return as ordered to Proletarskaja, the Russians attacked again. *Sturmgeschütze* and *Panzergrenadiere* once more turned around and chased the Russians out of the village one more time. *Kampfgruppe Lohmann*, including all *Sturmgeschütze*, then disengaged and returned to Proletarskaja after a difficult night march.

On 15 January, while *9.* and *11.*/"*Nordland*" were fighting for Krasnoje Snamja as part of *I. Bataillon*, the staff of *III.* (*finnisches*)/"*Nordland*", as well as *10. Kompanie* and *12. Kompanie*, marched from Donskoje to Proletarskaja at 1300 hours. They occupied the *Bataillon's* designated sector on the far right of the bridgehead that was forming in Proletarskaja. The *III. (finnisches)/"Nordland"* had contact with *II. Bataillon* on the right and was positioned next to the Manytsch River on the left.

The Proletarskaja bridgehead blocked the important Manytsch crossing between Proletarskaja and Salsk. River crossings are important military objectives, just as are mountain passes, and have to be taken into account when planning strategy. A bridgehead may be a jumping-off point for an offensive, but also a barrier as part of a defence. And the Proletarskaja bridgehead blocked the advance of the Russians for some time. There, all three regiments of "*Wiking*" were adjacent to each other in the following order, from left to right: "*Nordland*", "*Westland*", and "*Germania*".

While "*Germania*" and "*Westland*" repelled powerful enemy attacks on 17 January, it remained relatively quiet in the sector of *Regiment* "*Nordland*". The *Pionier-Bataillon* from "*Wiking*" repelled an enemy attack south of Proletarskaja, at Stalinskij, and threw the Russians back to the east in a counterattack.

Because the Soviet 28th Army was unable to eliminate the Proletarskaja bridgehead due to the energetic defence of regiments "*Germania*" and "*Westland*", its commander, General Gerassimenko, ordered the 99th Rifle Brigade to cross the frozen Manytsch southeast of Proletarskaja, and take out the German bridgehead from the rear. The attack was launched through Jekaterinowka against Salsk. Salsk was a rail and road intersection approximately 20 kilometres south of Proletarskaja. Ju-52s were still flying resupply missions from Salsk to Stalingrad. A group from *Jagdgeschwader 52* still started and landed there but it was becoming evident that that would not be possible for much longer. With the evacuation of Proletarskaja and Salsk, the resupply flights to Stalingrad would also have to be terminated and Stalingrad would finally be lost.

Jekaterinowka

During the night of 18/19 January the Soviet 99th Rifle Brigade crossed the ice of the Manytsch River and penetrated Jekaterinowka with its lead elements. With that, the withdrawal route of "*Wiking*" from the Proletarskaja bridgehead was immediately threatened. The *17. Panzerdivision*, which had been transferred south of the Manytsch River during the occupation of the Proletarskaja bridgehead to screen the area east of Salsk, was deployed in widely-separated defensive strongpoints and could not prevent Soviet entry into Jekaterinowka.

Division "*Wiking*" was immediately threatened. Messages carrying bad news arrived rapidly, one after the other. The commander, *Brigadeführer* Gille, and his *Ia*, *Sturmbannführer* Schönfelder, could see what was coming toward them: threat to the withdrawal route at a sensitive point, the Manytsch bridges and the long dam between Proletarskaja and Salsk. Gille and Schönfelder agreed to withdraw the Finnish *Bataillon*, which was under less pressure on the left wing of the bridgehead, and transfer it to Jekaterinowka. The *I.*/"*Nordland*" had to additionally take over the sector of *III. Bataillon*. The Finnish *Bataillon* departed Jekaterinowka on 18 January at 2130 hours and arrived two hours later at Schablijewka.

On the morning of 19 January 1943 the *9. Kompanie* remained as village security and *Bataillon* reserve in Schablijewka. The other companies of the Finnish *Bataillon* entered the positions held by *Schützenregiment 40* of

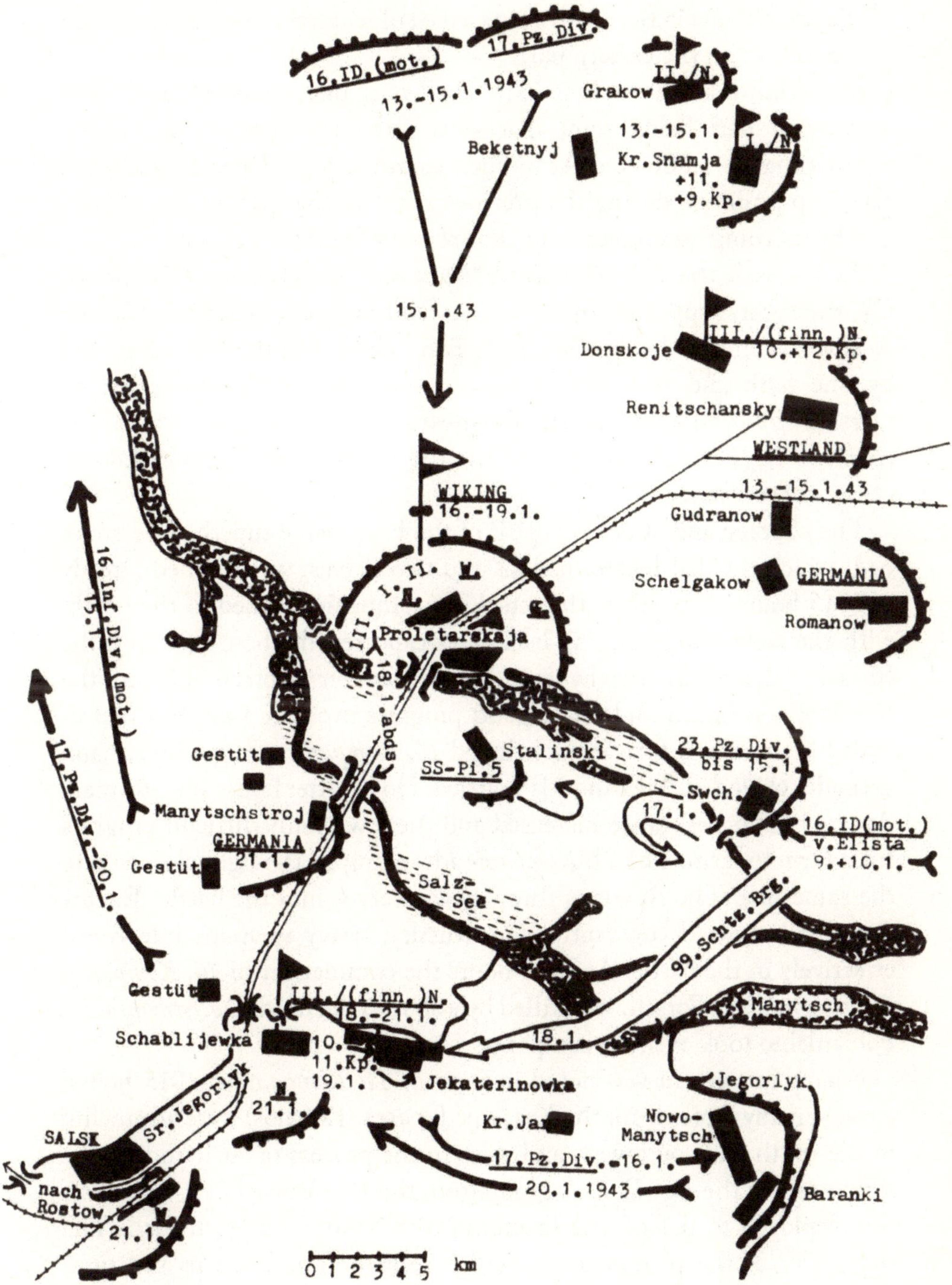

Kalmyk Steppe and the Proletarskaja Bridgehead.

17. Panzerdivision in the southwestern part of Jekaterinowka and prepared for an assault on the eastern part.

Jekaterinowka was a long, stretched-out, one street village, with its eastern part being somewhat away from the rest of the village. Approximately 1,000 Red Army men from the 99th Rifle Brigade had taken up positions during the previous night in that part of the village, and by morning had brought up "*Ratschbumm*" and heavy mortars.

As ordered, the *III. (finnisches)/"Nordland"* attacked at 0900 hours. On the right, supported by two tanks and one *Sturmgeschütz,* was *11. Kompanie* commanded by *Obersturmführer* Deck. On the left, supported by one tank and two *Sturmgeschütze,* was the *10. Kompanie* led by *Obersturmführer* Porsch. In the foremost line was also a *VB* of *12./SS-Artillerie-Regiment 5*, who guided the fire of the battery against known centres of resistance.

The courage and attacking spirit of the Finns were superb. The brook bed, which divided Jekaterinowka into two halves, was reached already at 0915 hours. After that, the attacking companies turned to the north, with the right wing hanging back, and captured the houses, which the Russians defended, one by one. *Obersturmführer* Porsch utilized the Russians' confusion and made good progress over the first 800 metres with his somewhat forward-echeloned *10. Kompanie.* Everywhere, hand grenades exploded, MG and MPi rattled. House after house was stormed. At 0945 hours resistance increased and there was only difficult progress from farm to farm. The *11. Kompanie* advancing on the right closed up to the same line. The Russians threw new reserves into the battle. Enemy strength increased constantly. The Russian heavy weapons intervened effectively in the battle. At 1000 hours the commander of *10. Kompanie, Obersturmführer* Porsch, was killed by a shot to the head. *Obersturmführer* Pohjanlehto took over the company.

Enemy movement was noted in front of *11. Kompanie* at 1015 hours; strong enemy forces from the Krasnoje Jar area (Kolchos) were advancing to the south and southwest, and were in the process of surrounding the right wing of the *Bataillon.* A group from the *Pionierzug* of *12. Kompanie* was deployed to defend the Jekaterinowka-Nowo Manytsch road. The remainder of the platoon remained in reserve. The front passed right through the centre of the stretched-out village of Jekaterinowka.

At 1030 hours 600 Red Army soldiers attacked the *10. Kompanie* with loud shouts of "urrah", but the Finns, under the leadership of their countryman Pohjanlehto, did not yield. Cold bloodedly they let the Russians approach very close to their positions before they opened fire and destroyed them. There was hand-to-hand fighting in some places. The attack was repelled with heavy losses for the enemy. And then the Finns counterattacked. An enemy mortar position, which affected the counterattack significantly, was overrun.

The commander of the Soviet 28th Army, General Gerassimenko, pressured the 99th Rifle Brigade to achieve success and sent them new reserves. At 1130 hours new waves attacked the *10.* Kompanie and *11. Kompanie*. The Finnish losses increased. The *Pak* and *lIG* of the *12. Kompanie* fired non-stop. The barrels of the machineguns were glowing hot. The salvoes of the *12. Batterie* of the "*Wiking*" artillery regiment repeatedly smashed into the densest enemy assemblies; the *VB* proved himself to be a master of his profession. At 1130 hours the remainder of the *Pionierzug*, held in reserve, was sent to the hard-pressed *10. Kompanie*.

At 1215 hours a new wave of 400 Red Army soldiers attacked from the northeastern part of Jekaterinowka. That wave was also forced to go to ground and the remnants withdrew at 1245 hours.

At 1300 hours a *Pionierzug* of *Schützenregiment 40* from *17. Panzerdivision* was sent to reinforce the left flank of *10./"Nordland"*. There followed a number of additional attacks against *10. Kompanie*. However, they did not have any force or penetrating power. All attacks were already destroyed a long distance in front of the *HKL* by the heavy weapons. By evening the number of enemy dead had risen to 300, the number of prisoners to 159; amongst them were a battalion commander and a communications and an engineering officer of the 99th Rifle Brigade. The Finnish war booty consisted of: two wagons with communications equipment, five super heavy mortars, two heavy MGs, five light MGs, and many hand-held weapons.

The Finnish *Bataillon* had nine dead and 24 wounded. Amongst the dead were *Obersturmführer* Porsch, *Chef* of the *10. Kompanie*, and three NCOs.

During the night of 20 January 1943 the Soviets moved new forces into the northeastern part of Jekaterinowka; they wanted to continue the attacks on the next day. To forestall them, *Sturmbannführer* Collani ordered a counterattack.

20 January 1943: The order for the attack reached *10. Kompanie* and *11. Kompanie*. Both companies were extremely weak, truly having only the

strength of a platoon. Attack preparations? What was there to prepare? The Finns knew where the Russians were. A *VB* from the artillery was briefed on the enemy centres of resistance. Two German tanks rolled up. *Obersturmführer* Pohjanlehto, the new *Chef* of the *10. Kompanie*, quickly assembled a combat patrol; the *pionier* group under the command of *Unterscharführer* Toivo Vainio and nearby members of *10. Kompanie* and *11. Kompanie*; amongst them the medical orderly Valtonen and messengers Forss and Silfverberg from the company troop of the tenth. Pohjanlehto briefed the men of the combat patrol with a few sentences. Then it started.

While the artillery suddenly laid salvoes onto recognized enemy-occupied farms and houses, and one part of the Finnish infantry forces fired onto the flanking enemy centres of resistance with MGs and rifles, the eleven men of the strong combat patrol and *Obersturmführer* Pohjanlehto ran as agreed, at 0755 hours, at a sprinter's speed across the open area toward the northeastern part of Jekaterinowka. At the same time, the two tanks rolled along the village street firing from all barrels.

Pohjanlehto's combat patrol reached the northeastern part of the village without any losses and then let their MGs, MPis, and hand grenades do the talking. Everything happened lightning-fast. The Russians were completely surprised; as it turned out later, they were soldiers that had just recently been drafted into the Red Army and had very little fighting experience. A short time before they lived at the estuary of the Volga estuary and along the shores of the Caspian Sea. They were drafted and then were brought up in forced marches from Astrakhan. Then the war hit them with all its violence. Instead of leaving the houses and finding cover outside, they remained in the houses to defend themselves. The tank shells burst inside the houses and reaped a bloody harvest.

Pohjanlehto was at the front, encouraging his men on, for each house one, two hand grenades, and then onward. The men from the combat patrol behaved as if they have lost their minds. They could not hesitate. They had to take full advantage of the enemy's confusion before he could organize a defence. That ensured success and saved their blood.

Pohjanlehto was still leading from the front. He shouted brief instructions to his men. Russians were coming out of basements and houses and surrendered. More and more Russians threw their rifles away.

A few men from the combat patrol took them to the rear so that the combat patrol was covered from the back.

Five men of the combat patrol were still with Pohjanlehto when it finally reached the outskirts. The others were "collecting" the prisoners. Two *pioniere* placed a captured sMG in position and fired on the fleeing Russians with it. A small daring group, born during the hour of desperation, assembled around one of the lightly-wounded Finns, had destroyed the fighting spirit of a numerically-superior enemy who could already taste victory, and kept the rear of the division free and safe.

The cleaning up operation was carried to completion, and by 0900 hours the entire northeastern part of Jekaterinowka was in the hands of the Finns. Over 100 dead covered the battle ground and 73 Red Army soldiers went into German captivity. The booty consisted of three super heavy mortars, one *Pak*, three sMGs, two lMGs, 30 MPis, and 200 rifles, as well as one field kitchen and 17 wagons with ammunition and equipment.

According to statements by prisoners, the 99th Rifle Brigade's mission was to capture Jekaterinowka and, in a further advance, block the Proletarskaja-Salsk road to cut off the withdrawal route of *Division "Wiking"* in the Proletarskaja bridgehead. It was thanks to the deployment of the courageous Finnish *Bataillon* that that did not happen.

Under the protection of the Finnish Bataillon, the regiments of "*Wiking*" evacuated the Proletarskaja bridgehead during the night of 20 January 1943 and drove across the Manytsch bridge and the dam to take up a new defensive positions in a great semi-circle around Salsk. The *I.* and *II./"Nordland"* transferred for a brief time to Schablijewka and Jekaterinowka to give some support to the Finnish *Bataillon*, which at that time was grappling with the Russians in Jekaterinowka.

The schedule of the German withdrawal was calculated and timed exactly. The individual stages guided the formations rapidly to the rear. One intermediary position after another was occupied. The troops of *1. Panzerarmee* also withdrew slowly out of the eastern Caucasus and would soon establish contact with *LVII. Panzerkorps*. The *17. Armee* was directed from the western Caucasus into the Kuban bridgehead, from where the Caucasus was again to be attacked during the following summer. However, events and developments of the over-all situation nullified those plans.

From Salsk to Jegorlykskaja

The men from "*Wiking*" left the Kalmyk Steppe behind them when they crossed the Manytsch River. South of the Manytsch, between Salsk and Rostov, the villages were again closer together. There were also better roads there. Gentle hills and valleys, clumps of trees and fruit orchards, brooks and large grain fields gave the landscape a different character. In the villages there were small industries, and kolhozes and horse breeding farms, where good horses were bred, were distributed across the landscape. Only cold and snow remained and, as before, the cold east wind forced the defensive lines to be again anchored in the villages.

On 21 January 1943 Russian attacks were repelled by all formations at the front in the vicinity of Salsk, including the Finnish *Bataillon* in Jekaterinowka. The "*Wiking*" disengaged once more during the night of 22 January. On the next day, the defence was aligned as follows: *SS-Regiment "Nordland"* with *I. Bataillon* in Gigant, the *II. Bataillon* around Petschakowskij, and the *III. (finnisches) Bataillon* in Zelina. The *II./"Westland"* was in Adranow with loose contact to the north, to the *23. Panzerdivision*, and the *I./"Westland"* was in Zelina. *SS-Regiment "Germania"* moved the farthest and constructed a new defensive line on both sides of Nesselyj. The open southern flank was guarded by armoured reconnaissance troops from the *Aufklärungs-Abteilung* of "*Wiking*". The *I./"Nordland"* positioned in Gigant on the Salsk-Rostov main road was exposed to strong pressure. There was an indication of a northern encirclement of the *Bataillon*.

At 1500 hours *III. (finnisches)/"Nordland"*, carrying out village security in Zelina, was ordered to drive to Verchnij Chutor (between Gigant and Zelina) to construct a *Aufnahmestellung* (Tr: there is no good equivalent English term for this. It is a prepared line or position into which withdrawing units retreat, where units provide cover for the withdrawal as well as having a prepared defensive line ready, which is then reinforced by the retreating troops) for the *I. Bataillon* under pressure in Gigant. The ordered movement was carried out at 1615 hours. Zelina was defended only by *I."Westland"*.

By evening the enemy had outflanked *I./"Nordland"* to the north and blocked its withdrawal route. *Bataillon Lohmann* was able to leave Gigant by going across the open fields and bypassing the Russian barrier, reaching the main road farther to the west, and passing through the *Aufnahmestellung* created by the Finnish *Bataillon* at Verchnij Chutor, between 1945 and 2130 hours. Already at 2300 hours, an advanced reconnaissance patrol from the Finnish *Bataillon* reported tank noises coming from the direction of Gigant. As no more friendly forces were arriving, the Finnish *Bataillon* evacuated Verchnij Chutor soon after midnight and drove to Zelina to occupy a new defensive sector.

As on the day before, on Sunday evening, 23 January 1943, the enemy *schwerpunkt* was also against the road to Rostov. On the morning of 23 January, after a difficult night march across roads covered with snow drifts and being exposed to severe cold, the *grenadiere* climbed out of their vehicles. All the men, except those absolutely necessary for guard duty, disappeared inside the houses to get warm and clean weapons. During that murderous withdrawal, caring for weapons and vehicles came before eating. The drivers took care of any small damage to their vehicles and refuelled them. The diesel motors of the heavy "Klöckner-Deutz" could not stop because motor and transmission would quickly freeze up and be damaged. At the beginning of the campaign vehicles had to be destroyed for that reason.

The Russians pursued relentlessly and occupied the villages that were evacuated by German units. The Finns already knew the time when they had to be in the new defensive lines. That was the routine. Every day, at around noon, the Finnish reconnaissance patrols returned and reported precisely the approach of the Russian forces.

At 1130 hours Russian formations, including some tanks, had closed up to Zelina and, after a short preparatory period, attacked the village in several waves. The *schwerpunkt* was along the rail line and south of the road.

A red flare hissed skyward into the clear winter sky. Quite suddenly, German defensive fire opened up and forced the Russian attack to ground. All attempts to reignite the attack were smothered in its infancy by fire from machineguns and 2 cm quad antiaircraft guns.

Strong forces then bypassed the village and strove toward a kolhoz three kilometres north of Zelina. In an effort to pre-empt the enemy occupation, and to maintain loose contact with *II./"Nordland"* in Petschakowskij, the 9./"*Nordland*" was ordered to occupy that kolhoz. Here is a report by company commander Ertel on that action:

At 1300 hours I received the order to occupy the kolhoz three kilometres northeast of Zelina. My company was very weak because *Zug Elmgren* had not yet returned from a reconnaissance patrol and therefore was not available to me. The company started out soon. With me was a 5 cm *Pak* of the twelfth.

Directly after crossing the rail line, the column already received fire from the right, probably from the Russian attack waves that were stuck east of Zelina. The firing came from a long distance and was quite ineffectual. I drove at the front with my *Kfz 70* and kept an eye on the kolhoz that we were to occupy. As we got closer, I noticed suspicious movements near the kolhoz.

'Dismount!' was my first reaction. The men jumped from the vehicles and took cover on both sides of the road leading to the kolhoz. Our dismounting resulted in heavy fire from the kolhoz. We initially observed and identified several MGs and a 7.62 cm *Pak* position, which betrayed themselves by their muzzle flashes. The Russians probably expected us and wanted us to drive into a trap.

That was not the first time the men from my company had dealt with such a difficult situation. While the group was getting organized for the attack, my driver and the motorized vehicle detachment leader of the company moved the vehicles out of the danger zone, mostly by driving in reverse.

The gun commander of the *Pak* was killed by a head shot. A tracer round set on fire a fuel container on the *Pak* prime mover and the crew lost its head for a moment. I addressed them energetically and ordered: 'A bit to the right of us is an enemy occupied kolhoz. From the long building, left window, MG fire. *Pak*, high explosive rounds onto the designated target-fire at will!' In no time at all, the *Pak* was in position and opened fire.

In the meantime, our mortar squad in the road side ditch (more of a channel) was in position and intervened in the firefight. Our artillery, which guarded our advance, had also obviously recognized the situation and fired on the kolhoz. It then fired barrier fire to make observation difficult for the Russians.

The company attacked – what company?! Barely thirty men attacked and worked themselves forward in leaps and bounds. It was about 800 metres to the kolhoz – 800 metres as sitting ducks. I only recognized that later.

After the company had gained about 100 to 200 metres of ground, the *Ordonnanzoffizier* of the *Bataillon*, *Untersturmführer* von Scholz, raced up on a motorcycle with an order from the *Bataillon* commander: 'Stop the attack and return to the departure position. The *9. Kompanie* is to take up a defensive position north of the railroad embankment!' *Untersturmführer* von Scholz must have taken off suddenly because he was without his cap, coat, or belt.

The *Bataillon* order was quickly carried out. The company returned and went into position at the railroad embankment. One MG squad remained in front as a battle outpost. *Zug Elmgren* also returned to the company at the railroad embankment – but then again, what '*Zug*': Twelve guys with two machineguns.

We had barely established ourselves at the railroad embankment when the regimental *Ordonnanzoffizier* showed up with an order to again attack the kolhoz. That time we were to be supported by two of our tanks. Fortunately, the commander of the *Panzerabteilung*, *Sturmbannführer* Mühlenkamp, arrived, and we explained the situation to him. Mühlenkamp also considered the attack meaningless and reported that to regiment. The attack was cancelled. We remained in position at the railroad embankment. During the withdrawal movement that started at dusk, we became the rearguard and were supported by two tanks. We learned later from statements by prisoners that the kolhoz, which we were supposed to attack with 40 men from 9./"*Nordland*", was occupied by approximately 400 Russians.

During dusk, Russian forces supported by tanks once more attacked the positions of *I./"Nordland"* at Zelina from the east, along the rail line and the road. That attack also collapsed once one enemy tank was destroyed by an 8.8 cm *Flak* located in the northern part of Zelina.

The men from "*Wiking*" disengaged from Zelina once darkness had set in. *Untersturmführer* Ertel and his 9./"*Nordland*" formed the rearguard. The next move took the Finns to Jegorlykskaja. The Finnish *Bataillon* took up quarters at 2230 hours in the northern part of the village.

Jegorlykskaja

Jegorlykskaja, a larger village between Salsk and Rostov, was to be held for two days. Contact was to be established south of Jegorlykskaja with the formations of *1. Panzerarmee* coming from the eastern Caucasus.

Division "*Wiking*" rushed through Jegorlykskaja on 29 July 1942 during its offensive toward the south and then captured Jegorlyk and Belaja Glina. Then it was the most beautiful of summers, this time it was a dreary winter. At that time the men from "*Wiking*" were the hunters and the Russians were the hard-pressed enemy – this time the reverse was true.

Again, as before, "*Wiking*" was attached to *LVII. Panzerkorps* of *General* Kirchner. At that time German formations advanced seamlessly to the south – this time the *Korps* had no contact to the south and the southern wing was up in the air. But that was no basis for concern. Equipped with radios, reconnaissance patrols from the *Aufklärungs-Abteilung* of "*Wiking*" guarded the open southern flank of *LVII. Panzerkorps* with mobility and skill. They reported the precise strength, composition, and direction of march of the pursuing Russian formations.

Consequently, the division and corps were always in the picture about enemy movements and could take the corresponding defensive measures. It was not only from Salsk that Russian formations, amongst them also armoured units, were pursuing. From the southeast were approaching Russian infantry, cavalry, and armoured formations, which were to meet with the initially-mentioned formations in Jegorlykskaja. As a result, strong formations of "*Wiking*" were ordered to Jegorlykskaja.

During the night of 24 January 1943, regiments "*Westland*" and "*Nordland*", the *Pionier-Bataillon*, and the *Panzerabteilung* of *Division* "*Wiking*", arrived one after the other in Jegorlykskaja. The companies that arrived dismounted and warmed themselves in the houses. All believed that the Russians would close up, as usual, only during the next morning. Jegorlykskaja was full of life and movements during this night. Companies arrived continuously. Vehicles were parked and refuelled. Supplies and ammunition were replenished. Many men, completely exhausted from the difficult night march, jammed themselves into some warm corner and slept. Alertness and security were a little on the short side. All believed that the Russians would only attack on the next day.

However, at 0200 hours on 24 January 1943 Russian tanks fired on Jegorlykskaja and 45 minutes later penetrated into the village. Most of the men from "*Wiking*" did not recognize the approaching danger. They did not pay attention to the few tank shells, and did not even know from where they were coming from. Who in the dark could distinguish between the arriving German units and the pursuing Russians?

At the same time 9./"*Nordland*" was approaching Jegorlykskaja as the rearguard of the withdrawal movement from Zelina. With the company were the two tanks that had remained with them in Zelina to the end. The company commander, *Untersturmführer* Ertel, reported about that as follows:

> During that winter night Jegorlykskaja showed up as a dark shadow in the snowy landscape in front of us. Our two tanks, which were driving at the front, suddenly created a commotion, which I could not immediately explain.
>
> Suddenly, a mighty fireworks display started when we reached the first houses of Jegorlykskaja. Enemy tanks had reached the village, somewhat to our flank, at the same time as we. Shells with tracers swept across the company column. The steely clank of the shells followed shortly by the dull sound of firing indicated that the firing was taking place from very short distances. My first thought: Get off the street! I jumped out of my *Kfz 70* and directed the company vehicles to the right, where they were parked behind the houses. Then I ran into a house, where I met *Sturmbannführer* Lohmann, the commander of *I. Bataillon*. I subordinated my company to him, which in the meantime had gotten ready for battle.
>
> As suddenly as the battle noise had arisen, so quickly did it die out. No one knew what was really happening. When my driver and I returned to my *Kübelwagen* we found our company medical assistant dead. A tank shell had passed through the car radiator and killed our medic. My driver later fixed the hole with the usual Russian construction material, clay and cow dung, and drove the vehicle until we got a new radiator.
>
> I searched for my *Bataillon* still during the night and delivered my company to it.

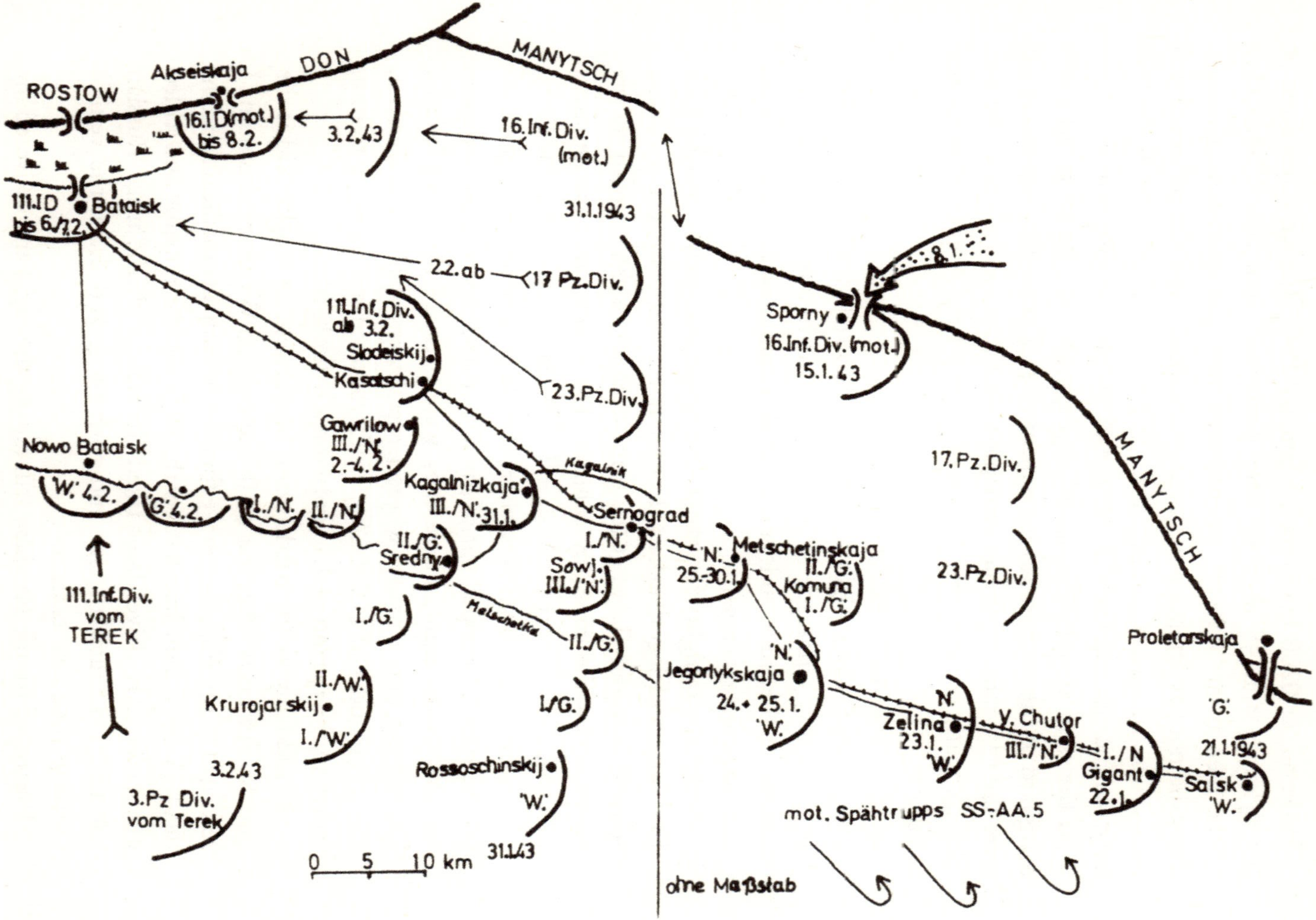

Fighting withdrawal to hold open Rostow for 1. Panzerarmee, January to February 1943.

The *III. (finnisches)/"Nordland"*, alerted in the meantime, took up defensive positions in the northern part of Jegorlykskaja.

During the wild confusion the Russian tanks had penetrated into the centre of the village with mounted infantry and set up an all-around defence. Mühlenkamp silently sent his tanks against the Russian ones; he directed each one into a good firing position. He stressed to each tank commander that he was only to fire on his command, which he would give by radio. The command to fire would be given when daylight arrived.

In the meantime, it was quiet again in Jegorlykskaja. Each unit held its sector. Nerves were tense and there was an unbelievable cold-bloodedness during individual actions. With foresight and guile, one attempted to approach the enemy, evaluate his strength, weigh his own chances, gain oversight of the situation, and from that make plans for actions on the next morning. The *Bataillon* commanders briefed the company commanders but could not tell them all that much. So contact was made, defensive positions were occupied in total silence, and the Russian hedgehog was surrounded. A report by *Sturmmann* Silfverberg, messenger with the company troop of *10./"Nordland"*, illuminates the situation during that night of 24 January 1943:

> Around midnight, after a three hour night drive, our company rolled into Jegorlykskaja. After we had refuelled the vehicles, we wanted to occupy the accommodations that we had scouted out, where we planned to get a bit of sleep. However, Russian tanks suddenly fired along the street. Initially, there was a considerable bit of confusion. Tracer shells had set some houses on fire and lightened up the winter night. The *Gruppen* quickly departed from the accommodations and assembled. Directives and orders were issued. The company advanced toward the outskirts of the village. Under the command of the *Kompaniechef*, *Obersturmführer* Pohjanlehto, in a thin line, we moved like ghosts past housing alcoves.
>
> Suddenly, a young *Untersturmführer* from the artillery appeared out of the darkness. He had just returned from leave and was looking for his battery. As is common with people returning from leave, he wore a peaked cap with shining silver cord and a flawless coat, and on his belt a small pistol. He was a crazy contrast to us, who were

in fur-lined anoraks and felt boots. His armament consisted of a small pistol; we had machineguns and most of the riflemen carried Russian MPis. Comprehension set in rapidly:

'Where are you from?'

...

'Ah so, Finns! What are you planning?'

'We are going to try and crack a few tanks!'

'What! – May I join?'

'Of course!'

The answer to his second question was a bit of an exaggeration because, in addition to a few hand grenades and a flare pistol, we had only one magnetic hollow-charge. Why shouldn't one introduce an artillery man into the daily business of fighting, even at night, by *Panzergrenadiere*?! He joined us enthusiastically and remained for several hours.

After a while the line of skirmishers reached a large house. We carefully snuck around the building and determined that it was the village school. Then, 30 metres from the door, we saw a tank in the school yard. It had to be a Russian one. In the darkness we could not even determine in which direction his gun was pointing.

Undecided, we stood at the corner of the house and quietly discussed what to do with the tank. There was suddenly a noise to the left of us and the tank's machinegun fired a burst in that direction. From the muzzle flashes, we then knew in which direction the turret was pointing.

After a while two telephone operators arrived behind us, laying out a line. They asked us if we knew where the command post of *I./"Westland"* was.

'Probably to the right of us! But be careful, there is a Russian tank 30 metres in front of us!'

The telephone operators continued to sneak to the right, quietly unrolling their wire. The Russian tank drove off and we occupied the school house. It was cold and dark inside.

The chronicler has entered in his diary: 0000 hours one tank, 0200 hours two tanks, 0600 hours four tanks, 0800 hours eight tanks. At the present in Motti (von motittaa = surround).

We had occupied the school house and kept an eye on the Russian tanks. When dawn arrived, the Russian tank crews became nervous and drove around the village with their tracked vehicles, covering one another. We saw one T-34 hit the supply wagon, parked behind a house, dead on with a tank shell, and the bread and other goodies fly through the air. Some of us fired from the windows on the Russian tank commanders, who were sticking their heads out of the turret hatches. Our house was fired on twice with armour piercing shells instead of high explosive shells, indicating that their ammunition was getting short.

In one classroom, some youth from the *10. Kompanie* were squatting on the floor and telling jokes. After a while one of them went to the window to look out but immediately ducked his head and said to one of his comrades, the tall flag carrier of the *Bataillon*: 'Katso Henry, tuolla ulkonasataa lunta!' (Have a look Henry, it is snowing outside). Henry lifted his head and looked out but ducked down again lightning fast; Henry had looked into the mouth of a 7.62 cm tank gun; distance two metres.

Never during that night did we have the feeling that we were inferior. We knew that Jegorlykskaja was full of men from "*Wiking*" and that as soon as it got light the Russian tank apparitions would be taken care off. And that is how it came to be.

Once it got light enough to open fire, *Sturmbannführer* Mühlenkamp ordered his tanks to open fire. With one blow, all hell broke loose. Most of the Russian tanks flew into the air within one minute of the German order to open fire. What the German tanks did not accomplish, was completed by the close-combat antitank troops of the *Panzergrenadiere* and those of the *Pionier-Bataillon*. All Russian tanks, thirteen by count, were destroyed in Jegorlykskaja. Consequently, the Russians lost interest in attacking Jegorlykskaja and passed north of the village to the west. There they ran into *SS-Regiment* "*Germania*".

From Metschetinskaja to Rostov

On 25 January 1943 the *III.* (*finnisches*)/"*Nordland*" was withdrawn from the defence of Jegorlykskaja and transferred to Metschetinskaja to oppose a Russian northern encirclement effort. At 1130 hours a reconnaissance patrol from the *Bataillon* established contact with *SS-Regiment* "*Germania*", which was in position at Komuna. At 1500 hours *I./"Nordland"* was also brought up for the defence of Metschetinskaja. By evening a contact reconnaissance troop from the Finnish *Bataillon* already reported Russian infantry and armoured forces southeast of Komuna. On the next day Russian forces were again reported as closing up. The Russians left Jegorlykskaja to the left and advanced south of *SS-Regiment "Germania"* against Metschetinskaja. They chose the path of least resistance.

By 27 January it began. Early in the morning, strong enemy forces already assembled between the Jegorlykskaja-Metschetinskaja road and the Metschetka valley for the attack. At 0615 hours they attacked the *I./"Nordland"*, which was positioned by the road. North of there, *11./"Nordland"* opened flanking fire against the attackers. Two super-heavy captured mortars (12 cm) were brought into position and the 400 rounds belonging to it were used up in firing on the attacker. The attack came to a halt. Two German ground-attack aircraft intervened in the ground battle. German tanks arrived at 1115 hours from the direction of Jegorlykskaja. The enemy then fled in haste to the east.

In the meantime, Jegorlykskaja had been evacuated. *SS-Regiment "Germania"* evacuated the area around Komuna. All formations took up new defensive positions farther to the rear.

On 28 January, *III. (finnisches)/"Nordland"*, in position in the northern section of Metschetinskaja, reported massive enemy movements in front of its sector. On 29 January a reconnaissance troop brought in 11 prisoners from the Metschetka Valley; 17 defectors were added to that total. The left neighbour (elements of *23. Panzerdivision*) withdrew to the positions of *9./"Nordland"* at the Metschetinskaja rail station. Kagalnitschek, evacuated by them, was occupied by the Russians.

The railroad station two kilometres northeast of Metschetinskaja was held by *9./"Nordland"* (Ertel). It formed an independently operating *kampfgruppe* with a 8.8 cm *Flak* battery from *Flak-Abteilung "Wiking"* and one battery from *Artillerieregiment "Wiking"*. Commanded by *Obersturmführer* Pleiner, it dominated the terrain to the north with its far-reaching guns.

On 30 January 1943, one reconnaissance patrol sent out by the Finnish *Bataillon* from Metschetinskaja to the northeast brought back 22 prisoners. The reconnaissance determined that the kolhoz three kilometres east of the Metschetinskaja rail station was enemy-occupied.

At noon a horse-drawn column approached the defences of the Finnish *Bataillon* on the northeastern outskirts of Metschetinskaja. The Russians were unsuspecting. Had they become confused, or had they been wrongly informed? The Finns immediately decided to let them approach. They remained absolutely quiet and permitted the Russian trains column to enter its defensive area.

A great shock was expressed by the Russians as they were suddenly surrounded by Finns. They had no chance and surrendered. Twenty Red Army soldiers, seven horses, four camels, five wagons, one field kitchen, one car, 50 rifles, seven MPis, and a large amount of supplies were captured. American canned goods were a welcome improvement to the Finnish menu.

On 30 January, as part of the fighting retreat by *LVII. Panzerkorps*, the German defences were once more moved to the rear. In the *"Wiking"* sector, *SS-Regiment "Nordland"* continued its withdrawal to the west, and took up new defensive positions on both sides of Sernograd. *SS-Regiment "Germania"* took up positions to the right of it (south) and defended the farms and small villages on both sides of the Metschetka Valley. *SS-Regiment "Westland"* moved to the extreme right wing of the division in a line south of Nowo Bataisk, where it made contact with the *3. Panzerdivision* coming from the Terek.

As part of that movement *III. (finnisches)/"Nordland"* left its positions at 1730 hours (30 January) as ordered near Metschetinskaja, and occupied a new defensive line at 2000 hours at a kolhoz southwest of Sernograd. Sernograd was defended by *I./"Nordland"* and *II./"Nordland"*.

It was quiet in the *III. (finnisches)/"Nordland"* sector on 31 January 1943. Reconnaissance patrols established contact with the neighbours on both sides. Russian forces moved up to Sernograd by noon and fired on the positions of the Finnish *Bataillon* at the kolhoz with two "Ratschbumm".

However, even that defence line was not held for very long and already started moving on the afternoon of 31 January. At 1600 hours *III. (finnisches)/"Nordland"* moved to Kagalnizkaja as ordered and became regimental reserve. At 1700 hours *10. Kompanie* was attached to *II./"Nordland"* as village security for Kagalnizkaja. It was quiet on the Kagalnizkaja front on 1 February 1943. The Russian were in the process of closing up.

A reconnaissance patrol from the Finnish *Bataillon* traveled to *SS-Regiment "Germania"*, which was located eight kilometres southwest in the Metschetka Valley. There, in the south, the Russians had not yet closed up.

Powerful Russian forces had assembled for the assault in Kagalnizkaja by noon. A short time later *I./"Nordland"*, in position at the railroad station, was attacked by enemy forces. At 1205 hours the *9./Kompanie* (Ertel) was sent as reinforcement to *I. Bataillon* and intervened in the defensive battles.

At the same time *II./"Nordland"*, in position on the outskirts of Kagalnizkaja, was attacked frontally by powerful Russian forces. The strength of the Russians amounted to approximately 1,500 men and six tanks. The situation became critical. The *10./"Nordland"*, attached to *II. Bataillon* and holding its position as an isolated outpost, was already attacked in the rear by enemy infantry and armoured forces at 1400 hours. The company established a hedgehog defence in a kolhoz and repelled all enemy attacks. Silfverberg from the tenth wrote about that:

> At 1200 hours an attack by the Russians that none of us will forget. The 35-man-strong company was surrounded for six hours by enemy infantry and armoured forces. Since that time Kuutti, Nyrke, Mansikka, Syreeni, and Aalto are missing, killed or captured?

And Latra-Pantilla wrote later about it:

> We ran quickly before the Russian tanks, very quickly. That day was the most difficult. I don't want to write more about it.

The Finn Erkki Liukkonen also wrote about the battle for Kagalnizkaja:

> The situation was unfavourable for us because the Kagalnik, located behind Kagalnizkaja, had to be crossed on a bridge, the eye of the needle, and an adjacent long, open, frontal slope, which made all of our withdrawal movements visible to the enemy. He could see our vehicle stream flow to the rear in the early afternoon, with tanks and heavy weapons joining in, and attacked even more violently in all places. The *10. Kompanie* was surrounded in the kolhoz. There,

> enemy tanks were driving around the straw barn-sheds and the few kolhoz buildings. Company commander 'Poku' Pohjanlehto demanded help and reinforcements from *Bataillon*, but there were no more reserves available and the heavy weapons were already withdrawing. The company received the order to fight its way through to our own lines once it got dark.[12]

At the same time, as *10. Kompanie* under the command of *Obersturmführer* Pohjanlehto made it difficult for the Russians to gain territory through their desperate defence, it was also "burning" on the southeastern outskirts of Kagalnizkaja. There, as the last reserves, at 1430 hours were deployed the *11./"Nordland"* (Deck) and one *Pak* from *12./"Nordland"*. At 1630 hours, the company in position in front of the village was pulled back to its outskirts. As soon as the battle for Kagalnizkaja became critical, *Hauptsturmführer* Ladau, the *Chef* of *12./"Nordland"*, began to move all unnecessary vehicles of *III. (finnisches)/"Nordland"* back to Gawrilow.

The front at Kagalnizkaja and the Kagalnik was abandoned by the evening. Erkki Liukkonen, seconded as messenger from *10. Kompanie* to *Bataillon*, was given the assignment to wait for the *10. Kompanie* and guide it after the *Bataillon*. He wrote about it:

> The Kagalnik bridge is to be blown up at 1800 hours. I wait with quaking heart for a long, long time for the company. Nothing is to be heard from company Pohjanlehto as the bridge flies into the air. According to my estimates, an eternity has passed when I finally hear the knocking of the diesel motors of the 'Klöckner-Deutz' and soon after that the three vehicles from *10. Kompanie* appear. I brief *Obersturmführer* Pohjanlehto and we drive across the ice of a small river at a flat river bank and follow the *Bataillon*. Five men from *10. Kompanie* remained at the kolhoz, presumably dead.

The final act of the fighting retreat of *LVII. Panzerkorps* took place on 2 February 1943 south of the Manytsch and the Don. A bridgehead was formed slowly around Bataisk, south of Rostov. As part of that process,

12. Mauno Jokipii, loc cit, page 619.

III. (finnisches)/"Nordland" drove to Gawrilow and occupied a new defensive line there.

In the meantime, large sections of *1. Panzerarmee* had crossed the dam and the bridges of Bataisk and were moving west. The forced march through cold and snow storms was over. The *1. Panzerarmee* was saved. A second Stalingrad did not take place. But north of Rostov, on the Donez, new thunder clouds were already on the horizon: In the process of continuing to develop their success at Stalingrad, the Russians planned to encircle all of the southern wing of the *Ostfront*. The Armoured Group Popow had already crossed the Donez at Isjum and strove toward the southwest. To counter that danger, the forces of *LVII. Panzerkorps* would also be needed. The Bataisk bridgehead was thinned out. During the night of 3 February 1943, the *17. Panzerdivision* and the *23. Panzerdivision*, which were carrying out a fighting retreat north of "*Wiking*", were withdrawn from *LVII. Panzerkorps* and transferred through Rostov for new deployment in the Stalino area. In the eastern front of the bridgehead, north to south, were the following units: *16. Infanterie-Division* (mot.), south of there arrived the *111. Infanterie-Division* coming from the Terek, and "*Wiking*" at the *schwerpunkt* on the road and rail line from Salsk to Rostov, with its southern wing bent toward the west.

Heavy fighting raged on 3 February 1943 along the entire sector of the bridgehead. Substantial enemy forces, which had followed *1. Panzerarmee* on foot, combined with forces that had been pressuring *LVII. Panzerkorps* for weeks. The Russians absolutely wanted to achieve success. After smashing German forces at Bataisk, they wanted to advance south to attack in the rear the *17. Armee*, which was withdrawing from the western Caucasus into the Kuban bridgehead. *Sturmbannführer* Mühlenkamp had to repeatedly send out his few remaining tanks to launch counterattacks, which, however, only provided temporary relief.

The *III. (finnisches)/"Nordland"*, in position at Gawrilow, had deployed the *9. Kompanie* on the left and the *11. Kompanie* on the right, in the foremost line, which in reality consisted of only a thin chain of strongpoints. To the left, there was loose contact with *111. Infanterie-Division*, to the right gaped a large hole of four kilometres to *II. Bataillon*, which was located in the Metschetka Valley at Wassiljewo-Schamschewo. An attack on Gawrilow during the afternoon of 3 February was already repelled far in front of the positions of *III. (finnisches)/"Nordland"*.

The Finn Mansikka from *10. Kompanie*, who had been reported missing during the fighting at Kagalnizkaja (2 February), returned to the *Bataillon*. That is a special story:

The Finn ended up in Russian captivity but was able to escape during the night. He made his way to the west, where he suspected the German positions would be. He reached the German lines on the morning of 3 February at Slodeiskij. There, instead of men from "*Wiking*", he met the east Brandenburgers from the *111. Infanterie-Division*, which had occupied that sector during the night of 3 February. Around noon, an officer from *111. Infanterie-Division* called the right neighbour, *9./"Nordland"*. He reported to the company commander, *Untersturmführer* Ertel, that a man in German uniform, speaking broken German, had entered their lines and claimed to be a Finn. That seemed ridiculous to a good Prussian officer, because he could not figure out how a Finn could show up there. *Untersturmführer* Ertel confirmed the Finn's statements and explained the situation. Mansikka was then sent to *Bataillon* in Gawrilow, where he was greeted joyfully by his comrades from the *10. Kompanie*.

The Bataisk bridgehead in the south was withdrawn to the small Kagalnik River on 4 February 1943. There was another regrouping within the "*Wiking*". While *SS-Regiment "Westland"* moved close to Nowo Bataisk, *SS-Regiment "Germania"* was inserted between the town and *SS-Regiment "Nordland"*, and defended in the Kagalnik Valley at Iwanowo-Schamschewo.

According to the plan, the bridgehead was to be held on 4 February and then withdrawn during the coming night to a narrow bridgehead south of the Don crossings at Rostov. The "*Wiking*" and the *16. Infanterie-Division* (*mot.*) were also to be withdrawn during that last movement. Consequently, the *111. Infanterie-Division* was to defend the bridgehead on its own for several days.

The "*Westland*", "*Germania*", and *I./"Nordland"*, in position on farms on the Kagalnik, were already attacked by strong enemy forces in the morning hours of 4 February. The fighting swung to and fro all day, but the men from "*Wiking*" held; they had to hold.

The *III. (finnisches)/"Nordland"* was also attacked heavily at Gawrilow. Already in the morning, approximately 150 Red Army men infiltrated between the two strongpoints of *11. Kompanie* positioned at the right

Bataillon sector. If the entire bridgehead was not to be endangered, the German defence had to hold, as was the line of the *11. Kompanie.*

Therefore, a counterattack was required to throw the Russians back and seal the frontline again. At 0500 hours *Obersturmführer* Deck assembled with 20 men from *11. Kompanie* for the counterattack. The small fighting force bypassed the enemy forces and attacked them suddenly from the flank. In the process, three Russian antitank guns were destroyed, 50 prisoners were captured and 30 Russian dead remained on the glittering snow surface.

At 0800 hours 7 Russian tanks and 400 Red Army men attacked the right strongpoint of the *11. Kompanie.* In the process, a "Mark III" tank (probably a British lend-lease) was destroyed by the Finnish *Pak.* The strongpoint group (about 15 men) withdrew to the kolhoz northwest of them and reinforced the defenders that were holding out there.

At 0830 hours, tanks and *Sturmgeschütze* from "*Wiking*" entered the defensive battle. They surrounded the enemy group and attacked it in the flank and rear. Three tanks were destroyed in no time at all; the others drove off at high speed. The fleeing Russians were hit by the on-board weapons of the tanks; 300 enemy dead remained on the battlefield.

The *Chef* of *9. Kompanie, Untersturmführer* Ertel, deployed on the left, wrote about that:

> The encirclement of the enemy by our tanks was a tactical masterpiece by Mühlenkamp (commander of *Panzerabteilung 'Wiking'*). We followed with concern the march direction of an enemy force approaching from slightly to the right. My right lMG, an MG 42, fired a few bursts against the Russians passing about 600 metres in front of us, who also had some tanks with them.
>
> The direction of the Russian advance aimed to pass the southern wing of my company. Suddenly we saw more tanks behind the Russian force. We were becoming uneasy because we believed that the Russians would advance with additional forces. But then we experienced a drama: The following tanks were our own.
>
> There were crashes, flashes, and clanking. The Russians were completely surprised. In a very short time our armoured group, excellently led, destroyed the entire enemy force. There were no holes, no cover on that frozen, flat plain. The Russians were delivered defenceless to our tanks and *Sturmgeschütze.*

The right strongpoint, given up earlier, was reoccupied by *11. Kompanie* shortly after 0900 hours. Six lMGs, six sMGs, four antitank rifles, and two mortars were captured by the *11. Kompanie. Obersturmführer* Deck's company suffered one dead and eight wounded.

The *III. (finnisches)/"Nordland"* had two companies from *Grenadierregiment 50* (*111. Infanterie-Division*) transferred to Gawrilow and attached to it. There was a gap to the northern neighbour, *Grenadierregiment 70*, in position at Kasatschi.

During the evening hours of 4 February 1943 units from the "*Wiking*" gave up their last positions in the Caucasus. At 1700 hours, *III. (finnisches)/"Nordland"* and the two attached companies from *Grenadierregiment 50*, as well as a 8.8 cm *Flak*, disengaged and withdrew as ordered toward the northwest. Whereas *111. Infanterie-Division* once more occupied a narrow bridgehead around the approach to the Bataisk bridge, units from "*Wiking*" continued on over the dam and the bridges to Rostov. The Don, which was crossed half a year before in a triumphant procession into Caucasia, was left behind by the Finns, the Germans and the European volunteers. These days it still lives in their conversations as the fateful Don, on whose banks the city of Rostov was the gate to the Caucasus.

Division "Wiking" and all its units, with men from all of Europe, as part of the *LVII. Panzerkorps* of *General der Panzertruppen* Kirchner, contributed to the fact that Rostov did not become a second Stalingrad, leading to the destruction of *General* von Mackensen's *1. Panzerarmee.* The volunteers from Finland contributed substantially to those defensive successes.

In conclusion, an order of the day honours the deployment of the "*Wiking*":

> The commanding general K.G.St., 4 February 1943
> of *LVII. Panzerkorps (mot.)*
> To *SS-Pz.Gren.Div. "Wiking"*
> The *SS-Pz.Gren.Div. "Wiking"* leaves today the formations of my *Panzerkorps*. The division has from the first to the last day of its attachment caused severe damage to the enemy and achieved admirable results through its spirited attacks, its dogged defence, in uninterrupted, week-long battles, under unfavourable weather

> conditions and always against a numerically-superior enemy, and always showed an outstanding fighting spirit. Thanks to the outstanding conduct of the division, the enemy's goal -breakthrough and encirclement – was not achieved. And so I see the men from *SS-Pz.Gren.Div.* "*Wiking*" leave my formations with a heavy heart. My thanks and full recognition go out to the leadership and the troops.
>
> signed Kirchner

"Stop Armoured Group Popow!"

Stalin wanted more than Stalingrad. It soon became obvious that the fighting retreat of *LVII. Panzerkorps* and the saving of *1. Panzerarmee* in no way banished the crisis on the southern sector of the *Ostfront*. After the Soviets broke through the Italian 8th Army's lines on the upper Don, they separated it from *Armeeabteilung* Fretter-Pico. They then continued their major offensive against the rear areas of the 2nd Hungarian Army during Christmas of 1942, forcing it out of the Woronesch area, and south of it, to the west. Russian formations streamed to the west through the 500 kilometre-wide gap. Their goal was to surround large formations and to destroy the entire German southern front. After they recaptured Charkow, the Dnjepr crossings at Saparoshje and Dnjepropetrowsk were the declared Soviet objectives. *Heeresgruppe* Don, later *Heeresgruppe Süd*, commanded by *Generalfeldmarshall* von Manstein, fought with *Armeeabteilungen* Fretter-Pico and Hollidt, as well as parts of *Heeresgruppe A* (von Kleist), which were able to just make it through the gap at Rostov, to gain some time, which would permit the arrival of reinforcements and the construction of a new defensive line. The defence of the area west of Charkow was assigned to *Armeeabteilung* Kempf. Into that area flowed from the west *SS-Panzerkorps Hausser* with *SS-Panzergenadier-Divisionen* "*Leibstandarte*", "*Das Reich*", and "*Totenkopf*". Later they would fight in the battle for Charkow.

While one part of the Russian offensive forces advanced on Charkow, another part, after crossing the Donez, swung to the southwest with Armoured Group Popow as its lead element. Isjum was captured by the Russians on 5 February 1943, and the Donez River was crossed on a broad front in that area. One other Russian offensive group advanced on Dnjepropetrowsk through Losowaja and Pawlograd, with the mission of blocking the important Dnjepr crossings. The goal was clear: Encirclement and destruction of *Heeresgruppe Süd.*

In weapons and numbers, the Russians were far superior to the Germans. Stalin urged his formations to speed up because he believed that he could deal a death blow to the Germans. Hitler behaved according to his old maxim: Hold at all cost! However, *Generalfeldmarshall* von Manstein, one of the ablest German strategists, wrestled freedom of action from Hitler and moved his formation like chess figures to and fro in the threatened area. It was a race with time, which von Manstein finally won with his *Heeresgruppe*. Constantly being spurred on to greater speed by their commanders, the German formations struggled in severe cold and over snow-covered roads to reach their deployment areas. The drivers were exhausted. There were traffic jams, blockages, and long halts at bridges and other road obstacles, which the *feldgendarmerie* and *pioniere* had to remove in great haste.

Generalfeldmarshall von Manstein transferred his command post to Saporoshje. From there he followed every Russian move and replied with counter-moves. Finally, a new, somewhat solid (with many gaps) front, was created from the southern sector.

Armeeabteilung Hollidt assembled north of Rostov. It occupied and held the Mius line, which had already been part of the German *Ostfront* in the south during the winter of 1941/42. The decimated formations of *General* von Mackensen's *1. Panzerarmee*, which had just arrived from the Caucasus, assembled in the Stalino area. *General* Breith was to attack Popow in the flank from the Slawjansk area with his *III. Panzerkorps*, while the *XXXX. Panzerkorps*, under *General* Heinrici, was to prevent any further advance by Armoured Group Popow. The *4. Panzerarmee* of *General* Hoth, assembling in the Pawlograd area, was to attack northward later to establish contact with *Armeeabteilung* Kempf, which was in position southwest of Charkow, and thereby close the gap between that city and Pawlograd. To carry out that plan, it was necessary to first stop the Russian advance.

On 11 February 1943 Armoured Group Popow reached the village of Grischino, and a little later Krasnoarmejskoje. As a result, the most important supply line of the southern wing of the German *Ostfront*, the Dnjepropetrowsk-Stalino-Rostov rail line, was blocked.

At that time, *Panzergrenadier-Division "Wiking"*, which protected the withdrawal of the Caucasus troops at Rostov until the end, found itself on the march to the Stalino area to be available to *III. Panzerkorps* (Breith). Initially, the division was supposed to have a few days of rest to carry out absolutely necessary refitting. However, when divisional commander Steiner, (driving ahead on February10 for a briefing by the *Generalkommando* of *III. Panzerkorps*) arrived north of Stalino, he found a new deployment order waiting for him:

> *Pz.AOK 1* to Division "*Wiking*" – Urgent!
> Strong enemy, Armoured Group Popow, advancing south to Krasnoarmejskoje after crossing Donez at Isjum. Division "*Wiking*" to immediately turn to the west. Attack Krasnoarmejskoje. Assignment: Stop Armoured Group Popow.
> signed v. Mackensen

The extremely weak *XXXX. Panzerkorps* (Heinrici) had occupied Slawjansk with the *7. Panzerdivision* of *General* von Funck, but General Popow bypassed it west of there, advancing to the south into an area nearly devoid of troops. During that situation, the *Division "Wiking"* just arriving in Stalino, instead of turning north to the *III. Panzerkorps*, was turned to the west and attached to *XXXX. Panzerkorps*. It was to intercept Armoured Group Popow at Krasnoarmejskoje with a wide-sweeping movement. At the same time, the Slawjansk area was taken over by *III. Panzerkorps*. Funck's Thüringian *7. Panzerdivision*, and the Silesian *11. Panzerdivision* of *General* Balck located farther north, were deployed into Popow's deep flanks. The two *Panzerdivisionen* blocked Popow's rearward communications so that eventually no supplies reached Popow's fighting formations.

So much for the overall situation. But now let us turn to Manstein's actors, the innumerable soldiers. Within their squads, platoons, companies and battalions, they had to shoulder the difficult marches and the rigours of the weather, and to take upon themselves the hardships of battle.

The *III. (finnisches)/"Nordland"* had, as did all other formations of *Panzergrenadier-Division "Wiking"*, a difficult march from the Bataisk bridgehead, through Rostov to the Mius, behind it. From 5 to 8 February 1943, the *Bataillon* was located in Kiriloff to repair damage to three cars and 20 trucks. Those were difficult days for the drivers and maintenance detachments; overloaded with work under primitive working conditions.

From 9 to 12 February they travelled through old familiar places on the Mius. There were numerous reunions with former hosts (winter position 1941/42). *Hauptscharführer* Pape, company troop leader from *9./"Nordland"*, drove with his company commander and messengers to his "Chosaika", where he had his quarters. It was a happy reunion. There was much to talk about. Where there should have been enmity, friendship flared up brightly. But from the reports of the women and elders, it became obvious that the German civil administration had made many errors after the front line troops left, and did not win the hearts and minds of the population.

Commanded by *Obersturmbannführer* Joerchel, *SS-Regiment "Nordland"*, as the lead element of Division "*Wiking*", reached the Stalino area on 10 February 1943. Because of the new order to stop Armoured Group Popow, the regiment was immediately brought forward. Its first elements drove through Galluzinowka-Selidowka to Datschanskij and constructed a defensive line there. With that, an anchor point was secured for additional arriving "*Wiking*" units,

During the night of 11 February 1943, when the lead elements of *SS-Regiment "Nordland"* were already defending the area south of Krasnoarmejskoje, the Finnish *Bataillon* in Gorlowka received the newest situation report and the order to move up on the following day.

On 11 February, at 0600 hours, the *III. (finnisches)/"Nordland"* departed Gorlowka, passed Stalino in the direction of Datschanskij, and at 1050 hours formed up in battle-march formation. The lead element was the *9. Kompanie*, with an attached *Pak* and *lIG* platoon from the *12. Kompanie*. Crowds of Italians, who were apparently trying to win as much territory as possible at the rear, met the advancing units. Germans and Finns shouted "Avanti, Avanti!" to them. At 1300 hours Datschanskij, defended by weak German forces, was reached and village security was taken over. Reconnaissance patrols were sent out. Reconnaissance yielded the following results: Four enemy tanks four kilometres north of our own defensive line on the road to Krasnoarmejskoje. At 1400 hours the security west of the Datschanskij-Krasnoarmejskoje road was taken over by the arriving *II./"Nordland"*.

The *III. (finnisches)/"Nordland"* received the order to advance to Nowo Pawlowka and to reach the assembly area for *SS-Regiment "Nordland"* for the attack on Krasnoarmejskoje. The unit continued in the motorized battle-march formation because Gubin was supposed to be occupied by weak friendly formations. *Untersturmführer* Ertel's *9. Kompanie* formed the lead element.

Ertel's company drove, widely separated, toward a long slope. A motorcycle/side car combination carrying *Obersturmführer* Deck and Pohjanlehto raced past the column. In a youthful and high-spirited manner, Deck and Pohjanlehto waved to the men of the *9. Kompanie* and *Untersturmführer* Ertel. A short time later some firing was heard from the direction of the slope, behind which the motorcycle had disappeared. The company snuck up even more slowly and carefully to the hilltop. When Ertel, his company commander, and his messengers reached the hilltop, they were already suspecting what had happened. Deck and Pohjanlehto came racing back in leaping bounds. When they reached Ertel they reported: They had believed that Gubin was free of the enemy and wanted to reconnoitre the best possibilities for their companies to attack the village of Nowo Pawlowka. In the process, they were fired on by Russians. The driver of the motorcycle, Pöntinen, was killed.

Ertel had his *9. Kompanie* dismount and go into position on both sides of the Datschanskij-Gubin road. The *10. Kompanie* and *11. Kompanie* were brought up under its protection and readied for the attack.

The *III. (finnisches)/"Nordland"* started the attack at 1605 hours. Gubin was reached in a rapid advance. Weak enemy rearguards withdrew toward Nowo Pawlowka. The Finns pursued them. By 1730 hours the Russians were also thrown out of Nowo Pawlowka. The Finnish *Bataillon* occupied and secured the village.

The *9. Kompanie* defended at the left wing of the *Bataillon*, along the Nowo Pawlowka-Ignatiewskij road. An sMG group of the company was located directly on the road, at the exit from Nowo Pawlowka. At 1830 hours, it was already dark, a vehicle approached the MG position from the direction of Krasnoarmejskoje with its headlights on full. The group leader kept his cool and transmitted his calmness to his men. When the vehicle had approached to within 20 metres of his position he ordered:

"Continuous fire – open fire!"

Two heavy machineguns barked at the enemy vehicle like two angry dogs. The crews worked with precision, even though it was dark. Tracers bounced off the armour plate and sprayed bright light, like a fireworks display. The enemy vehicle stopped. The engine was running. No shot was fired from the opposing side. The sMGs stopped firing. Their crews approached the dark object very carefully. It turned out to be a Russian armoured reconnaissance vehicle. The vision slit was open. Three men of the crew were dead – caught by the machinegun bursts. Chance and fate for one side, bad luck for the other. The war found its victims in such an unpredictable manner.

The 9. *Kompanie* used its new trophy for a few days. Then it turned over the Russian armoured reconnaissance vehicle to regiment because it used too much fuel and oil.

Apparently the situation was not clear to the Russians either. A half hour after the incident with the armoured reconnaissance vehicle, which had in the meantime been brought to the rear by an experienced driver, at approximately 1900 hours, four Russian tanks followed by two trucks with infantry rolled toward Nowo Pawlowka. Hours before that, STAWKA, the Russian supreme command, had issued orders to its "South West Front" to prevent the withdrawal of the Germans to Dnjepropetrowsk and Saparoshje, and to throw them back into the Crimea, where they would be starved out and forced to surrender. In compliance with STAWKA's directives, Colonel General Watutin, supreme commander of the "South West Front", also pushed Armoured Group Popow to greater speed. But STAWKA and Watutin were wrong. The Germans were not retreating. Rather, they were reorganizing to carry out Manstein's brilliant plan; hitting with the backhand, and wresting a victory from the forward-storming Russian formations drunk with victory by smashing them in a great pair of pincers. But everything was not yet ready. German formations were still striving desperately to get to their departure positions. That resulted in situations where German formations, and many times small formations, already in contact with the enemy, had to master crises because everything was being staked on one turn of the cards.

One "trump" in the hand of *XXXX. Panzerkorps*, of *Division* "*Wiking*", was the Finnish *Bataillon*, which was pushed far forward to Krasnoarmejskoje and was in position at Nowo Pawlowka. The *II./SS-*

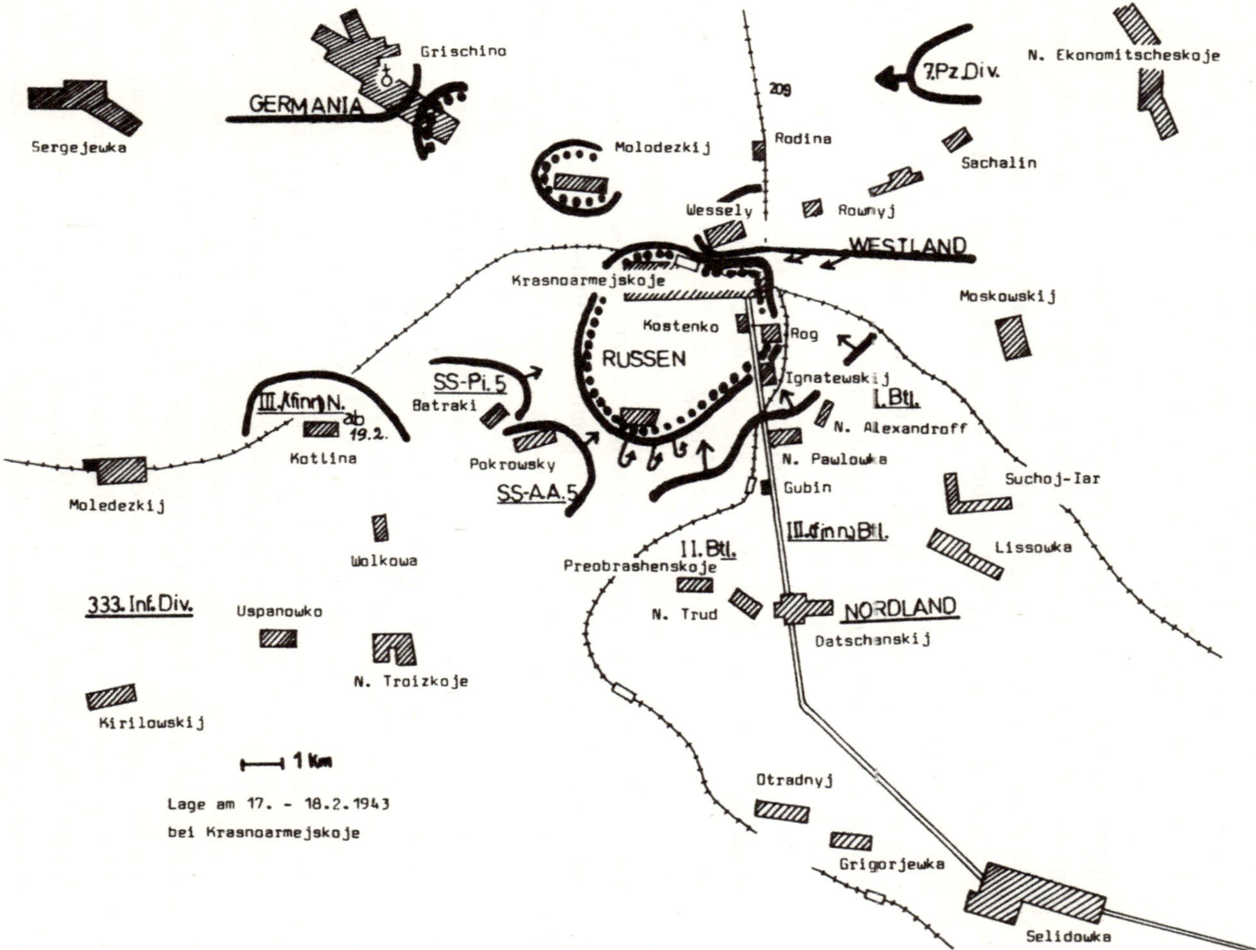

Destruction of Armoured Group Popow at Krasnoarmejskoje, February 1943.

Regiment "Nordland" was unable to close up on the left and *I. Bataillon* on the right. The leading enemy tank elements with accompanying infantry rolling toward Nowo Pawlowka at 1900 hours were greeted by the Finns with fire. A *Pak* from the *12. Kompanie* fired, but was already destroyed by Russian tanks after firing only five rounds. Simultaneously, those tanks took the edge of the village under heavy fire. The new order from STAWKA and from the supreme commander of the "South West Front" contained the directives to bypass strong resistance and gain as much territory as possible. West of Nowo Pawlowka, the Russian tanks rolled to the south, toward Preobrashenskoje, where *II./"Nordland"* was defending under the command of *Sturmbannführer* Krügel.

Because the enemy situation was not clear, the *III. (finnisches)/"Nordland"* was withdrawn from Nowo Pawlowka to Datschanskij, where the *12. Kompanie* arrived at 0400 hours on 12 February, and was integrated into the village defence.

Additional units from "*Wiking*" closed up during the night of 12 February. *SS-Pionier-Bataillon 5*, commanded by *Sturmbannführer* Schäfer, positioned behind the blocking line of *SS-Regiment "Nordland"* on both sides of Datschanskij, was brought up to Swerow, so as to encircle Krasnoarmejskoje from the southwest. The *Aufklärungs-Abteilung* from "*Wiking*" was brought up still farther to the west and, after passing through Nowo Troizkoje, reached the large village of Sergejewka, 15 kilometres northwest of Krasnoarmejskoje. *SS-Regiment "Westland"* was turned sharply to the north from Selidowka and, during the same night, after passing through Lissowka, reached the village of Rownyj, four kilometres east of Krasnoarmejskoje. *SS-Regiment "Germania"*, the last battle group from "*Wiking*" arriving in Selidowka, marched in the early morning of 12 February 1943 through Nowo Troizkoje-Sergejewka to Grischino, to help encircle Krasnoarmejskoje from the west. As a result of those moves, Armoured Group Popow sat in a trap. However, the trap could not yet be completely closed because, in relation to its frontal width, the forces available to "*Wiking*" for the encirclement were relatively weak.

Only artillery could have helped there. It became the decisive issue on the scales of the God of War and ultimately found Armoured Group Popow wanting. *Brigadeführer* Gille, an artillery man by profession, organized "*Wiking's*" artillery for the decisive deployment. Regiments "*Germania*" and "*Westland*" were each assigned one *Abteilung*, while the mass of the artillery regiment and the division's *Flak-Abteilung* went into position behind *SS-Regiment "Nordland"*. Added to those forces were also the heavy infantry howitzers of *SS-Regiment "Nordland"*, whose fire was controlled from observation positions of the artillery. The howitzers and cannons, as well as the cannon battery from "*Wiking*", fired on Krasnoarmejskoje from all sides and at different times. *Brigadeführer* Gille proved himself to be a master of his profession. The salvoes of the German artillery, in a constantly alternating pattern and strength, fired into Krasnoarmejskoje and slowly ground down the Russian resistance.

On 12 February the Finnish *Bataillon*, as part of the overall process of compressing the encirclement, once more attacked Nowo Pawlowka from the east with the *9. Kompanie* and *11. Kompanie*. The companies started the assault at 0900 hours and were soon in possession of the village. Enemy counterattacks, supported by heavy artillery fire, collapsed in the defensive fire of the Finns. Pohjanlehto's *10. Kompanie* was brought up from Datschanskij to Nowo Pawlowka because new enemy assembly areas had been identified.

And once again a new Russian attack on Nowo Pawlowka was launched! The Russian infantry was forced to go to ground by the Finns; at 1530 hours four T-34s penetrated into Nowo Pawlowka. A cat and mouse game began. The T-34s covered each other and drove around between the houses. The Finns kept the Russian infantry at a distance while waiting for a good opportunity to destroy the T-34s. In the late afternoon one T-34 drove into a mud hole to the left of the village entrance and remained stuck. In the meantime it had gotten dark. *Unterscharführer* Zinnöcker and *Sturmmann* Silfverberg from the *10. Kompanie*, a company troop leader and a messenger, discovered the immobilized tank while combing through the village. The moon had already formed a half crescent in the night sky. They snuck up to the tank in the pale moon light. The turret hatch was open and the instrument light glowed weakly. Zinnöcker and Silfverberg ran up to the tank like cats and threw hand grenades inside. There were dull detonations and the onboard ammunition exploded. Bright jets of flame indicated the end of the T-34. The crew had probably left the tank earlier.

There were further attempts by Armoured Group Popow to carry out its assignment to advance to the southwest. West of Armoured Group Popow, General Charitonow's 6th Army gained territory to the southwest and approached the Dnjepr River. The push for speed was passed from Stalin to Watutin and on to Popow's smaller formation. In addition to firing on other areas, the Russian artillery also fired on Datschanskij and the Finnish *Bataillon* position north of there. All attacks by Popow's forces were suffocated in their infancy. The German artillery fired concentrated barrages and changed the *schwerpunkt* often, thereby giving the impression of much greater strength. The clamps applied by "*Wiking*" held.

On 14 February 1943 the time had come to unleash the attack on the "wasp's nest" that was Krasnoarmejskoje. While "*Germania*" captured the greater part of Grischino and "*Westland*" took additional ground between Rownyj and Krasnoarmejskoje, *SS-Regiment* "*Nordland*" attacked Krasnoarmejskoje from the south.

The SS-Regiment "*Nordland*" attack fornation was arranged as follows: right *I. Bataillon*, centre *III. Bataillon*, and left *II. Bataillon*.

The simulated strength of the artillery, the *Flak*, and the heavy infantry howitzers of "*Wiking*" resulted in false conclusions being drawn by the Soviet command staff. Popow radioed to his superior command, the "South West Front":

> Am being attacked by five *SS-Panzer Divisions*. Can only maintain my resistance with great difficulties. Help is urgently needed. Long live Stalin!

In reality, it was only division "*Wiking*" that was attacking. Its regiments and battalions were extremely weak. On average, the fighting strengths of the companies consisted of only 40 men. The units had been greatly worn-out by the deployment in the Caucasus and the Kalmyk Steppe. Totally insufficient replacements had arrived at the division.

On 14 February, at 1100 hours, *III.* (*finnisches*)/"*Nordland*", as part of the general attack on Krasnoarmejskoje, once more attacked Nowo Pawlowka with the *10. Kompanie* and *11. Kompanie*. The *9. Kompanie* formed the reserve. During the assault, a tracked vehicle from the *Panzerjäger-Abteilung* was destroyed by a T-34. Nowo Pawlowka was defended by numerous Red Army soldiers and three T-34s.

The *VB* from the *8.* and *9./Artillerieregiment* "*Wiking*" achieved precise and outstanding results; they controlled the fire from their batteries with such efficiency that the Russians were forced out of Nowo Pawlowka. The Finnish *Bataillon* captured the village and reached the heights one kilometre north of Nowo Pawlowka at 1500 hours. A new *HKL* was constructed on the ridge. It was defended against tanks from the direction of Krasnoarmejskoje with *Teller* antitank mines.

The *I. Bataillon*, attacking on the right of *III. Bataillon*, was supported by an armoured train which travelled along the Stalino-Krasnoarmejskoje line. *Sturmbannführer* Lohmann's *I. Bataillon* encountered an especially strong defence and suffered painful losses, especially from mortars and artillery fire, which found plenty of victims on the frozen, coverless snow surface. The *3. Kompanie* lost its last officer and nearly all remaining NCOs. The *II. Bataillon* (Krüger) experiencesd a similar situation. It turned out that the Russians were more battle-capable than had been assumed. The attack by *SS-Regiment* "*Nordland*" was halted.

In the morning a reconnaissance troop from the Finnish *Bataillon* established contact with *I. Bataillon* northeast of Nowo Pawlowka. Another one made contact with the *II. Bataillon* west of the Gubin railroad station. At 1030 hours, the reserve company, the ninth, was brought up and defended the small locality of Nowo Alexandroff on the right wing of the Finnish *Bataillon*.

On 16 and 17 February the front was relatively quiet at Krasnoarmejskoje. Friend and enemy remained passive. On the German side, efforts were being made to grind down Armoured Group Popow with artillery fire and by choking off its supplies. Popow's supply routes were becoming increasingly more insecure. His weakly-defended eastern flank was being attacked by *General* Fuch's *7. Panzerdivision* from the Nowo Ekonimischeskoje area. Popow's fuel and ammunition supply vehicles were knocked off one after the other. Farther north, *General* Balck's *11. Panzerdivision* was doing the same thing so that Popow's supply dried up completely. Popow's offensive group was sitting in a trap from which there was no escape. The radio intercept platoon from the *XXXX. Panzerkorps* had cracked the Russian code on 18 February and deciphered a radio message from Popow to his "South West Front", beginning with the words:

"All wheels are standing still…"

and reported that soon no tanks would be driving or firing because there was a lack of fuel and ammunition. The supply routes through Slawjansk had been interrupted by the Germans.

Ignatiewskij was occupied by strong Russian infantry forces. Three T-34s formed the backbone. Popow waited in vain for reinforcements and resupply so that he could continue his advance toward the south. The reinforcements and resupply were stopped by the German *7. Panzerdivision* and *11. Panzerdivision* and shot to pieces. It appeared that it was the time to administer the death blow to Armoured Group Popow.

On the afternoon of 18 February 1943 *SS-Regiment "Nordland"* again took part in the attack by Division "*Wiking*". At 1500 hours *9./"Nordland"* captured Ignatiewskij against tenacious resistance. The Russians flowed back to Krasnoarmejskoje. The attack by the *9./"Nordland"* was hindered by a dug-in tank firing on the company from the flank until it was finally taken out by a shell. The company suffered one dead and several wounded. A telephone troop laid a wire from the *Bataillon* command post in Nowo Pawlowka to the advanced company, but the wire ran out just before reaching Ignatiewskij. While the men were building new positions on the southern outskirts of Ignatiewskij and alternately warmed themselves in the houses, the company commander , *Untersturmführer* Ertel, remained in the open field 30 metres from the southern outskirts of Ignatiewskij so that he could remain in constant contact by telephone with *Bataillon*. When a Russian counterattack was recognized and Ertel reported that to *Bataillon*, the *13./"Nordland"* immediately started its defensive fire, which partially landed on the positions of the *9./"Nordland"*. Fortunately, the company had no losses. Were the calculators at the *sIG* malfunctioning due to the cold?

Untersturmführer Ertel remained near the field telephone during the cold night so that he could be in constant contact with *Bataillon*.

Hauptscharführer Heinkes, the *Spieß* of *9. Kompanie*, drove onto a mine and was killed as he brought warm and cold food to the front. Heinkes was always touchingly concerned with the welfare of his company and brought forward the noon meal under even the most difficult of situations. *Oberscharführer* Pape became the new *Spieß* of the company.

As the *9. Kompanie* was attacking Ignatiewskij, a reconnaissance troop from the *Bataillon* staff at the northern outskirts of Nowo Alexandroff reported at 1745 hours the approach of 60 Red Army soldiers. The *Stab*

III./"Nordland" and the reserve company opened fire on the Russians and expelled the ones that had entered the village. The killed Russians were wearing civilian clothing under their uniforms. They presumably wanted to get into the houses during the night to warm themselves up.

Hauptsturmführer Ladau, *Chef* of the twelfth, was wounded through a mine explosion. The Finnish *Obersturmführer* Tenomaa took over the heavy company of the Finnish *Bataillon*. The *Bataillon* had two dead and eight wounded on 18 February 1943.

The battalion's mines were picked up by the *Pioniere* during the morning of 19 February. The concentric attack by "*Wiking*" on Krasnoarmejskoje began at 0830 hours. *SS-Regiment "Nordland"* attacked from the south. The first attacking goal of *II.* and *III. Bataillon* was Rog, directly southeast of Krasnoarmejskoje. The *I. Bataillon* exerted pressure on the eastern outskirts of Krasnoarmejskoje from its position by the rail line from Stalino, west of Moskowskij. By 0945 hours, the initially-strong Russian defence collapsed and the survivors retreated hastily to Krasnoarmejskoje. Armoured Group Popow was in a hopeless situation and had no chance of surviving. The fighting became senseless, the units were disintegrating, and chaos spread everywhere. There was no fuel for an escape and any options for a retreat were frustrated by the Germans.

The *II.*./"Nordland" and *III./"Nordland"* captured Rog. The Finnish *Bataillon* alone captured there 15 trucks, two T-34s, and large amounts of war materiel. *SS-Regiment "Germania"* exerted pressure from the northwest and *SS-Regiment "Westland"* from the northeast. The roads to the north were blocked by the *7. Panzerdivision*. Armoured Group Popow was wiped out in Grischino and Krasnoarmejskoje; during the night, only remnants fought their way out across the fields and woods toward the north, and to the Russian formations on the Donez.

The defence of Rog was taken over at 1600 hours by *II. Bataillon*; the *III. (finnisches)/"Nordland"* was transferred to Kotina and employed as village security.

The end of Armoured Group Popow came on 19 February 1943. Stalin, his supreme commanders of the "South West Front" and "Woronesch Front", Generaloberst Golikow and Watutin, still did not recognize Manstein's brilliant strategy of the backhand blow, the attack from a retreat. They still directed their formations to reach the Dnjepr as quickly as possible. They either did not recognize the traps that Manstein was setting, or they did not want to see them.

Although Armoured Group Popow had 145 T-34s when crossing the Donez, its strength was reduced to only a very few combat-ready tanks. Did Stalin know that? There was no arguing against his orders. Only his word and his orders counted. The Army commanders and supreme commanders knuckled under and passed his orders on; from one superior command to the next lower one. And so fate took its course; it began with the destruction of Armoured Group Popow, was followed by the destruction of the Soviet 6th Army, and ended with the recapture of Charkow by the Germans and the creation of a solid front in the south of Russia. The "larger Stalingrad", the destruction of the entire southern wing of the German *Ostfront*, did not happen during those February days in 1943, not yet!

Based on prisoner statements and overheard Russian radio messages, Professor Jankuhn, the *Ic* of "*Wiking*", compiled a report about Armoured Group Popow, its strength, and its battles and destruction. It was added as Enclosure No. 1 to the division order to "*Wiking*" on 21 February 1943, which already assigned new goals to it:

> The enemy had occupied, on 18 February 1943, Krasnoarmejskoje with five formations (the 9th, 12 th and 14th Guards Armoured Brigades, the 3rd Guards Motorized Brigade and the 7th Ski Brigade). Our own attack in the morning of 19 February caught the Russians completely by surprise. Unclear about the strength of our attacking forces, the opposing leadership issued an order on 19 February to destroy the German forces that had penetrated into Krasnoarmejskoje, without however providing the necessary reinforcements to the IV Guards Armoured Corps fighting in Krasnoarmejskoje. Group Popow, on the contrary, ordered the assembly of X Armoured Corps on 19 February in the Dobropolje area (25 kilometres northwest of Krasnoarmejskoje) and ordered at the same time the withdrawal of III Armoured Corps from Krasnoarmejskoje. It was only on the morning of 20 February that Group Popow gained knowledge of the loss of the villages of Krasnoarmejskoje (by "*Nordland*" and "*Westland*") and Grischino (by "*Germania*"). At the same time, the assignment of III Armoured

> Corps to march through Alexandrowka (25 kilometres southwest of Kramatorskaja) to Stepanowka was made unfeasible by the attack of *11. Panzerdivision* (Balck). The renewed advances by *7. Panzerdivision* on 21 February from the Dobropolje area toward the north and northwest and the *11. Panzerdivision* from the area west of Alexandrowka toward the north into the Lawrowka-Oktjabrskij area (25 kilometres northwest Kramatorskaja) forced the enemy today to change its initial decision, to prevent the escape of the German *Kampfgruppe* to the west by a sudden advance in the Slawjanka-Petropawlowka area. Instead, Group Popow has now, in the afternoon (21 February) ordered all its formations, which are already at this time having great difficulties with the supply of fuel and rations, to retreat into the Gniluscha area, while the remnants of 7th Ski Brigade and 9th Guards Armoured Brigade are going toward their destruction in the western part of Krasnoarmejskoje.

On 23 February 1943 the divisions of *XXXX. Panzerkorps* broke Armoured Group Popow's last resistance at Krasnoarmejskoje and north of there, and advanced on a broad front toward the north. Popow pleaded for help from Watutin over the radio. Instead, he ordered Popow to halt the enemy, the German *XXXX. Panzerkorps*, in the Barwenkowo area, and destroy it.

The Donez was the Goal

The crisis situation at *Heeresgruppe Süd* seemed to be winding down on 21 February 1943. The front at the Mius had held. The pressure on the cornerstone of the *Heeresgruppe*, between the Mius and the Donez, had been successfully intercepted by *Armee-Abteilung Fretter-Pico*. Armoured Group Popow was going to its doom in the sector of *1. Panzerarmee*. The *4. Panzerarmee* had recaptured Pawlograd, encircled the Russian forces of the 6th Army in that area, and was then on its way to the Donez. The Russian offensive forces had begun to wane.

With that, *Heeresgruppe Süd* wrested the initiative for itself and could then get down to business of destroying the enemy forces between the Dnjepr and Donez or throwing them back across the Donez because the new solid front is to be constructed on the Donez. From that development came the recapture of Charkow by *SS-Panzerkorps* Hausser.

The "*Wiking*", after destroying Popow's armoured spearhead on 22 February 1943, got ready for the attack to the northwest as part of *XXXX. Panzerkorps* (Heinrici).

On 22 and 23 February, *III.* (*finnisches*)/"*Nordland*", brought up through Kotlina, defended Andrenowka on the left flank of the division. As the attack by the *4. Panzerarmee* was still far back, the left flank became constantly longer. From Andrenowka were seen Russian forces advancing from the Selenyj area to the south. While Manstein's forces were in the process of attacking to the north to close the large gap in the German front at the Donez, Stalin was exhorting his forces toward the south, to the Dnjepr; a fateful error!

The Finnish *Bataillon* worked closely with the *Aufklärungs-Abteilung* of the "*Wiking*" in screening the left division flank. That was an assignment that Steiner delegated to the Finns because he wanted to keep the *Bataillon* as the motorcycle *Bataillon* or the *Sturmbataillon* of his to be newly-created *Korps*.

The advance was endless torture for "*Wiking*" and all other German formations because the temperature hovered around the zero point and then the thaw was followed by a frost. However, the men from "*Wiking*" were in a good mood because they were finally moving again.

On 24 February *SS-Regiment* "*Westland*" met up with Popow's last remaining battle-capable formation in the Bogdanowka area, the X Armoured Corps, which defended itself tenaciously. The subsequent battle resulted in heavy casualties for both sides. As part of that action, and to screen the open flank, on that day the Finnish *Bataillon* was deployed as security in Kriworoshje and at the Tscherwona Sirka kolhoz, and one day later at Schewtschenka.

After defeating the enemy at Bogdanowka, "*Wiking*" advanced on the Suchoj-Torez sector. In the process, *SS-Regiment* "*Germania*", advancing on the right, relieved some of the pressure on *7. Panzerdivision* (Funck) to its right with an attack on Bogdanowka. *SS-Regiment* "*Germania*" then captured the villages of Podolje and Archangelskaja. *SS-Regiment* "*Westland*", in the centre of division "*Wiking*", reached the heights at Zyglerowka, which the enemy defended somewhat more strongly. The commander of *SS-Regiment* "*Westland*", *Obersturmbannführer* Reichel, was severely wounded during the beginning of the subsequent battle; he died several days later at the field hospital in Dnjepropetrowsk.

In the left divisional sector, *SS-Regiment "Nordland"* and *"Wiking's" Panzerabteilung* attacked in the flank the enemy force that was holding up *SS-Regiment "Westland"* and *SS-Regiment "Germania"*, forcing it to retreat to the north.

In the meantime, there were always new defensive assignments for the Finnish *Bataillon*. On 26 February 1943 it marched through Nowo Alexandrowka-Gawrilowka to Bugajewka. The march continued on 27 February, with continuous defensive assignments in Danilowka, Krasnoje Dolina, and Molotschnyj.

On 28 February, *III. (finnisches)/"Nordland"* defended Molotschnyj. At 0815 hours, strong enemy movements from the southwest toward the village were brought early under the division's well-aimed artillery fire. The enemy turned away and left behind three damaged trucks, two guns, and a T-26 tank.

All of Popow's remaining forces and the Soviet 6th Army, which had escaped the fighting farther south, concentrated in the vicinity of the Donez River.

On the German side, no one knew whether Stalin had approved the retreat of his armies across the Donez or whether he was assembling new formations for an assault in the direction of the Dnjepr. In other words: was there to be an assembly for a new attack or cover for the forces crossing back over the river to the north?

On 1 March 1943 *III. (finnisches)/"Nordland"* marched with *"Wiking's" Aufklärungs-Abteilung* through Wodjany-Dmitriewka to Petropolje. The roads and pathways were only mud tracks because of the thaw. The Finnish *Bataillon* remained in Petropolje for the night.

On 2 March, with its heavy weapons, the *Bataillon* supported the attack by *Aufklärungs-Abteilung "Wiking"* against the heights near Andrejewka, in front of the Donez. The river banks fell into German hands.

The weather changed again during the night of 3 March. Heavy blowing snow, following the thaw, aided the retreat of the dispersed Russian forces. In the grey of morning, at 0600 hours, the security elements of the Finnish *Bataillon* noticed enemy movements at Petropolje in the direction of Sawodskoj.

Soon after, they heard a powerful explosion – the Russians had blown up the bridge across the Donez. At 0700 hours, reconnaissance patrols, which had followed the Russians, reported that Sawodskoj was free of the enemy. After resupplying and refuelling, the companies of the Finnish *Bataillon* continued to advance and reached Andrejewka by noon. There, they took up quarters and organized for defence.

At nearly the same time, all battle formations of the "*Wiking*" and the *XXXX. Panzerkorps* reached the Donez on a broad front, west of the Donez loop at Isjum.

The commander of the "*Wiking*" honoured the achievements of his soldiers on 4 March 1943 in an order of the day:

SS-Panzer-Grenadier-Division "*Wiking*" — Div.Gef.St., 4 March 1943

Comrades!

After long and hard withdrawal battles, which were necessary due to the difficult situation on the Don front, the division has once again suddenly turned around, when the barely-hindered enemy attempted to carry out the decisive blow.

Initially, the division held up the strongest part of the Russian operational group at Krasnoarmejskoje, the Armoured Group Popow, and then as part of *XXXX. Panzerkorps*, side by side with the comrades of the *7.* and *11. Panzerdivision*, destroyed the enemy formations one after the other. Today we stand again on the Donez, the Russian Armoured Group Popow has been destroyed, and the Russian 1st Guards Army and 6th Army are in the process of dissolution. German military tradition has once more been victorious.

The division has once again, as always, done its duty, fought victoriously at decisive places and won new glory.

During these days you truly struggled for the fate of our homeland and were victorious. It will someday thank you for it. Today, you will have to be satisfied for now with my thanks and highest recognition, as well as pride in your achievements.

(signed) Steiner[13]

13. Straßner, "Europäische Freiwillige", Munin Verlag Osnabrück, page 201, 202.

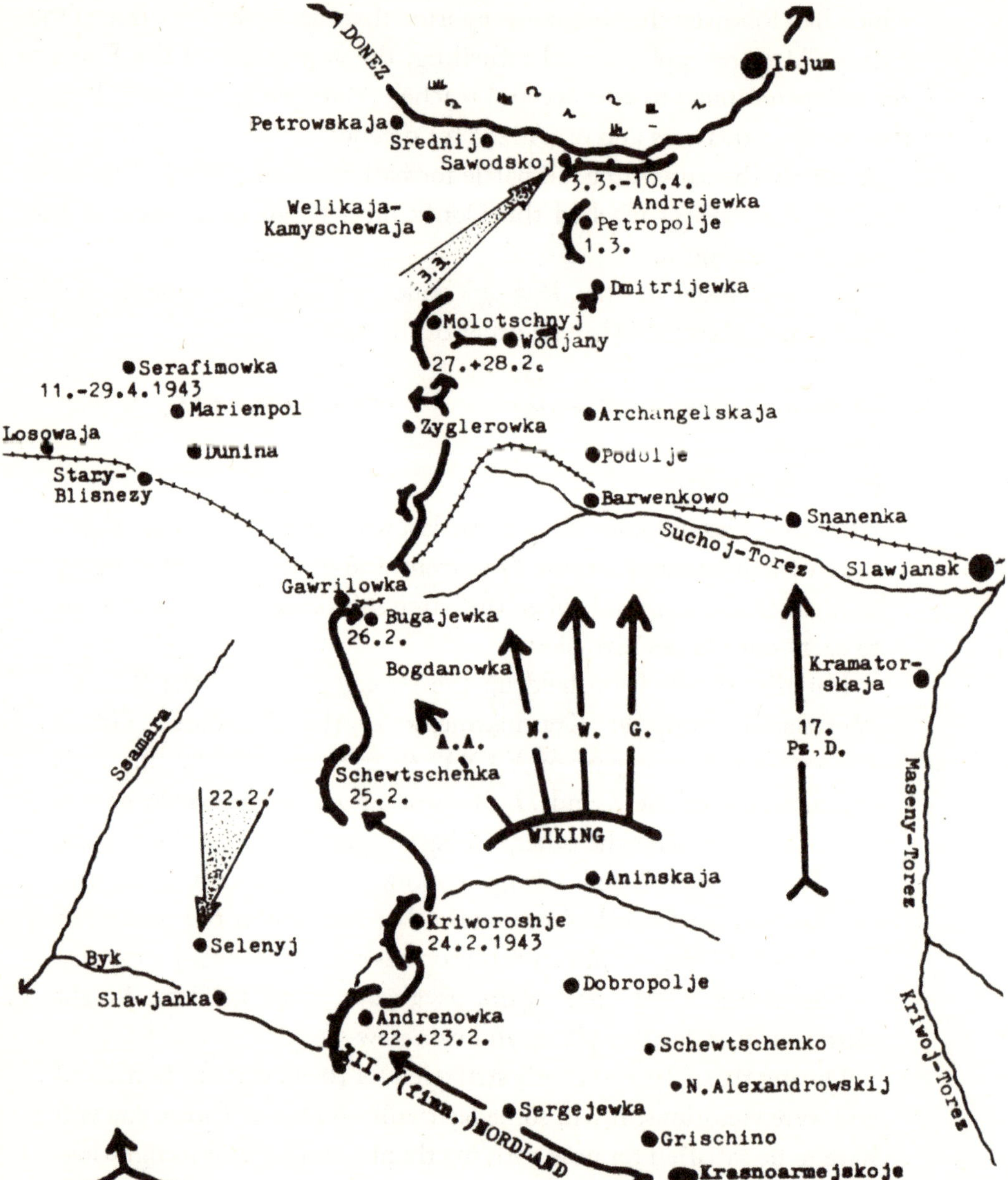

Advance up to the Donez, February–March 1943.

Last Position and Farewell to Russia

The *III. (finnisches)/"Nordland"* had reached the Donez as part of *Division "Wiking"* and had taken up quarters in Andrejewka. The companies went into position on the Donez. The first operational goal of *Heeresgruppe Süd* had been reached. The city of Charkow was recaptured on 16 March by *SS-Panzerkorps Hausser* during the second operational phase.

The companies of *SS-Panzer-Grenadier-Division "Wiking"* had been decimated during the long weeks of battle and needed to be rested and refitted. Because the Donez provided a certain security to the new position, as had all positions behind river barriers, the division was able to rest its weakened formations in the rear area, one *Bataillon* at a time.

The terrain of the new position favoured the defence. South of the Donez are gentle hills, a coherent raised area, which slopes down to the river and permits a clear view of the landscape. On the other side of the Donez, on the enemy side, were thick woods and bushy terrain, poorly suited for tanks and the deployment of large infantry formations. That position offered the Germans a great degree of security because the ice had already broken up by March. Only the harassing artillery fire and the activities of snipers, who were hiding in all the river bank undergrowth, forced the soldiers from "*Wiking*" to take precautions.

From 4 March on, *III. (finnisches)/"Nordland"* was engaged in the construction of a new position in the Andrejewka section of the *HKL*. Trenches were dug and accommodation bunkers were created. Obstacles, mines, and wire entanglements were placed at threatened positions.

On 10 March the Russians attacked the *7. Panzerdivision* from a bridgehead at Isjum. As a result, *Division "Wiking"* also made defensive preparations: The *10. Kompanie* of the Finnish *Bataillon*, in reserve in Andrejewka, was assigned to *I./"Nordland"*, which was in Dmitrijewka as *Korps* reserve (*XXXX. Panzerkorps*). The crisis at Isjum was mastered by the *7. Panzerdivision* on its own so that *Bataillon Lohmann*, with its attached *10./"Nordland"*, did not have to intervene.

During the next few weeks there was an exchange of positions within the division. One after the other, the positioned regiments and battalions were given an opportunity to rest and to replenish, and to replace weapons and equipment. As new German divisions arrived, there were rearrangements within the *Armeekorps* and the *Armeen* from the middle of March on. The *Panzerdivisionen* were mostly replaced by *Infanterie-Divisionen*, which were then equipped in the homeland with new tanks and vehicles. As other divisions were inserted, the widths of some sectors were reduced.

And so, with the exception of the isolated artillery barrage and the activities of snipers, the Finnish *Bataillon* spent a few relatively quiet days in the Donez position until 7 April 1943. The *Chef* of *10. Kompanie*, *Obersturmführer* Pohjanlehto, was wounded on 12 March and *Obersturmführer* Ingerö took over the command of the company. The *Chef* of the *12. Kompanie*, *Obersturmführer* Tenomaa, became ill on 26 March and the *12.* was taken over by *Obersturmführer* Sartio.

Rumours persisted that the *Bataillon* was to be withdrawn and transported to Germany. The two-year obligation of the Finns was running out. On the German side, efforts were made to extend the contract. Understandably, the Finnish state and military leaders took their time because a final German victory no longer appeared certain. They wanted, and who can fault them, to maintain the unity of Finland and the peoples' cohesion amongst all the confusion of the time.

At the beginning of April it became certain that the Finnish *Bataillon* would be withdrawn from the "*Wiking*" formation and transported to Germany.

All unnecessary trains and vehicle detachments of the *Bataillon* were transferred back to Blinezy. An advance commando from the Berlin-Brandenburg *257. Infanterie-Division* (*General* Püschler) arrived and was briefed on the positions of the Finnish *Bataillon*.

During the night of 10 April 1943 the *III.* (*finnisches*)/"*Nordland*" was relieved by *II./Grenadierregiment 457.* Next morning it was transported from Andrejewka to Petropolje, and one day later into the new Serafimowka-Marienpol-Dunina bivouac area. On 12 and 13 April weapons, vehicles, and equipment were cleaned and repaired, and readied for transfer to the Estonian volunteer *Bataillon* "*Narwa*" arriving at the front.

The *SS-Freiwilligen-Bataillon* "*Narwa*" was previously the *I. Bataillon* of the 1st Regiment of the Estonian Legion. It was commanded by *Hauptsturmführer* Georg Eberhardt. *Bataillon* "*Narwa*" consisted of active officers and NCOs from the former Estonian army, which, after the Soviet occupation of Estonia, was disbanded in 1939. The *Bataillon* already had frontline combat experience and was also employed in anti-partisan operations. On 14 April 1943, the Estonian *Bataillon "Narwa"* took over the weapons, equipment, and vehicles from the Finnish *Bataillon* and moved to the front.

With the expansion of the *Waffen-SS* through the creation of new divisions, and even its own *Armeekorps*, it became clear that *SS-Regiment "Nordland"* would have to leave "*Wiking*" because of the reorganization of *Division "Wiking"* into a *Panzerdivision*; which, according to the war time structure, was to have only two *Panzergrenadierregimenter*. The regiment was to be expanded into a division.

The "*Nordland*" and the *Legion "Nederland"*, which was also to be expanded to a division, were to form the *III. (germ.) SS-Panzerkorps*.

Felix Steiner was considered as the commanding general and was to turn over command of "*Wiking*" to *Generalmajor der Waffen-SS* Herbert Gille. The former regimental commander, *Generalmajor der Waffen-SS* Fritz von Scholz, was to be the commander of the to-be-formed *Division "Nordland"*.

There was a mood of "getting ready to move" in the accommodations of *III. (finnisches)/"Nordland"*. It had gone through sixteen months of deprivations and the toughest battles in sweltering heat and icy cold. Sixteen months of combat deployment, far from home. It was a difficult path and many simple field graves remained behind as a sign of the fighting; fighting also for the freedom of Finland. Faith is everything. It moves mountains, the belief in a good cause, as they thought of it. You have to give them that! And they, the Finnish volunteers, experienced the community of like-minded men, the comradeship which trivialized country borders, which included all of the European volunteers of *Division "Wiking"*.

On 20 April 1943 the commander of *III. (finnisches)/"Nordland"*, *Sturmbannführer* Collani, was promoted to *Obersturmbannführer*. With that, recognized were the services of a man who, with his energy, prudence, courage, and his ability to empathize, had led the Finns entrusted to him from success to success.

The frontline deployment of the Finns was recognized on 22 April 1943 by the awarding of the Finnish Medal for Bravery I. and II. Class to 112 soldiers of *III. (finnisches)/"Nordland"*.

General der Waffen-SS Felix Steiner, who wanted to retain the *Bataillon* as a nucleus for his motorcycle rifle or assault battalion in his new *Panzerkorps*, said his farewell to the Finnish *Bataillon* as commander of *Division "Wiking"* in Serafimowka on 24 April 1943. He memorialized the dead and recognized once more the deployment of the *Bataillon*:

> Every one, even the most difficult of assignments, was carried out by you in an exemplary manner!

All Finns serving with other units of *Division "Wiking"* were transferred to the Finnish volunteer *Bataillon*. The time had come on 29 April 1943: 16 officers, and 353 NCOs and enlisted men got onto a troop train at the Stary Blisnezy railroad station and were transported to Germany. On 7 May they arrived at the Grafenwöhr troop training area, where the *III. (germ.) SS-Panzerkorps* was forming.

In Germany and Return to Finland

The *III. (finnisches)/"Nordland"*, the Finnish volunteer *Bataillon* of the *Waffen-SS*, took up accommodations at the Grafenwöhr troop training area on 7 May 1943. The *Ersatz-Bataillon* arrived a day later and was combined with the front *Bataillon*.The total strength then was: 18 officers, 194 NCOs, and 546 enlisted men. The *Ersatz-Bataillon* was stationed in Graz and had the task of accepting replacements from Finland and, after training them, passing them along. It also looked after wounded soldiers of the *Bataillon* after they were released from hospitals and then sent them back to the front *Bataillon*.

From 11 to 27 May, the *Bataillon* recuperated in the Bavarian resort of Ruhpolding. When it arrived at the railroad station it was greeted by a large group of friendly people and heartily welcomed by the mayor of the town. The soldiers were accommodated in private homes. Great friendships were quickly established with the population. The Finnish volunteers were good emissaries of their country. There followed excursions into the beautiful surroundings of the Alpine landscape. Press, radio, and film recorded the meetings between the Finns and the Germans, and focused especially on their comradeship-in-arms. A movie was made about the *Bataillon*, with *Kompanie Ertel* being the "movie company". Interviews were recorded for propaganda broadcasts. The officer corps of the *Bataillon* was invited by Dr. Degener, the resort director, to meet for an amicable drink.

On 23 May 1943 the foreign countries section of the NSDAP held a social evening for the *Bataillon*. Internationally-known artists participated. Amongst them were Gretel Theimer, Petre Munteanu (tenor), Mary Hanikainen, and the Leo Eysoldt orchestra. Also participating in the social evening were *General* Steiner, personalities from the *Wehrmacht*, the field clergy, and the liaison officer of the *Bataillon*, Kurkiala, and a representative of the city.

On 27 May the companies were issued rifles and marched in a closed *Bataillon* formation through Ruhpolding to the city's Sportsplatz. The population took an active interest in the proceedings. The *Bataillon* lined up in parade position in a square and *General der Waffen-SS* Felix Steiner inspected it.

On 28 May the Finnish volunteer *Bataillon* left Ruhpolding for their homeland. The rail journey took the *Bataillon* through Munich – Regensburg -Hof – Chemnitz – Cottbus – Tilsit – Riga – Taps to Reval, where it arrived at 0500 hours on 1 July 1943. It marched immediately to the harbour and boarded the transporter "Warthe". At 0700 hours the ship left the Estonian harbour of Reval and sailed for Finland. At 1400 hours the *Bataillon* arrived on the west coast of Finland, in the harbour at Hangö. The men then marched to their accommodations.

On 2 June 1943 the *Bataillon*, drawn up in parade formation, was greeted by *General* Steiner, who flew to Finland by aircraft, and the commander of the Finnish replacement army, General Malmberg, and was welcomed in their homeland. Subsequently, both generals reviewed the *Bataillon* in a march-past.

Especially with respect to foreign policies, the Finnish government was making a great effort to quietly absorb the *Bataillon* in Finland. After the march-past, the *Bataillon* had to turn in all the weapons it was issued in Ruhpolding. That annoyed many of the volunteers. They had fought with German weapons and wanted to enter Finland with German weapons. The special train carrying the *Bataillon* left Hangö at 1600 hours and arrived in Tampere on the morning of 3 June.

The arrival of the Finnish volunteers had spread through the country like wild fire. The population and the relatives of the *Bataillon* members prepared an overwhelming reception. The *Bataillon* lined up for a roll-call for the last time on Tampere's Sportsplatz. *General* Steiner turned the *Bataillon* over to the commander of the Finnish replacement army, General Malmberg. In their speeches they paid homage to the frontline deployment and the achievements of the *Bataillon* and the German-Finnish comradeship-in-arms.

Amongst the numerous Finns, also present was the Baroness Ruth Munck. As a nurse, she had already cared for the Finns of *Jägerbataillon Nr. 27* during the First World War, and now was the head of the Finnish Lotta organization, an auxiliary formation of the Finnish army. Two Finnish nurses, Lisa and Laine-Marie, who looked after their countrymen in German hospitals, were also in attendance. There was great sympathy for the Finnish volunteers and the German members of the *Bataillon*.

By 1700 hours, all the formalities for leave-taking were finished. The Finnish volunteers left for their home areas for four weeks leave, until 2 July. The German members of the *Bataillon* were invited by the Finnish army to a sight-seeing trip through southern Finland. The trip lasted from 4 to 9 June 1943. They visited the Vierumäki sports school, which was run by the first liaison officer of the *Bataillon*, Oberst Leválahti.

Then the Germans drove to Jyväskylä, where wreaths were laid at the monument for the Finnish dead and at the monument for the fallen German of the *Ostsee-Division* of 1918; *Obersturmführer* Ertel gave a brief commemorative speech. Then the German members of the *Bataillon* drove through the beautiful Päijannejärvi lake area to Lahti, where they visited the long-wave transmitter, one of the most powerful in the world at that time. Then they were guests of the Finnish garrison at Lahti. From there they travelled to Helsinki, which was normally closed to Germans.

The German *Bataillon* members experienced some unforgettable days in Helsinki. In the usually austere Finland's capital city, they were met everywhere with hospitality. The Finns served their German friends a supper in true Finnish style and tradition at the Hotel Kemp.

During one of his walks *Obersturmführer* Ertel found himself directly in front of the Stars and Stripes, which was flying over the US embassy, and Finnish reality got a hold of him again.

In the meantime, by agreement with the German military attaché in Helsinki, a support base had been created for the *Bataillon* under the command of *Untersturmführer* von Scholz. It was to accept the German *Bataillon* members after their sight-seeing trip. From there, they drove on 9 and 10 June to Germany for leave. On 1 July 1943 all officers of the *Bataillon* assembled in the German camp at Hangö and on 2 July they were joined by all the other members of the *Bataillon*.

In the meantime, the dice had fallen after negotiations. Marshal Mannerheim demanded his Finnish countrymen back so that he could absorb them into the Finnish armed forces. The soldiers of the *Bataillon* remained in the German camp in Hangö until all the formalities were completed.

On the morning of 10 July, a beautiful summer day, the Finnish *Bataillon* assembled for the last time for roll call. *Obersturmbannführer* Collani said farewell to his Finnish men with a handshake. A comradeship-in-arms in the truest sense of the word, a comradeship which was formed during the most difficult days of the war-time deployment, came outwardly to an end, but it continued as a mediator between two greatly tried nations.

The war diary of the *Bataillon* closed with the following entry:

> 10 July 1943:
> At the request of Marshal Mannerheim, release of all Finns from the *Waffen-SS*. 0800 hours farewell of the Finnish SS-members through a handshake from the commander, *Obersturmbannführer* Collani.
>
> Transferred to the Finnish replacement organization: 14 officers, 234 NCOs, and 534 enlisted men. 11 officers and 27 enlisted men will be released later, after additional medical treatment.
>
> The Finnish volunteer *Bataillon* has existed from 15 June 1941 until 11 July 1943. Fighting spirit and fighting power were outstanding and were recognized by all superiors. Germans and Finns are joined by the band of comradeship.
>
> Concluded on 11 July 1943.
> F.d.R.d.A. (certified)
> signed Hirt, *Obersturmführer* and *Adjutant*
> signed Collani, *Obersturmbannführer* and *Kommandeur*

Already by the end of 1941 the competent Finnish military personnel were aware that the war against the Soviet Union would not be over as quickly as hoped for. Yes, even the first doubts were raised as to whether Germany could even win that war.

The Finnish government and the Finnish military became increasingly reticent, and there was an increased effort, especially by Generalleutnant Talvela[14], to remove the Finnish volunteer *Bataillon* from its association with the *Waffen-SS*. in which it was more associated with the nationalistic Germany than it would have been in the *Heer*.

Those efforts were started because a number of contractual agreements were not kept by the Germans; for example, the *Bataillon* was not an "independent unit" with its own officers. Those, and other contractual violations, created justified concerns and many personal disappointments amongst the affected Finnish volunteers, who participated in the various formations of "*Wiking*" only as "guests" in the campaign against the Soviet Union.[15]

To counter those efforts and to continue to have the Finnish volunteers *Bataillon* as part of "*Wiking*" (and to organize for replacements because otherwise the *Bataillon* would be bled white and its disbanding would have to follow), at the urging of *Chef* of *SS-Ergänzungsamt*, Berger, a new Finnish committee was created under the leadership of the principal of the Helsinki University, Professor Nevanlinna.[16]

However, the new committee hardly got to work because by the fall of 1942 the military situation had once again worsened for the Germans. From those points of view, the preparation in March 1943 for the creation of the *III. (germ.) SS-Panzerkorps*, and the suggestion by Himmler to combine all Finns in a German-Finnish regiment with the name "*Kalevala*" (after the Finnish national epic by Elias Lönnrot), became meaningless.

A new attempt to form a new Finnish formation at the turn of 1944/45 from Finnish prisoners of war captured by the German *Lapland-Armee*, and from Finns living in Germany, failed due to lack of personnel.

14. Note appendix, document No. 4, from 4 November 1942.
15. Compare appendix, document No. 2, from 10 February 1942.
16. See appendix, document No. 3, from 28 April 1942.

The Disbanding of the Finnish SS-*Bataillon* during 1943

by Professor Dr. Mauno Jokipii

As the two-year contractual time of the *Bataillon* was approaching an end the Germans were starting to talk, already at times in March 1943, of a continuation of the agreement. The *Bataillon* had a symbolic value, a propaganda value from the point of view of the Germans. From the Finnish point of view, there was no rush. The Finnish government, its Prime Minister after the presidential vote in February 1943 was professor Edwin Linkomies, and his foreign minister, Dr. Henrik Ramsay, sent an unofficial representative, the principal of the University of Helsinki, Professor Rolf Nevanlinna, to Berlin in the spring of 1943 to find out the German wishes. He dealt with the *Chef* of the *SS*-Replacement office, *General* Gottlob Berger, and passed along the resultant information and negotiating results to Finland.

On 1 July 1940, the committee for foreign issues of the Finnish parliament decided that Finnish conscripts could not serve in a foreign army if Finland was engaged in a war. The contents of that decision were not published so that we do not know whether it related to other contracts that were then in force. In any case, because of that, after the beginning of the war with the Soviet Union there was no replacement organization established for the Finnish *SS-Bataillon*.

During the new negotiations in the spring of 1943 the Finnish government limited the length of a new contract of the Finnish *Bataillon* to six months. Mannerheim agreed to a limit of one year.

After the contract time had expired the Finnish *Bataillon* was quietly transported from Reval to its homeland, and was unloaded in Hanko. It was decided against unloading in Helsinki in order not to invoke any enemy air raids. The *Bataillon* was permitted to hold a parade on 3 June 1943 in the inner part of Finland, in Tampere. The men received a one month leave, their future still undecided.

Mannerheim, the Marshal of Finland, then intervened. At the end of the volunteers' leave, on 27 June 1943 he handed over to the German *General* at his headquarters, Waldemur Erfurth, a letter for Hitler. In it he rejected a new contract for the *Bataillon* by explaining his own difficulties of finding replacements. However, in discussions he moderated his position in that former members of the *Bataillon*, if they so desired, could again serve, but would receive no replacements. Some Finns associated with the *Bataillon* considered that as unwise and attempted to have President Ryti and Prime Minister Linkomies influence Mannerheim's position. However, Ryti and Linkomies refused to do that. Linkomies and foreign minister Ramsay had already explained to Nevanlinna, when he drove to Berlin during the spring, that they were striving for the disbanding of the *Bataillon*. Nevanlinna was the chair of the committee that was responsible for the *SS* volunteers.

After the situation had taken such an "unfriendly turn of events" (Erfurth) on the Finnish side, Hitler, the *OKH*, and the *Reichsführer-SS* decided to do "without the *Bataillon* to spare the volunteers conflicts of conscience" (Jodl). That message reached the Finnish headquarters by telephone on 4 July 1943 just as the transhipment of the *Bataillon* volunteers, who were returning from leave, was being prepared.

The *SS* organization that was tasked with the disbanding of the *Bataillon* wanted to carry that out without any demonstrative festivities; the corresponding directives arrived at Helsinki on 9 July 1943. However, generals Erfurth and Heinrichs pushed through the idea that the *Bataillon* would be disbanded with modest ceremonies on 11 July 1943 in Hanko.

From the diplomatic point of view, the disbanding of the *Bataillon* was a clear indication that the relationship between Germany and Finland was going in a new direction. On 5 July 1943 the Privy Councillor from the foreign affairs department wrote to Foreign Minister von Ribbentrop:

> Finland was showing tendencies not only to not intensify its relations with Germany but rather to distance itself from Germany slowly and carefully.

The disbanding of the *Bataillon* was one of the first indicators of a great change that was in the offing in Finland's politics.

Finland between the Great Powers – Detachment from Germany

After the fortunes of war turned away from Germany, there grew in Finland discomfort at cooperation with Germany. Far-sighted Finnish politicians pushed increasingly openly for a detachment from Germany. The final decision for a separation from Germany and a cautious contact with the Western Powers was taken on 3 February 1943 at a meeting of Ryti, Mannerheim and other representatives of the Finnish general staff, as well as the Finnish government. A few days later a Finnish colonel gave a detailed report to a secret meeting of the Finnish parliament on the overall war situation. He advised his listeners to become acquainted with the idea of a renewed peace agreement with Moscow.

On 15 February 1943 the Finnish Social Democrats issued a declaration with the important article:

> Finland does not participate in the war between the great powers. The circumstances that Finland fights on the side of Germany against the same enemy does not change anything about this fact. From this it follows that Finland, when there is a suitable situation, has the option of deciding to get out of this war.[17]

On 5 March the Finnish President formed a new government, with no German-friendly members included. In August of 1943 there followed a memorandum, which had a great effect on Finnish public opinion. It demanded the rejection of Germany and the initiation of an active peace policy; it was signed by 33 representatives from the political and cultural life of the nation and directed at the Finnish President.

This background makes it clear why Field Marshal Mannerheim considered the removal of the Finnish volunteer *Bataillon* from the *Waffen-SS* as the first step in the solution to the problem. The two-year contractual obligation ran out. The *Bataillon* returned to Finland and was disbanded, its members distributed to the Finnish armed forces. Many young Finns went to officer and troop training schools. The Finns that had already served as officers with the Germans received the same rank in the Finnish army.

The Finnish exploratory talks and peace feelers went through the Soviet embassy in Stockholm; they did not remain hidden from the German military and government observers because the Swedish press reported on that quite often. Then the Germans, especially Foreign Minister Ribbentrop, pressed for the conclusion of an alliance in which the partners committed themselves to not signing a separate peace.

17. Dieter Aspelmeier, loc cit, page 128.

That contractual commitment was constantly put off by the Finns and Germany ceased supplying armament and food help to the Finns.

Finland's gradual separation from Germany was based on the fact that it had no contractual alliance with Germany. When the war against the Soviet Union began on 22 June 1941 the Finnish government informed all relevant governments through their representatives that Finland would continue to be neutral. Finnish troops did not take part in the march into the Soviet Union.

The so-called neutrality phase lasted from 22 to 25 June 1941. Only then did Mannerheim permit his troops to return fire against the Soviets. That was to prove that Finland was no appendage of Germany, and that it carried out its politics independently.

In fact, the competent military and political leaders constantly strove to keep as great a distance as possible from Germany; amongst them was especially Mannerheim, who had the survival of the Finnish people under his cool and calculating gaze, and who, once already in 1918, turned Finland's politics around by 180 degrees.

It was also he that constantly prevented a closer cooperation between German and Finnish forces. He declined when the Germans offered him the supreme command of the entire Finnish front. He insisted that *General* Dietl command the Finnish northern front (20. German Mountain Army) while he, Mannerheim, commanded the Finnish southern front with mainly Finnish forces. Mannerheim was basically inclined to be on the defensive. He did not want to advance beyond previous Finnish territory. Only parts of the Finnish forces initially took part in the German offensives.

The Finns avoided the term "ally" and usually spoke of the German "brother-in-arms".

> This was to prove to the world that Finland had no political agreement, no official alliance with Germany and that the military command structures of the two countries collaborated only to coordinate the military operations, which were very complicated in Finland due to outside influences, and these led to it becoming Germany's cobelligerent against the USSR."[18]

18. Dieter Aspelmeier, loc cit, page 117.

On 9 June 1944 the Russians unexpectedly launched a major offensive in the Karelian land narrows and broke through the Finnish front at several places. All political considerations took a back seat. On 11 June the Finns requested German military help; the German *122. Infanterie-Division* and *Sturmgeschütz-Brigade 303*, as well as weapons and ammunition, were sent to help the Finns. The grain deliveries to Finland were started again. Once more the collapse of the Finnish front was prevented with German help, although then with the price of the so-called Ribbentrop Pact that was signed by Ryti on 22 June 194 that contained the important passage:

> In consideration of the military help which Germany has given Finland in the present situation, I declare as President of the Finnish State that I will only negotiate peace with the Soviet Union with the agreement of the German Reich government and will not permit the designated government officials or other personalities to carry out cease-fire or peace negotiations or negotiations related to this, without the agreement of the German Reich government.[19]

The Ribbentrop agreement became invalid when Finnish President Ryti resigned and Finland obtained a free hand to carry out cease-fire discussions with the Soviet Union. It was probably not an easy decision for Mannerheim, but he only saw a chance for Finland's survival in a settlement with the mighty Russian neighbour. That meant a total rejection of the former brother-in-arms Germany.

Mannerheim justified his decision in a letter to Hitler; in it is still the same old song of comradeship and brothers-in-arms. On 2 September Mannerheim gave the letter to *General* Waldemar Erfurth, German liaison officer at the Finnish general staff, which Hitler received on 3 September. The letter contained the following:

> During this hour, because serious decisions are imminent, I feel the need to enlighten you about the decision that I have arrived at, which the duty of saving my nation has forced upon me, to find a quick exit out of the war.

19. ibid, loc cit, page 135.

The unfavourable development in the overall military situation increasingly limits Germany's ability (particularly during the hours of our greatest need, which are most likely yet to come) to provide help at the right time and in sufficient amounts, which we urgently need and which Germany sincerely wishes us to receive. Alone, the deployment of a single division to Finland, takes so much time that our resistance against the enemy's superior strength could collapse in the meantime. I believe that the situation does not permit keeping sufficient divisions constantly in Finland for such an eventuality. The experiences from the previous summer also confirm these assumptions.

The evaluation of the military situation by me, as given to you, is shared by a growing majority of the representatives of the Finnish people. Even if I were of a different opinion, it would no longer be compatible with our constitution, where I could ignore the emerging will of the majority of the people.

When *Generalfeldmarshall* Keitel visited me on your behalf he stressed that the Greater German people, if fate demanded it, would fight the war for another ten years. I replied that one could hope that this was correct for a nation of ninety million but that it was physically impossible for us Finns to sustain a long war. The large Russian offensives in June have already exhausted my reserves. We can no longer afford a similar blood letting without further endangering the existence of the tiny Finnish nation.

I would like to especially point out that should fate prevent your weapons from gaining victory, Germany would still survive. No one can give a similar assurance to Finland. When this country of barely four million is defeated militarily, there can be no doubt but that it will be expelled or eradicated. I can not expose my people to this possibility.

Although I can barely dare to hope that you will agree with my point of view and reasoning, I still wanted to write to you before the decision is made.

Our paths will most probably separate soon. But the memory of our German brothers-in-arms will live forever. In Finland the Germans were certainly not a representative of a foreign domination but helpers and brothers-in-arms. But even then the position of the stranger is difficult and requires much.

I can assure you that during the past few years in Finland nothing happened that could lead us to see the German troops as intruders or oppressors. I believe that the behaviour of the German army in northern Finland, with respect to the local population and the local authorities, could be considered, under similar circumstances, a unique example of correct and cordial relations and enter our history as such.

I consider it my duty to extricate my people from this war. I can and will not use our weapons, which you gave us so freely, voluntarily against Germans. I foster the hope that you also, even when you disapprove of my step, will just as I and all Finns, have the wish to endeavour to conclude our previous relations avoiding any sort of aggravation of the situation.

In admiration and thankfulness

signed Freiherr Mannerheim, Marshal of Finland,
State President of the Finnish Republic[20]

At the same time, on 2 September 1944, as Mannerheim's letter to Hitler was on its way, the Finnish Reichstag voted, with 113 votes for and 46 votes against, to accept the Russian cease-fire conditions. Diplomatic relations with Germany were broken off. The German Ambassador, von Blücher, left Helsinki with his co-workers on 10 September 1944 for embarkation in Turku.

When the first signs of the Finns exiting the war appeared at the end of 1943, two operations had already been formulated in September; "*Birke*" was the withdrawal of the German *20. Gebirgsarmee* from northern Finland to northern Norway, and "*Tanne*" was the occupation of the Aland Islands. The latter plan was formalized through a directive from Hitler on 8 April 1944 and sub-divided into plans "*Tanne-West*" and "*Tanne-Ost*", the occupation of the island of Suursaari (Hogland). Suursaari had special importance because, located between the Finnish eastern south coast and the Estonian city of Narwa, it could prevent sorties of the Russian "Baltic Red Banner Fleet" from its bases near Leningrad and could secure the sea flank of the German *Heeresgruppe Nord* in Estonia. The *OKM* (*Ober-*

20. C.G. Mannerheim, "Erinnerungen", Atlantis Verlag, Zurich 1952, Pages 526–7; and P.E. Schramm, "Kriegstagebuch des Oberkommandos der Wehrmacht", Verlag Bernhard & Graefe, Frankfurt/main 1965, Band IV, 1. Halbband, Pages 894–5.

Kommando-Marine – Supreme Command of the Navy) initiated its own preparations for "*Tanne-Ost*" because *Heeresgruppe Nord* was unable to provide any forces for it. During a Führer discussion "*Großadmiral* Dönitz had pointed out the war decisive importance of the Estonian coast."[21]

On 3 September, when Mannerheim's letter to Hitler arrived, the negotiations for the transport of German troops out of southern Finland had already begun. The Soviet demands that Finland had to be clear of German troops by 15 September 1944 could not be met by the German Lapland army.

The *OKW* gave the initial order for "Operation Tanne" on 4 September. The *23. Infanterie-Division* had to make ready parts of its *Füsilier-Regiment 68*, as well as naval forces, for the first landing wave.

On 5 September Hitler approved the proposal by *Heeresgruppe Nord* (Schörner) of the creation of a new Finnish *Jägerbataillon Nr. 27*. The *Bataillon* was to become the holding unit for all Finns who opposed the capitulation of their country; under those conditions, they would be deserters. However, that new *Bataillon* existed only on paper.

A Finnish delegation flew to Moscow on 6 September to negotiate the cease-fire conditions. On the same day, the German liaison staff under *General* Erfurth left the Finnish headquarters in Mikkeli for Helsinki.

Sturmgeschütz-Brigade 303 was the first unit of the German troops stationed in southern Finland to already embark on 7 September at the Helsinki harbour. The Finns helped with the difficult loading of the ships. On 9 September the ships left with the German service organizations on board and *General* Erfurth left Helsinki harbour on 13 September on the last German evacuation ship, the steamer *Lapland*. With that, the withdrawal of the German troops from southern Finland was completed.

Simultaneously, Hitler ordered that "*Tanne-Ost*" be carried out because it seemed unlikely, based on Soviet cease-fire conditions, that the island of Suursaari would be turned over voluntarily. A German naval fleet formation under *Kapitän zur See* Mecke departed from Estonian harbours on 14 September and set course for Suursaari (Hogland). When approaching the island at 2300 hours, the formation, consisting

21. W. Haupt, "Heeresgruppe Nord", Podzun Verlag, Bad Nauheim 1967, page 231ff.

of artillery, landing, mine clearance, and torpedo boats, came under accurate fire from Finnish coastal batteries.

Nonetheless, the torpedo boats managed to get through and put *Füsilier-Regiment 68* ashore. The coastal batteries under Lieutenant Colonel Miettinnen, and the Russian air attacks during the day, prevented the bringing up of the main German forces. The German landing forces were split up and laid down their weapons on 15 September. Operation *"Tanne-Ost"* had cost the Germans 400 dead and 1,056 prisoners. *"Tanne-West"*, the occupation of the Aland Islands, was not carried out. Later on, Finnish batteries on those islands fired on passing German naval forces.

Leaving northern Finland in 14 days could not be done due to the long distances and difficult road conditions involved. *Generaloberst* Rendulic already alluded to that during his previous visit with Mannerheim on 2 September 1944. Mannerheim wrote about this:

> *Generaloberst* Rendulic was...courteous and obliging, but as it appeared hard and not approachable... explained to me that he had to express his serious concerns due to the turn-about which events had taken. During his brief time in Lapland (the previous commander of *20. Gebirgsarmee, Generaloberst* Dietl, had lost his life in a plane crash) he had been able to determine that the Finns were tough fighters, but nobody could deny that the Germans were also unafraid and, if it had to be, would proceed ruthlessly in conducting the war. A collision between Finns and Germans would undoubtedly develop into a gruesome bloody war.[22]

A considerable intensification of the situation arose when the Finnish transport chief stated hat the Finnish rail system would only be available to the German *20. Gebirgsarmee* until 14 September. On 11 September, as the liaison officer from the Finnish headquarters, Lieutenant Colonel Haahti flew to *Gebirgs-AOK 20* in Rovaniemi to negotiate. *Generaloberst* Rendulic was able to negotiate for the Salla-Kemi rail line to be available to Germany until further notice.

On 19 September 1944, the Finnish delegation signed the cease-fire agreement in Moscow. The German withdrawal movement had already started.

---

22. Mannerheim, loc cit, page 527.

The difficulty of the withdrawal rested on the fact that the troops had to be moved north, to northern Norway, because they were not allowed to enter neutral Swedish territory. The southern wing of *20. Gebirgsarmee* had to first evacuate the Oulu and Kemi supply bases at the northern end of the Gulf of Bothnia. The evacuation of Oulu was completed on 15 September, that of Kemi on 21 September. Then the fighting formations of *XVIII. Gebirgskorps*, those that were stationed farthest south, moved north in stages. Amongst them was *6. SS-Gebirgsdivision "Nord"*.

On 24 September the *XXXVI. Gebirgskorps*, in the centre of the *20. Gebirgsarmee*, was withdrawn westward from the Kandalaschka sector into the line west of Salla. A few days later the *XIX. Gebirgskorps* in the Murmansk sector also disengaged from the Russian enemy.

Kampfgruppe West, with motorized parts of *6. SS-Gebirgsdivision "Nord"*, held the Pudasjärvi road intersection from 28 to 30 September against pursuing Finnish formations; there was intense fighting on 2 October at Ranua.

The 3rd and 11th Finnish divisions landed by sea at Tornio, at the Swedish-Finnish border, to cut off the German retreat. There was intense fighting at Kemi.

Rovaniemi was evacuated by German forces on 16 October. The *6. SS-Gebirgsdivision "Nord"* reached Muonio on 28 October and on 5 November the Keresuando position on the Norwegian border. With that, operation "*Birke*" was also concluded.[23]

That it came to fighting between the former brothers-in-arms, Finns and Germans, was due to the harsh conditions of the cease-fire and the intervention of Soviet officers and commissars of the cease-fire commission. Finland had to fulfill the demands of the Soviets to have any chance of survival.

In those difficult days, when a nation existed and did not exist, the former soldiers of the Finnish volunteer *Bataillon* of the *Waffen-SS* also acknowledged its people and its leadership, and carried out their duty loyally, even when it pitted them against their former brothers-in-arms.

That of course caused bitterness in the German soldiers in Finland; they felt themselves betrayed and were able to carry out their retreat to Norway

23. Franz Schreiber, "Kampf unter dem Nordlicht", Munin Verlag Osnabrück 1969, page 284ff.

only through ruthless military determination. The Germans applied the "scorched earth" tactic to keep the pursuing enemy at a distance; everything that could have been of use to the enemy was destroyed. All bridges were destroyed, and, in the Lapland, nearly all the houses.

One has to look at both sides to understand the tragedy between two former friendly countries, expressed by the behaviour of their soldiers. One has to also see that Mannerheim's words in his letter to Hitler had come true; which simply expressed the fact that after a Soviet victory the large German people would continue to exist, but the small Finnish country would disappear if it did not lay down its arms in time. That Mannerheim had taken Finland out of the war at the last minute, proved to be correct.

With the surrender of Finland, the Germans also gave up the Narwa area and withdrew through northeast Estonia to the southwest (operation "*Aster*"); amongst them the staff of *SS-Freiwilligen-Panzergrenadierregiment 49* "*De Ruyter*", which had been formed from the former staff of the Finnish volunteer *Bataillon* of the *Waffen-SS*. On 29 July 1944, the former commander of the *Bataillon*, *Obersturmbannführer* Collani, was killed as the commander of *Regiment* "*De Ruyter*" in the "*Tannenberg* position". He was promoted to *Standartenführer* and awarded the Knight's Cross posthumously.

After Germany's defeat, the "Big Three", Stalin, Truman, and Churchill, decided to offer peace, initially to Italy, Bulgaria, and Finland, and instructed their foreign ministers to prepare the peace agreements. The negotiations took place from 29 July until 15 October 1946 in Paris. The peace agreements were signed at the same place on 10 February 1947.

Although Finland got back its sovereignty, it was with a certain dependence on the Soviet Union; it was not turned into a people's democracy under Soviet influence, as were Poland and Czechoslovakia. The territorial losses agreed to in the cease-fire agreement were confirmed. The strength of the Finnish armed forces was limited. It had to lease Soviet bases on Finnish territory and pay 300 million dollars in reparations. Those were harsh conditions, but Finland retained its independence. This was also due to the fact that Finland was not of great importance to the Soviet Union, as were Poland, Czechoslovakia and central Germany.

In addition, the change of Finland to a people's democracy probably would have forced Sweden into the western alliance. In the friendship agreement with the Soviet Union of 6 April 1948, Finland agreed not to conclude or join any coalition that was directed against the Soviet Union. And so Finland stands today between two power blocks. Because it is exposed to an immediate intervention by the Soviet Union, it must avoid any action that could be construed as an unfriendly act.

Former German soldiers from the Second World War fondly remember the comradeship-in-arms with their Finnish comrades. Many contacts exist even today and by now include the families. The good relationship is not disturbed by Finland's rejection of Germany in 1944, which resulted from the necessities of the geographic situation; living next to a powerful neighbour. The distancing from Germany between 1944 and 1948 did not mean a distancing of the heart.

All peace-loving people look with admiration at the tiny country in northeastern Europe, whose self-assertiveness and battle-readiness awakened and grew whenever freedom and independence were threatened. They look with admiration upon the Finnish people, whose love for their homeland provided many instances of courage and self-sacrifice for Europe's history, that has learned from painful times, and today keeps to a strict course of neutrality and acts as an intermediary between the great power blocks.

Biography of the Commander

Hans Collani was born on 13 December 1908 as the son of a professional officer in Stettin. He attended the Dom-Gymnasium in Schleswig and took his school-leaving examination in a Gymnasium in Flensburg.

He then learned the trade of a merchant with a shipping firm. In that profession he undertook several trips to other countries, including Latvia, Murmansk, and Leningrad.

He joined the *Allgemeine SS* on 13 April 1931 in Schleswig-Holstein and, on 17 March 1933, was seconded to Hitler's *Stabswache* (headquarters guard), from which "*Leibstandarte Adolf Hitler*" was soon formed. After attending an officers' course in Zossen, he became a company commander and was promoted to *SS-Hauptsturmführer* on 1 October 1933. In February 1935 the commander of *Leibstandarte*, Sepp Dietrich, requested him as regimental adjutant. Collani held that position until November 1939.

Collani took part in the Western Campaign in 1940 as an *Ordonnanzoffizier* of *1. Regiment* of *SS-Division "Totenkopf"*. In February 1941 he was transferred to the newly-created *Division "Wiking"* and was employed initially with the division staff. He then formed the *Finnische Freiwilligen-Bataillon der Waffen-SS* and commanded it as part of *SS-Division "Wiking"* in Russia. On 21 December 1941 Collani was promoted to *SS-Sturmbannführer* and on 20 April 1943 to *SS-Obersturmbannführer*. With respect to awards, he won both classes of the Iron Cross, the German Cross in Gold, and Finnish awards for bravery. *Obersturmbannführer* Collani turned over his *Finnische Freiwilligen-Bataillon* to the Finnish army in July 1943.

As part of the creation of *III. (germanischen) SS-Panzerkorps*, Collani formed the *2./niederländische SS-Freiwilligen-Panzergrenadier-Regiment Nr. 49* ("*De Ruyter*") of the *23. SS-Freiwilligen-Panzergrenadier-Division "Nederland"*, with which he went to the *Ostfront* at the end of 1943.

Collani commanded *Regiment Nr. 49* in the Narwa bridgehead; there it participated in an outstanding manner in the defence of the bridgehead.

When the *I. Bataillon* of his regiment was cut off during the withdrawal movement into the "*Tannenberg* position", he decided on his own to bring up the *II. Bataillon*, which was already in the position, and free-up the *Rollbahn* for the cut-off *Bataillon*.

During the heavy battles in the "*Tannenberg* position" Collani was severely wounded by an artillery barrage on 29 July 1944 and took his own life when the enemy appeared in front of his command post. Collani was awarded the Knight's Cross and was promoted to *SS-Standartenführer* posthumously.

Appendix

Organizational Structure of the Finnish *Freiwilligen-Bataillon der Waffen-SS*

Bataillon Kommandeur:

Hauptsturmführer/Obersturmbannführer Collani

Adjutant:

Untersturmführer Hinrichs, until 9 February 1942

Obersturmführer Helmut Hirt

Ordonnanzoffizier:

Untersturmführer Karl-Heinz Ertel, May–October 1942

Untersturmführer Helmut Scholz, April 1942–July 1943

Administrative officer:

Obersturmführer/Hauptsturmführer Erwin Kaatsch, 15 February 1943 transferred to *SS-Panzer-Grenadier Division "Wiking"*

Untersturmführer Herbert Fuchs

Medical officer:

Obersturmführer Dr. Gerhard Bumke

Untersturmführer/Obersturmführer Dr. Olli Somersalo (F=Finn)

Assistant medical officer:

Untersturmführer Dr. Necker

Untersturmführer Dr. Olli Somersalo (F)

Dentist: *Obersturmführer/Hauptsturmführer* Dr. Wilhelm Franke

Technical officer motorized vehicles (*TFK*):

Untersturmführer/Obersturmführer Konrad Bläss

1./9. Kompanie:

Kompanie Führer:

Obersturmführer Karl Hoy, 15 June 1941–16 September 1942, took ill

Hauptsturmführer Heinz Troiker, 16 September 1942–13 October 1942, took ill

Obersturmführer Pallesche, 13 October 1942–17 October 1942, killed

Untersturmführer/Obersturmführer Karl-Heinz Ertel, 17 October 1942–11 July 1943

2./10 Kompanie:

Kompanie Führer:

Obersturmführer Pallesche, 15 June 1941–31 January 1942, transferred to regiment

Obersturmführer Karl-Erik Ladau (F), 1 February–26 March 1942, wounded

Obersturmführer Werner (Bobby) Hilker, 11 April–13 August 1942, killed

Obersturmführer Hans Joachim Porsch, 14 August–8 October 1942, wounded

Combined with *11. Kompanie* under the command of chef of *11. Kompanie* from 8–17 October 1942

Untersturmführer/Obersturmführer Tauno Pohjanlehto (F), 17 October–13 December 1942

Obersturmführer Hans Joachim Porsch, 13 December 1942–19 January 1943, killed

Obersturmführer Tauno Pohjanlehto (F), 19 January 1943–12 March 1943, wounded

Obersturmführer Kauko Ingerö (F), 12 March 1943–11 August 1943

3./11. Kompanie:

Kompanie Führer:

Obersturmführer Hartmann, 15 June–23 November 1941, suicide;

Obersturmführer Theodor Schnabel, 25 November 1941–13 August 1942, killed

Untersturmführer Lüttgens, 13–16 August 1942, killed

Obersturmführer August Mühlinghaus, 16 August–17 November 1942, killed

From 17 November–8 December 1942 with the *10. Kompanie* under the command of company commander 10. *Kompanie* combined

Obersturmführer Eugen Deck, 8 December 1942–11 July 1943

4./12 Kompanie:

Kompanie Führer:

Obersturmführer Franz Pleiner, 15 June 1941–4 July 1942, transferred to *SS-Artillerie-Regiment 5*

Hauptsturmführer Brückner, 4 July–8 August 1942, severely wounded during a live fire exercise, died of his wounds in hospital

Obersturmführer Reus, acting deputy/*Zugführer* of light infantry howitzer platoon, 8 August–16 August 1942, killed

16 August–8 December 1942 the platoons were deployed by *Bataillon*

Hauptsturmführer Karl-Erik Ladau (F), 8 December 1942–18 February 1943, wounded

Obersturmführer Yrjö Tenomaa (F), 18 February–26 March 1943, took ill

Obersturmführer Lauri Sartio (F), 26 March–11 July 1943

Report from Generalleutnant Talvela to Field Marshal Mannerheim on his Visit to the Finnish *Freiwilligen-Bataillon* (III./"Nordland")

The representative of the Finnish army at German headquarters
Generalleutnant Talvela

OKH 22 October 1942

To the *Oberbefehlshaber*
Field Marshal Mannerheim

Field Marshal!

I inform you that today, at 1700 hours, I have returned from my trip to the Caucasus and hurry to send you a few lines about my impressions of the Finnish SS-*Bataillon*.

The *Bataillon* has been involved in indescribably hard fighting during the last three weeks; as has been the entire division to which it belongs. During this time the division captured the city of Malgobek and the oil fields during the most severe fighting in an open, hilly terrain. The Finnish *Bataillon* especially distinguished itself during this fighting and was praised by the division commander, as well as other German officers.

Unfortunately, the losses of the *Bataillon* are also very great. The commander of the *Bataillon* informed me that the total loss of men was 485 of which 80 were killed. This number also includes the German cadre, which, on a percentage basis, had similar losses to the Finnish section. In addition, since a number of men of the *Bataillon* had been transferred (e.g. 15 to officers training schools) and a number were ill, the fighting strength of the *Bataillon* consisted of only 132 men, as the *Bataillon* commander informed me. Fortunately, regarding the wounded, we are dealing mostly with light cases. The division commander mentioned the number of 350 lightly wounded.

Naturally, the mood was more or less depressed after these heavy battles, but under no circumstances anything like on my last visit to the *Bataillon* in the spring. Especially the officers, of whom only one did not belong to the group of those killed or wounded, were depressed to a certain extent. In contrast, the men in the most forward foxholes, where they had been transferred during the night, made a relatively cheerful impression.[24]

I also visited the men in a number of field hospitals and had to confirm that most of their wounds were in general not that severe. The men were very well looked after in the hospitals, especially in the splendid hospital in Kislowosk in the hills of the Caucasus. I will later describe this resort of the Bolshevik masters in greater detail in my formal report on my trip. I also met in the hospital two wounded officers, who will soon return to the front. In relation to this I would like to mention that the number of Finnish officers in the *Bataillon* is especially small, because there are only about 10 officers. Amongst other items, all the company commanders, the German as well as the Finnish ones, became casualties during the fighting and the division commander inquired of me the possibility of receiving two competent officers from Finland. I supported this suggestion heartily because our boys would feel much more comfortable under the command of Finnish company commanders than under German ones. Obviously, the division commander also aimed for this because he tried his best to look after the Finns, whom he said that he especially liked. I will permit myself to come back to this question later…

In my opinion, my visit to the *Bataillon* came at an especially favourable point in time because I hope that I was able to encourage our boys. I considered it an especially fortunate circumstance that on my trip I was able to hand over the decorations that the Field Marshal had asked me to award to the men, especially the wounded, with the greetings from the Field Marshal. The Field Marshal had given me

24. For the situation at the time of General Tavela's visit, see the report in the section "Quiet Front Sectors" page 141.

100 medals and 20 crosses to award to the men. Considering the *Bataillon's* high losses, I was forced to award all of them, even though the Field Marshal had demanded that I use strict criteria. The eyes of the men, especially the wounded, lit up from joy as I handed them the Finnish awards. I would have liked to have given every wounded man a medal. However, as there were over 400 wounded, the medals did not suffice for this. I awarded the Cross of Freedom in the name of the Field Marshal to the commander of the division, *General* Steiner, who then requested that I convey to the Field Marshal his sincere thanks and his most respectful greetings.

Generalleutnant Paavo Talvela[25]

Medical Treatment of the Wounded and Sick in the Finnish *SS-Bataillon*

by Professor Dr. Mauno Jokipii

The number of Finnish *SS*-men killed was approximately 250, of whom 80 were "division men", and about 170 were "*Bataillon* boys". According to the information from the *Bataillon* war diary, the losses were 520 wounded, of whom 401 were Finns and 119 Germans. The number of sick amounted to approximately 400; which meant that on the average the greater part of the *Bataillon* members required one medical treatment, as a wounded or sick person, during the one-and-a-half years of war-time deployment.

The medical care for the Finns was good. The *Bataillon* had its own doctor, Dr. Gerhard Bumke, and a dentist, Dr. Wilhelm Franke, both well liked, as well as an assistant doctor, and an excellently equipped medical first aid station. To minimize the language difficulties, an assistant doctor, Dr. Olli Somersalo, was brought from Finland in September 1942 for the *Bataillon*. He distinguished himself during the winter battles and then became the medical officer in February 1943 in place of Dr. Bumke.

There were differences in the organization of caring for the wounded and sick between the Finnish and German *Wehrmacht*. The Finnish system looked after the wounded very close to the frontline and therefore had a larger complement of personnel at the first aid station. The patients

25. Mauno Jokipii, loc cit, pages 561/562.

were treated medically well there, as well as in the field hospitals. In the German system every effort was made to bring the wounded back as far and as fast as possible. Therefore, the first aid stations were equipped more provisionally and only the most immediate problems were treated medically to insure that the patients could survive the trip to the nearest field hospital. The differences in the systems resulted in the Finnish volunteers, probably from a lack of information, being sharply critical, especially in relation to the first aid stations near the front. However, they did also admit that the hospitals of the home front were excellent.

From the examples taken from the diaries of the volunteers, it can be seen that it took from one half to two days to be transported from the first aid station to the field hospital (of division), and from there to the military hospital (*SS*-hospital) approximately one week. The transport to the military hospital usually took place in primitive trains (closed freight cars with straw bundles), which were officially named *behelfsmäßige Verwundeten*-Züge (*BVZ*) (makeshift wounded trains). The *SS*-hospitals (military hospitals) were located in the Polish cities of Lublin, Lemberg, and Cracow, where the wounded were taken in and looked after properly. A complete cleansing and de-lousing process took place there before the wounded were transported to beds covered in white sheets. On the average, it took approximately eight days for a transport from Rostov to Cracow in the *BVZ*. There, in the *SS*-hospitals (military hospitals), an immediate thorough medical treatment took place. If the wounded had no fever for three days they were transported in well-equipped hospital trains (D-trains with double tiered, white linen covered beds) to the homeland or reserve hospitals, which sometimes were specialist hospitals (brain or neural injuries, complicated fractures, etc.). There, intensive medical treatment and care was provided. The length of time for the transport of a wounded person from the field hospital to a homeland hospital varied and depended mainly upon whether the wounded was even fit to be transported.

To overcome the language difficulties two trained nurses were sent from Finland in October 1942 to the field hospitals of "*Wiking*" at Kislowodsk and later to Amwrosiewka. Later, in the spring of 1943, when approximately 40 Finnish wounded had been assembled in a Vienna hospital, an additional nurse and two trained representatives of the Lotta-

Svärd-Organization were sent. Those nurses carried out excellent work in the field hospitals, and in the homeland or reserve hospitals.

Major Riekki's committee, which had carried out the selection process in Finland, had, by autumn 1941, already sent Baroness Ruth Munck, a known leading figure in the Lotta-Svärd-Organization, to Germany, where she visited Finnish wounded in the various German hospitals. In total, Ruth Munck took five trips in the years from 1941 to 1943 and visited a large number of hospitals in Germany. Mrs. Alice Dahl also undertook a similar trip in the summer of 1942. Baroness Ruth Munck also became the beloved and honoured "nurse Ruth" for our "second *Jägerbataillon*".

Amongst other measures to cheer up and entertain the wounded, the lending library must be mentioned. Legation counsellor, Mrs. Marjatta Martola (now Mrs. Myrberg), managed it in her home in Berlin, from where books were sent to the hospitals for use by the wounded. She also organized three entertainment tours with some of her artist friends, who visited the hospitals with the greatest number of wounded Finns and the *Ersatz-Bataillon* in Graz, and spread joy with homeland offerings. Finally, it has to be mentioned that a number of Finnish-born women cared for the wounded in a laudable manner in hospitals in Breslau and Vienna.

To summarize, one can say that the above-mentioned activities of Finnish girls and women were well-suited to make life easier for Finnish wounded in a foreign land in which a foreign language was spoken.

Nearly a hundred of those wounded now live as disabled persons of various types and degree in Finland. After much reluctance, in 1956 the Finnish state, which had itself given the impetus for the formation of this *Bataillon*, at last declared itself ready to pay the normal pension for disabled war veterans.

Document No. 1

Foreign Ministry — Berlin W 8, 27 January 1942
Wilhelmstraße 74–76

Nr. Pol I M 425g

Secret

The German Legation in Helsinki wired on 24 January 1942:

The Finnish radio presented in its armed forces programme of 21 January at 1920 hours, an interview with three Finnish SS-men on leave. They reported about the fighting on the *Ostfront* and German attitude toward the Finns. In Germany one considers the Finns good soldiers. German discipline was quite different from that of Finnish discipline. The interviewer recommended German discipline of Finnish soldiers, especially those on leave. The attitude of the German population toward Finnish soldiers, as toward the Finnish people, was friendly. Furthermore, the respect toward disabled persons and soldiers on public transport in Germany was presented as exemplary. Food for German soldiers was excellent and substantial. The clothing was clean and good, even though Finnish high-boots were warmer. The greeting toward Finnish soldiers on leave was:

We are proud of you. We also fight for Finland in Germany because we are defending common interests. We hope that the German soldiers in Finland feel as content as the Finnish ones in Germany.

On behalf
signed signature (illegible)

To the *SS-Hauptamt*
to Hd. from *Obersturmbannführer* Dr. Riedweg
Berlin-Grunewald
Hagenstraße 39[26]

26. Source: From Archiv Vorpersal, from USA microfilm, Files RF and FHA, T 175/109.

Document No. 2

Copy

Reichsfuhrer-SS Berlin W 35, 10 February 1942
SS-Hauptamt – Amt VI Lützowstraße 48/49
VS-Tgb. Nr. 473/42 secret
VI 1 – Az.: 207/42 secret Dr. R./vB.
With respect to: Finnish war volunteers.
1. Remarks:
According to the report from the Finnish military attaché, *Oberst* Horn, from the head of the Lotta movement Baroness Munck, who had visited Finnish wounded in German hospitals, as well as from the communications of the liaison officer of Amt VI to the Finnish legation, the attitude within the Finnish volunteer group is so poor that they will not be serving German goals when they return home. According to the above, this is due to the fact that many Finnish officers were for the most part not deployed according to their positions, that there still wasn't an all-Finnish formation, and that good NCOs were serving as enlisted men with the *Ersatz-Bataillon* in Graz. The 18 officers and NCOs that returned to Finland a few weeks ago vigorously expressed their disappointments.

Baroness Munck informed the reporter that she wishes greatly for a close friendship between the Reich and Finland and is ready to do anything to promote it, but has been deeply disappointed by the inept way the Finnish volunteers were treated. The Finnish volunteers always held in front of them *Jägerbataillon Nr. 27*, which had been such a satisfactory deployment in every sense. She feared that increasingly more officers and NCOs would hand in their resignations and that there was a danger of the whole volunteer formation falling apart.

The Finnish legation, which doubts that the spirit of nationalism will be brought to Finland by the troops, supports the departure and has ordered that no one who has been released to Finland be allowed to report back.

It is urgently necessary that the Finnish officers and NCOs with the *Ersatz-Bataillon* are sent as soon as possible to its formation, and that, for political reasons, the Finnish volunteer formation be treated especially well.

2. To the *Chef* of *Hauptamt* m.d.B. (Mit der Bitte-with the request) to take note and include the addition to the remarks to the complete report for RF-SS (*Reichsführer-SS*).

VI 1
signed signature (illegible)

F.d.R.d.A.
signed signature (illegible)
SS-*Untersturmführer* and *Adjutant*[27]

27. Source: From Archiv Vorpersal, from USA microfilm, Files RF and FHA, T 175/109.

Document No. 3

Reichsführer-SS Berlin W 35, 28 April 1942
Chef SS-Hauptamt Lützowstraße 48/49
Post office box 43

OdSSHA/Be/Bo/Tgb.Nr.1471/42 secret
With respect to: Finland

To the
Reichsführer-SS
Führerhauptquartier

Reichsführer!
I wish to report the following, based on the report about the situation in Finland: (Chef of *Reichssicherheitshauptamt* [Reich main security department] has received the carbon copy).

The development of a new Finnish SS committee has led in the meantime to the following results.

The present principal of the Helsinki University, Prof. Nevanlinna, will take over the lead because it seems prudent, based on the Finnish mindset, to chose a neutral Finnish speaking personality for this position. Nevanlinna is the deputy chair of the Finnish-German society, known to be German-friendly, but at the same time not stamped with any political leanings. However, the actual preparations of the committee will in the future still be with Director Norrmen, who will later also exercise a significant influence on these activities.

Considered as additional members are:

1. Oberst Lindh, Leader of the Finnish Frontline Fighters Association (about 30,000 members);
2. Riekki;
3. Oberst Leander, war ministry, leader of the propaganda section of the "Waffenbrüder"-organization;
4. Veterinary Colonel Talvitie, member of the executive committee of the union of the former *Jägerbataillon Nr. 27*;
5. Rautala, IKL;
6. Oberstleutnant Levälahti, former liaison officer at Groß Born;
7. Baroness Munck;
8. Oberst Wihma, main staff of the home army.

The incorporation of Aaltonen, director Hedman, Captain Kalsta, and other personalities is still not completely clear. The number of people involved has for now been limited to 15. Some important personalities from the economy, e.g. Begrad Forsström, were also suggested.

Director Norrmen had a discussion with Foreign Minister Witting to sound out his position in the committee in relation to the volunteer situation. Witting basically expressed support but without taking a firm stand. He especially pointed out once more the basic opposition of Mannerheim to the volunteer situation. At the same time, Witting stated that with the termination of the volunteers the official government assignment for Riekki was concluded. Since that time Riekki has been acting as a purely private person without any official assignment. Related to this, a plan made its appearance that would retain General Östermann, at present armed forces inspector, as the official designated by the Finnish government in relation to all SS issues.

Director Norrmen will make the attempt to get the support of President Ryti through Witting. As to what degree of success this attempt will bring about cannot be predicted at this time. Östermann himself is very interested in the volunteer situation and, based on his attitude, would undoubtedly be the ideal personality for this. On the other hand, he is vigorously attacked by the centrist parties and is in opposition to Mannerheim. Amongst the nationalistic groups and circles, Östermann is seen as the next Finnish Führer personality, upon whom great hopes rest. Allegedly, Östermann is to have been in touch with the *Reichsführer-SS* in Rovaniemi during his brief Finland trip.

In any case, the designation of an official Finnish government representative would be desirable because there are still significant ambiguities in relation to all volunteer issues. As an example, it turned out from a discussion between Riekki and Aaltonen that the time served by the SS-volunteers would not be counted as time served in the Finnish army.

During the farewell visit by SS-*Obersturmführer* Gerlinger with ambassador Blücher, he mentioned the appearance of tendencies by the Finns that would make efforts to recall the volunteer *Bataillon*.

Minister von Blücher, who was obviously being influenced by certain one-sided Finnish circles, considered such a request not unreasonable (!) and leaned openly toward making these thought processes his. SS-*Obersturmführer* Gerlinger opposed these and pointed out that especially the member personalities of the SS-committee were totally in opposition to an early recall of the volunteers.

It was desirable that the embassy in Helsinki could have a clear directive from the foreign ministry with respect to this issue so that these demands put forth by certain Finnish circles would not be seriously discussed.

A discussion took place between Dr. Müller-Norden, chief editor Eichberg, and attaché Schneider, with respect to the Finnish broadcasts from the Königsberg radio station, whereby agreement was reached about the participation of the SS within the programme. As already mentioned in the earlier reports, there were to be sent special greetings and commentaries by Finnish volunteers. It is not possible to involve the Finnish press more closely with publicizing the volunteer spirit before the final constitution of the committee is completed. Typical of the previous, untenable treatment of this issue in the Finnish press was an article by the female representative of the newspaper *Uusi Suomi* in Berlin about three weeks ago on the occasion of the transit of 92 released Finnish NCOs. The female reporter, Saloma Simonen, presented the most trivial details, but without a single word being mentioned about the purpose of the deployment of the Finnish volunteers in the east. In another Finnish illustrated magazine, an article about the *Bataillon* gave only a lacklustre description of the Ukrainian landscape. A meaningless group photo of the Finnish volunteers served as the illustration. The systemics of these reports are obvious.

In conclusion, based on our experiences, the following points can be brought out. The internal, and especially the economic, development in Finland is at this time already difficult to determine. A relaxation of any noteworthy extent cannot be expected during the next few months. The great hope for the future, even though numerically small, is for the national socialist opposition, especially the Finnish *Waffen-SS*.

A political impact of the Finnish volunteer action, based on the relatively small numbers of the present contingent and its combination, can only be expected if a renewed recruiting campaign is started in Finland directly after the Finnish-Russian campaign. The mood for this is still, as before, very good amongst the Finnish youth, so that in this direction there is no reason to doubt success in recruiting. It is obviously more difficult in gaining the agreement of official circles. Nonetheless, by choosing an appropriate point in time, this agreement is attainable. It is of great importance to carefully observe developments in Finland over the next few months. Based on our past experiences, the establishment or maintenance of a permanent representation of the *SS-Hauptampt* in Helsinki is essential because otherwise resistance and difficulties created by the impact of negatively disposed groups can be effected without hindrance and, under some circumstances, result in a complete fizzling out of the SS-concept.

signed G. Berger
SS-Gruppenführer[28]

28. Source: From Archiv Vorpersal, from USA microfilm, Files RF and FHA, T 175/125,2.650-322-27.

Document No. 4

Reichsführer-SS Berlin W 35, 4 November 1942
Chef SS-Hauptamt Lützowstraße 48/49
CdSSHA/Be/Ge. VS-Tgb.Nr. 460/42
Secret military document

4 copies, copy 1
With respect to the Finnish Generalleutnant Talvela
Enclosures:-1-

To the *Reichsführer-SS*
and Chef of the German police,
Field-headquarters
Reichsführer!

I report:

1. Today I was awarded by Generalleutnant Talvela the Finnish Decoration I. Class with Swords of the White Rose. After that, there was an invitation to breakfast with the Finnish representative, Kivimäki.
2. I have already reported about General Talvela, a Free Mason and under the spell of Jews, who is secretly trying to sabotage *SS* activities in Finland. But it must not be ignored that Talvela is the confidant of Mannerheim and the exact opposite of Östermann.
3. Talvela will remain here in Berlin and carry out the business of a liaison officer from here to the Führerhauptquartier. The Finnish Major Dunker, who was a Captain in his corps that was created at the outbreak of the war, will assist him as his *Ia* and as *Generalstabschef*. His office is at Meinickestr. 4. The building itself is leased by the Italian armed forces. All the liaison officers from all the allied states are to be quartered here.
4. Oberst Horn will have his office in Hungary, where he is also accredited as a military attaché. As cover, he is to remain in Berlin as a military attaché for now. In this way General Talvela

will carry out his actual duties at the Finnish embassy unnoticed. Oberst Horn is to establish a close relationship with Hungary.

5. Major Wikmann will be transferred to Finland during the next 14 days. He is to be neutralized because of his friendliness to Germany. Kivimäki, but more so his wife, consider the transfer of General Talvela to Berlin as very unpleasant.
6. The invitation for General Östermann and Oberst Ekholm to visit Germany was not approved by Field Marshal Mannerheim.
7. The enclosed file[29] (Anlage -1-) gives the best information on the actual attitude of General Talvela toward us.

   The liaison officer to *Division "Wiking"*, SS-*Sturmbannführer* Kurkiala, a completely reliable man, received an order from Talvela never to travel to Finland without his permission and not to send any reports there without his knowledge.

   Reichsführer, here is the beginning of a great political game. There is no basis for any sort of apprehension. I request only that all offices of the *RF-SS* direct that discussions in any form, reporting of news, etc. must be coordinated.
8. The circles around Talvela count on the volunteer *Bataillon* of *Division "Wiking"* returning to Finland by the end of June 1943 because the time of their commitment will have expired. Therefore, from my point of view, at this time we proceed carefully with respect to replacements!
9. Oberst Horn spoke of the occupation of the area assigned to you by the *Führer*. You wanted to occupy all of Karelia and to do this with the intention of moving the "Finnish people" out of the Russian area. I have deliberately not said anything about racial deterioration etc., but only asked if you yourself were clear about the concept of these Finnish people. He recognized the point immediately and stated that he would discuss in detail this question with you.
10. Talvela then spoke of the creation of a *Reichskommissariat*, which should be positioned in front of this Finnish Reich toward the

29. The enclosure -1- shows a coincidental meeting of Talvela with Baroness Munck and the Finnish SS-Rottenfuhrer Tamminen of the Finnish liaison office in front of Colonel Horn's house in Helsinki on the evening of 26 October 1942, whereby Talvela completely ignored Tamminen.

east. I informed him that I knew nothing of this and that I could not assume under any circumstances from the simple fact that this "courageous Finnish people could have transferred to it this area in front of it as security". That was said deliberately by me because at this moment of time the SS is again the imperialist. Both became silent upon this declaration.

Signed, Berger
SS-Gruppenführer[30]

30. Source: From Archiv Vorpersal, from USA microfilm, Files RF and FHA, T 175/129.

Sources

Official Sources:

War Diary of the "*Finnisches Freiwilligen-Bataillon der Waffen-SS*" IV./*SS-Regiment "Nordland*"/*III.* (*finnisches*)/"*Nordland*"

War Diary No.1

Start: 1 November 1942 – Closed: 3 December 1942

The *Bataillon* was attached from 21 January to 15 February 1942 to *SS-Regiment* "*Westland*", from 16 February to 3 December 1942 to *SS-Regiment* "*Nordland*".

The KTB was kept

from 1 November to 23 November 1941 by *Untersturmführer* Hinrichs, Adjutant
from 23 November to 2 December 1941 by *Untersturmführer* Ertel
from 3 December 1941 to 9 February 1942 by *Untersturmführer* Hinrichs, Adjutant
from 10 February to 19 October 1942 by *Obersturmführer* Hirt, Adjutant
from 20 October to 31 October 1942 by *Untersturmführer* Scholz, Ordonnanzoffizier
from 1 November to 3 December 1942 by *Obersturmführer* Hirt, Adjutant

War Diary No. 2

III. (*finnisches*)/*SS-Panzergrenadierregiment* "*Nordland*"

Start: 4 December 1942 – Closed 11 July 1943

The *Bataillon* was attached

from 4 November 1942 to 1 January 1943 to *III. Panzerkorps*
from 1 January to 14 January 1943 to *SS-Panzergrenadierdivision* "*Wiking*"
from 15 January to 24 April 1943 to *SS-Panzergrenadierregiment* "*Nordland*" as the *Finnisches Freiwilligen-Bataillon der Waffen-SS*

The KTB was kept from 4 December 1942 to 11 July 1943 by *Obersturmführer* Hirt, Adjutant.

Bundesarchiv-Militärarchiv Freiburg:

Evaluated were the war diaries of *Heeresgruppe* A, of *17. Armee*, *1. Panzerarmee* and *LVII. Panzerkorps* from 1941 to 1943; The *III.*, *XIV.*, *XXXX.*, and *XXXXVIII. Panzerkorps* from 1943.

Archiv Vopersal:

Various official documents on the creation and recall of the *Finnisches Freiwilligen-Bataillon der Waffen-SS*.

Bibliography

Aaltonen, B.S.: "In den Spuren der 27. Jäger. Das Finn.Frw.Btl. der Waffen-S":, in "Waffenbruder Finnland". Ein Buch für den deutschen soldaten in Finnland. Finnland 1942.

Aspelmeier, Dieter: "Deutschland und Finnland während der beiden Weltkriege", Verlag Christoph von der Ropp, Hamburg 1967.

Biasi, de Mario: "finnlandia, Profil eines Landes". Tammi Verlag Helsinki (ohne Jahreszahl). Deutsche Fassung: Reinhold Dey. Druck: Conzett & Huber, Zürich.

Carell, Paul: "Unternehmen Barbarossa". Ullstein Frankfurt/M.-Berlin 1963; "Verbrannte Erde". Ullstein Frankfurt/M.-Berlin 1966.

Damerau, Helmut: "Die finnischen Jäger – Kgl. Prß. Jägerbataillon Nr. 27:, im "Deutschen soldaten-Jahrbuch" 1966. Schild-Verlag München.

Erfurth, Waldemar: "Der finnische Krieg 1941–1944". Limes-Verlag Wiesbaden 1950.

Ewers, W.: "Kleine Länderkunden-Suomi Finnland". Franckh'sche Verlagshandlung, W. Keller & Co., Stuttgart 1950.

Grieben-Reiseführer: "Finnland". Verlag Karl Thiemig KG, München 1971, Band 271.

Halter, Heinz: "Finnische Jäger erkämpfen die Freiheit" Ohne Angaben 1942.

Haupt, W.: "Heeresgruppe Nord", Podzun Verlag, Bad Nauheim 1967.

Hedin, Sven: "Ohne Auftrag in Berlin", Tübingen und Stuttgart 1950.

Jokipii, Mauno "Panttipaljona". Weilin + Göös, Helsinki 1968.

Klietmann, Dr. K.G.: "Die Waffen-SS". Munin Verlag Osnabrück 1965.

Klink, Ernst: "Der finnisch-sowjetische Krieg 1939–40", in "Wehrwissenschaftliche rundschau", Jahrgang 9, 1959, Volume 12.

Mannerheim, C.G.: "Erinnerungen", Atlantis Verlag, Zurich 1952.

Manstein, Erich vol: "Verlorene Siege". Athanäum Verlag Bonn 1955.

Paasikivi, Juho Kusti "Am Rande einer Supermacht" (The first edition appeared under the title: "My Moscow Mission 1939–41"), Holsten Verlag Hamburg 1966.

Sawjalow/Kaljadin: "Die Schlacht um den Kaukasus". Verlag des Ministeriums fü nationale Verteidigung, Berlin 1959.

Schramm, P.E.: "Kriegstagebuch des Oberkommandos der Wehrmacht", Verlag Bernhard & Graefe, Frankfurt/Main 1965, Band IV

Schreiber, Franz: "Kampf unter dem Nordlicht", Munin Verlag Osnabrück 1969.

Schybergson, M.G.: "Politische Geschichte Finnlands (1809–1919)". Verlag Friedrich Andreas Perthes AG, Gotha-Stuttgart 1925.

Sommer, William: "Geschichte Finnlands". Verlag von r. Oldenbourg, München und Berlin 1938.

Springenschmid, Karl: "Aktion Eisvogel". Verlag K.W. Schütz KG, Preußisch Oldendorf 1975.

Stein, George H.: "Geschichte der Waffen-SS". Droste Verlag, Düseldorf 1967.

Stein/Krosby, "Das Finnische Freiwilligen-Bataillon der Waffen-SS – Eine Studie zur SS-Diplomatie und zur ausländischen Freiwilligen-Bewegung", in "Vierteljahreshefte für Zeitgeschichte", 1966, Volume 4

Steiner, Felix "Die Freiwilligen", Plesse-Verlag Göttingen 1958;

. "Die Armee der Geächteten". Plesse-Verlag Göttingen 1962.

. Neuauflagen Verlag K.W. Schütz KG, Preußisch Oldendorf

Straßner, Peter: "Europäische Freiwillige", Munin Verlag Osnabrück 1968.

Telpuchowski: "Die sowjetische Geschichte des Großen Vaterländischen Krieges". Bernhard & Graefe Verlag, Frankfurt/M. (ohne Jahreszahl).

Tieke, Wilhelm: "Tragödie um die Treue". Munin Verlag Osnabrück 1968;

. "Der Kaukasus und das Öl". Munin Verlag Osnabrück 1970.

Wagner, Carl: "heeresgruppe Süd". Podzun-Verlag Bad Nauheim, ohne Jahreszahl;

. "Der Gegenangriff des XXXX. Panzerkorps gegen den Durchbruch der Panzerarmee Popow im Donezbecken im Februar 1943:, in "Wehrwissenschaftliche Rundschau", 1957, Volume 1.

Index

Index of Places

Index of Persons